UNIVERSAL HIGHER EDUCATION

Universal
Higher
Education

Edited by EARL J. McGRATH
Executive Officer
Institute of Higher Education

McGRAW-HILL BOOK COMPANY   New York · St. Louis

San Francisco · Toronto · London · Sydney

Foreword

All the papers presented here—except the final one—are, collectively, an exercise in forecast. As of the date of the meeting at which they were presented—November, 1964—it was not possible to predict the form of American education in 1980 or even in 1970. It could only be said that it was probable that the growth of what is loosely called "higher education" would, in years ahead, continue at the rapid and often surprising pace it had set since the close of World War II.

It was also certain that two new variables had been added to the traditional factors determining the size, form, and function of higher education. One variable was clearly described by Clark Kerr with his newly minted term "multiversity." The development since the war of a new form of institution, existing primarily for the creation and application of knowledge rather than for the transmission of the culture and the support of its institutions, means the opening of some doors—and the closing of others—in higher education. The multiversity frankly offers less opportunity to the underprivileged than did its predecessor institutions but places greater emphasis on achievement. It has less pity for those not selected, greater rewards for those who are.

The second variable is political, with moral overtones. It expresses itself in concern for the deprived, with emphasis on the Negro, and it seeks its principal remedy for the plight of the deprived through the uses of education. The remedy that is sought is greater opportunity for the underprivileged, an opportunity so full that it will excuse lack of achievement as merely an unavoidable deferment of hope.

The conference found itself forced to face the contradictions inherent in these variables—in other words, to accept the certainty of an expanding educational system with increasingly liberal standards at the point of access to higher education, as against the spectacle of an apex for the system becoming, at least to customary optics, even more restricted to a chosen few super-students than it has been in the past.

27613

It was the view of the conference that these contradictions could be and would be resolved. The resolution would begin with a massive enlargement of the definition of higher education, followed by changes in existing institutions and development of new institutions which would extend access to higher education to a majority of the nation's youth. The mass institutions of the new era of education would be those which stress the useful and the typical: former teachers colleges which would become state colleges; tuition-supported urban universities which have sprawling programs; technical institutes which would develop new forms of vocational and technical education; community colleges which may well be all things to all men. Beyond the mass institutions the present academic elite would continue in essentially its present pattern, drawing not only on its present clientele but also on products of the new mass education. The system, much enlarged, would present its problems, but most of them would be solved administratively. Intellectually, the accommodation would be possible.

The details of changes of this magnitude cannot be clearly seen at a distance of ten or fifteen years. The papers present an approximation of some of them, guess about others, and are discretely silent on others. But taken as a group they represent a first viewing from afar of a field which the next generation will come to know close at hand, and well.

Frank Bowles

Vice President
Fund for the Advancement of Education

Preface

The twelve chapters of this book are a report on a group inquiry [1] into the substance and implications of universal higher education, defined as opportunity for higher education utilized by more than half of the relevant (eighteen to twenty-two) age group.

Since universal higher education is not yet with us, the book is an exercise in prediction, and predictions as to the shape and mission of American education have proved to be dangerous business. Nearly all the studies and surveys which were made in the late 1940s and early 1950s to serve as the base for planning education for the following two decades have long since proved to be too conservative in estimate of enrollments; some were intellectually misleading in predictions of needs and expectations. Yet when the studies were made, all the preconditions for the present development of higher education already existed, and every student who is now in higher education had already been born. Therefore it was not for want of facts that the predictions turned out badly. It was rather a matter of the mood of the time when the predictions and plans were made.

So far as the educators were concerned, the late 1940s were an uncertain time. The GI Bill was certain to end, the swollen enrollments would drop, and the swollen institutions would shrink to pitiable conditions. The market for college graduates appeared to be poor, so there was little to attract students. The secondary schools had not yet even considered the possibility that half their products would wish to enter college, and it was still thought to be good form for secondary school principals to denounce the impossible rigidity of college requirements. No one knew where institutional support could come from: the formula of tuition increases made palatable by scholarship programs had not been evolved, and the successful fund-raising campaigns of the 1950s had not been considered. Projections showing enrollment increases were not disputed but their implications were ignored.

[1] A conference held under the auspices of the Institute of Higher Education, Teachers College, Columbia University, at the Dorado Beach Hotel, Dorado Beach, Puerto Rico, November 15–21, 1964. The 19 participants, of whom 11 presented papers, are listed on page xvii.

The prediction in 1950 was for continued financial stringency for education. There were no announced Federal programs to assist higher education, and, in the light of opposition within the government and from industry and many of the institutions of higher education themselves, there seemed little possibility that such aid would ever appear. The predicted enrollment increases were to be dealt with by slow and small increases in the size of major institutions and a gradual filling of the weaker ones. The formation of new institutions was not considered. The acknowledged shortages of scientists and engineers were to be taken care of by a program of exhortation and recruitment. The secondary schools were to remain in control of the college preparatory curriculum. The three major changes of the succeeding fifteen years—the emergence of the multiversity, the university recapture of control over entrance requirements, and the multibillion dollar annual Federal support for education—were unforeseen.

This is the history that lies behind whatever attempt we make to forecast the shape of education in 1980. Fortunately, the history has not inhibited valiant efforts to make forecasts, and these efforts have been supported by records and information about the current state of education that are far more accurate and complete than any we had in 1950. There is also recent experience in assessment and evaluation which makes predictions easier. We know what has happened to education, we believe that certain events are the results of education, and we have all been witnesses to successful efforts in prediction. Therefore we undertake the prediction for 1975 with some confidence.

The papers in this volume are based on the fact that for the past fifteen years there has been a steady annual increase in the percentage of youth attending college. It is assumed this will continue for the foreseeable future; hence there will be steadily growing pressure for admission to higher education.

There is less agreement beyond this point, an observation which reflects the sharp differences of opinion as to the controls which should be placed on the expansion of higher education. Since these differences are encountered in all policy discussions about the future of higher education, it is worthwhile to discuss them.

Broadly speaking, the differences sort themselves into two sets of views. One view, part of the philosophy of higher education from the time of the founding of universities, may be called "scholastic." It holds that higher education exists to select and form the relatively small group of individuals who in any society, large or small, will have the responsibility for making decisions. The formation is accomplished through study of the society. Two forms of learning are required in the study. The form of organization must be understood, whether it be feudalism, centralized autocracy, or decentralized democracy. And it is also necessary to acquire the knowledge and skills which the society requires for successful operation.

In its earliest expression this view limited education to the small group concerned with the philosophy and management of church and state—considerably less than 1 per cent of the population. As society became more complex, the view broadened to take in essential professions—medicine, engineering, finance, the military. This group was enlarged until, in our time, it embraces, if we are to judge from those societies which continue to honor the scholastic view, about 5 per cent of the population. The broadening has had cumulative consequences. The need for selection meant that the privilege of higher education could no longer be limited to a hereditary class but had to be offered, at least as an opportunity, to other classes. Thus, in order to select 5 per cent, it was necessary to form a group which amounted in its early stages to about 30 per cent of the population. This meant that higher education was opened to the middle class, who promptly took possession of it as a middle-class attribute.

The scholastic view brought up to date holds that opportunity for higher education has expanded with adequate speed and any large additional expansion would depreciate its value. As a hidden corollary, higher education is believed to be standardized in terms of the middle class; therefore it cannot be extended without disturbing the standards of the middle class, as well as its own. This view is obviously opposed to any such concept as universal higher education. Indeed, those who hold the view would say that universal higher education is first a self-contradictory phrase and second a threatening catastrophe.

The other interpretation of the purpose of higher education may well be called the "societal view," namely, that higher education exists to serve society as a whole and functions in two ways. For the individual it offers opportunity to move as far intellectually as his abilities will take him; for the society it undertakes to supply any type of trained individual required. The selection of the individuals who take the responsibility of making decisions for the management of society is left to competition and political process. However, selection at this level may be aided by providing specialized opportunities for those who wish to enter the competition.

This view opens education to any who can reach it, and in the process of supplying the diversity of education society may require, it offers a great range of choices to the individual.

Since there is no limitation on types of education, there is no limitation on the number of individuals who may be accommodated, and there is no standard selection procedure to control their entry. Thus, higher education may deal with 10 per cent of the population at one date, 20 per cent at another, and 50 per cent at another, depending on the current definition and the ability of society to pay for the required programs. Those who hold this view must believe that the expansion of higher education will continue so long as there are demands for new types of training and individuals who can follow the program.

The decision to hold a conference on the prospects of universal higher education was essentially a decision to explore the question of whether American higher education, already widely expanded, would continue to expand and, if so, what forms the expansion would take. It followed that those who were invited to participate in the conference were known to have explored the possibility of further expansion and were, in a broad sense, holders of the societal view. It should be clear, therefore, that the conference was not a confrontation between the scholastic and the societal views of higher education and was not intended to be.

It will be evident from the papers that the individuals who presented them differed in their definitions of the training that could be offered within higher education and their perceptions of the abilities that could profitably be utilized in the training process, but none of them wavered in their certainty that education has tasks for the future beyond those which it knows in the present.

The first mention of universal higher education to receive general public attention appeared in the 1947 Report of the President's Commission on Higher Education. The following excerpts are relevant: "At least 49 percent of our population has the mental ability to complete 14 years of schooling with a curriculum of general and vocational studies that should lead either to gainful employment or to further study at a more advanced level." In addition, "at least 32 percent of our population has the mental ability to complete an advanced liberal or specialized professional education." Converting these percentages into figures, the Commission estimated that "in 1960 a minimum of 4,600,000 young people should be enrolled in non-profit institutions for education beyond the traditional twelfth grade."

The report was not a prediction, but a statement of intellectual feasibility. The intellectual feasibility was converted into political feasibility by the 1964 Democratic platform which said: *"Our task is to make the national purpose serve the human purpose; that every person shall have the opportunity to become all that he or she is capable of becoming. . . . Regardless of family financial status, therefore, education should be open to every boy or girl in America up to the highest level which he or she is able to master."*

In a sense it may be said that these two statements, seventeen years apart in time, were the final affirmation of a goal our nation has always sought—not an intellectual goal, nor even a goal accepted by intellectuals, but the inevitable end product of or an aspiration deeply rooted in the American theory of human development. Henry Steele Commager has described this theory in the first chapter of this book:

> Sometime in the eighteenth century a new theory emerged—one which we can, with some propriety, designate "American," perhaps the *first* American principle. We can call it, for convenience, the theory of environmentalism, or of change, or even of progress. It was this: Man was not really depraved or virtuous but a creature of circumstances— a point of view which found support in the philosophy of "the Great Mr. Locke," and which seemed, besides, the common sense of the matter. Depravity, corruption, crime, vice, superstition, ignorance, folly—all these were products not of nature but of history. . . . Granted that in the Old World man appeared corrupt and ignorant, was that not because for centuries he had been weighed down by the tyranny of rulers, the might of soldiers, the superstition of priests; that for centuries he had been ground down in poverty, misery, and ignorance? . . .
>
> But in the New World all this might be changed. For it was *really* a New World—it took a long time for that to sink in. Here, for perhaps the first time in modern history, man could escape the tyranny of the past, the tyranny of power, superstition, poverty, and ignorance. . . . Here there would be no tyranny of state, for he was the state; no tyranny of church, for he made the church; no tyranny of the military and of war, for there was no military, and the New World was to be free of those wars so long the curse of the Old. And there would be no tyranny of want, for no people in history had ever enjoyed such abundance—room enough, as Jefferson said, for our descendants to the thousandth and thousandth generation, and all enjoying the rich bounty of nature. All this promised to take care of a good part of the problem of depravity.
>
> It did not, however, take care of the problems of ignorance and of folly. Those problems were to be taken care of by education. No wonder education so quickly became the American religion; no wonder all the Founding Fathers were educators—Franklin, Washington, John Adams, John Dickinson, Noah Webster, and, above all, Thomas Jefferson. Education was to be the instrument of change, change of nature (science was to make that possible) and of human nature. Education was to be what religion had been in a less secular age— the chief instrument for the regeneration of the human race.

With this view of education the schools were automatically defined as instruments of change, operated for the general welfare. As Commager says, later in the same essay: "To this day Americans expect their schools to do a very different job from that which

Old World schools perform; to this day they expect schools to do almost everything, which is one reason they are continually disappointed in them." With this expectation, it is no surprise to see universal higher education as a politically accepted fact in process of being transformed into an operating reality. But acceptance does not necessarily include explanation, and we may not be sure just why it is happening *now*.

The American theory, after all, has permitted gradualism for 200 years and has contributed to a comfortable rationalism which could accommodate changes as they come along. Why then is *this* the time when we must move to the outer limits of educational space and disregard the warnings of educational rationalists who see the move as a reckless discard of intellectual values and educational standards? Would it not, for example, be better to delay, to build our educational strengths and learn to deal with our known problems, which are bad enough, before searching for new ones? The question, asked so often in varying ways, can be answered only by examining and appraising the converging forces which are creating and forcing the reality.

The operating force which has brought higher education in America to its present size and status was the demand for trained manpower, continually rising throughout the century. This demand was the result of many factors: the manpower shortages created during the deficit years of the 1930s; the industrial response to a rising population and rising prosperity; the explosion of scientific knowledge; the creation of a major segment of industry—defense—which barely existed before 1940; and the demands for services coming out of the industrial and educational expansion. And this is not all of it—as is so often the case in manpower mathematics, the whole is greater than the sum of its definable parts.

The demand has gathered force from a succession of different forms of support. The GI Bill of Rights and other veterans' benefits brought money and students to the colleges during the difficult postwar years; the National Science Foundation provided direct support for facilities that would otherwise have been delayed; and the NDEA legislation, as a response to the uproar over Sputnik, provided aid for secondary schools and incidentally assisted higher education in reasserting control over the requirements for entry to higher education. Other forms of direct and indirect support, including a measure of corporate support, brought further strength. In addition, the educational system has itself learned to find and use new forms of support, including the simple expedient of increased income from student fees.

Another force operating upon the present establishment has been a rising level of aspiration on the part of prospective students and their families. This was partly because of the democratization of secondary education during the 1930s which produced a pre-war generation of high school graduates who urged their children to seek, in the postwar period, the higher education they, themselves, had not achieved. It was partly because of higher levels of family income, which provided a firm base for aspiration, and it was partly because of the evident fact that there were more and better opportunities for the products of higher education than there were for high school graduates.

It is these forces which produced increases in enrollments at an annual rate which, year in and year out, steadily exceeded the rate of population increase. It is the same forces which are producing increasing enrollments in the thirteenth and fourteenth grades, approaching, year by year, fulfillment of the observation by the President's Commission that 49 per cent of the population has the mental ability to complete fourteen years of schooling. It is the same forces which are steadily pushing toward meeting the Commission's further suggestion that 32 per cent of the population has the mental ability to complete an advanced liberal or specialized professional education.

Of course, other factors have operated in relation to these forces. Employers have encouraged formal education. Professional associations have consistently raised educational standards. Schools have become better, and they have been better articulated with higher education. The incentives for higher education have been publicized, and there has been much effective recruiting.

But these factors by themselves would not have produced the stimulus to open higher education to more than 50 per cent of the age group. This stimulus comes from another major force: the political decision to implement the words of the Democratic platform —in other words, to establish educational opportunity for all without regard to race, place of residence, ability to pay, or educational objectives.

Such a powerful decision brings in its train a whole new educational development which rests on the fact that most of those whom the decision affects have minimal educational opportunities. It is true that many of them would under normal circumstances complete an education, but the overwhelming majority of them either have no access to institutions, or could not or would not continue their education if they had the opportunity.

For such students—and their number includes many from bitter poverty—motivation and aspiration must be induced to avoid their otherwise certain candidacy for early dropout. Methods must be found to compensate for the educational deprivation which the environment of home and school have added to their other woes.

New institutions must be created, placed in the inner communities, near the students and the problems. This too will have an effect on student enrollments, for enrollments go up when institutions are near at hand. New types of programs, including some which will be outside the present definitions of higher education, must be planned. Teachers must acquire the patience and skill to deal with the fearful, the defiant, and the neglected as well as with the under-educated.

In this quick sketch of needs and probabilities, it is too easy to skip over the travail involved in accomplishing what will be re-quired. Even if the developments were to proceed under the ad-ministration of the educational system, as was the case with the quick expansion from 1945 to 1950, there would be problems enough to make life interesting. Education of teachers, construc-tion of buildings, curriculum reform for the lower schools, cur-riculum building in the new institutions, the development of learn-ing materials, the training of administrators, and the performance of other exercises too numerous to mention will all be difficult. But we add to them direct political intervention in the interest of creating totally new forms of higher education to deal with a new task—the task of educating those whom we have so far failed to educate, and bringing opportunity to those to whom we have so far denied opportunity.

Political intervention brings a new form of action to educational development—abrupt provision of money; demands for immediate results; pressures as to locations, staffing, and relationships to other institutions. These are special skills to be learned. We have ex-pected the arrival of universal higher education, but not so soon, and we find ourselves only beginning to plan even as we are on the eve of building.

The papers which follow, presenting a wide range of viewpoints on these crucial questions, are early contributions to the literature of planning and building. We may be certain that there will be others before we reach the date when the statistics of the Office of Education prove the achievement of universal higher education.

Earl J. McGrath

Contents

This book is the product of a conference on the implications of universal higher education, held in November, 1964, at the Dorado Beach Hotel, Dorado, Puerto Rico. The conference was planned and convened by the Institute of Higher Education, Teachers College, Columbia University, and supported by a grant from the Fund for the Advancement of Education.

The following individuals, of whom eleven contributed papers, attended the conference:

Dr. Paul R. Anderson, Vice President for Academic Affairs, Temple University

Dr. Frank H. Bowles, Vice President, the Fund for the Advancement of Education

Dr. Henry S. Commager, Professor, Amherst College

Dr. Leland C. DeVinney, Associate Director for Humanities and Social Sciences, Rockefeller Foundation

Dr. Clarence H. Faust, President, the Fund for the Advancement of Education

Dr. William J. Haggerty, President, New Paltz State College

Dr. Algo D. Henderson, Director, Center for the Study of Higher Education, University of Michigan

Mr. Harold Howe II, Executive Director, Learning Institute of North Carolina

Dr. Dexter M. Keezer, Economic Adviser, McGraw-Hill Book Company

Dr. Thomas R. McConnell, Chairman, Center for the Study of Higher Education, University of California at Berkeley

Dr. Earl McGrath, Executive Officer, Institute of Higher Education, Teachers College, Columbia University

Dr. Daniel P. Moynihan, Assistant Secretary of Labor, Department of Labor

Dr. C. Robert Pace, Professor, University of California at Los Angeles

Dr. Richard Pearson, President, College Entrance Examination Board

Mr. A. D. C. Peterson, Director, Department of Education, University of Oxford

Mr. Alan Pifer, Vice President, Carnegie Corporation of New York

Dr. Angel Quintero Alfaro, Secretary of Education, Commonwealth of Puerto Rico

Dr. James W. Reynolds, Professor, University of Texas

Dr. William G. Ryan, President, Seton Hill College

Dr. Nevitt Sanford, Director, Center for the Study of Human Problems, Stanford University

Social, Political, Economic, and Personal Consequences

HENRY STEELE COMMAGER, *Professor of History and American Studies, Amherst College*

One of the things that has struck all of us, again and again in recent years, is the way in which the obvious and the inevitable seem to take us by surprise. We have known for years that our population was moving to the cities and that our cities were not properly organized or governed to cope with the new population and its problems, but we have heretofore done nothing about it. We have known for years that the toll of our automobiles is as high as that of a major war—something like forty thousand lives a year—and that this recurrent catastrophe is caused by factors that are avoidable, but we have as yet done nothing about it. We have known for years that China would some day have the atomic bomb, but when that day arrived we acted as if it had all been the best-kept secret in history and as if we had to readjust our thinking all at once.

We have known for years, too, that the baby boom that set in shortly after World War II would surely reach the schools and the colleges, but we permitted ourselves to drift along and be taken by surprise with each new demand upon our educational enterprise, until now, twenty years after the war, we find ourselves unprepared to cope with even the material problems of education.

It is reassuring, then, that the groups and skills represented here should be taking thought for what is pretty clearly ahead in the next decade—the extension of schooling for almost everyone for an additional two years. Let us consider the historical background and the implications of this prospect.

I

Let us begin this inquiry with the observation that the eighteenth century took two things for granted about human nature: first, it was corrupt; and second, it was universal and stable. Man was everywhere corrupt and depraved, a creature of interests and passions, of ambition and greed, of selfishness and envy; man was everywhere irrational. This had always been true—history proved that—and it would continue to be true, for human nature did not change. That was the second great principle to which almost everyone subscribed: human nature was the same everywhere and had always been the same. It was for this reason that the philosophers and the historians were so ready to draw their illustrations from Persia or Greece, from the South Sea Islands or the forests of Canada, from Italy, France, or England—it was all one. There was no reason to suppose that nature would change and no reason to suppose that man would change. These were the fixed elements with which the philosophers started, and it was unsafe ever to get very far away from them.

Yet all was not desperate, not by any means, for the doctrine that man was everywhere the same, and everywhere ruled by immutable laws of nature, had its encouraging aspect. Man was a child of nature, but he was also a child of reason, for reason was part of nature. Progress was possible—the eighteenth century had really invented that concept—but it was possible only within the accepted pattern, for clearly nothing could break the pattern of nature or even the pattern of history. Progress was to be achieved by conforming to nature and nature's laws—a familiar phrase even in the New World. Reason could discover these laws, and persuade man to conform to them. The prospect, to be sure, was not particularly encouraging (that was Voltaire's conclusion in *Candide*), for although the philosophers and scientists could discover the laws, rulers were singularly unprepared to conform to them.

This was, in substantial measure, the philosophy which Europeans brought with them to the New World, and which, as Americans, they were presumed to subscribe to in the eighteenth century. It was not a philosophy which encouraged the belief that the American experience would differ in any marked degree from the European, or that America's fate would be more benign than that of other nations. It was still the same universe, controlled by the same laws. The great chain of being obtained in the New World as in the Old, and man's place in it was of course the same. Human nature, too, remained stubbornly the same. That was what John Adams argued in his magisterial *Defense of the Constitution;* that was what Hamilton made clear in *The Federalist Papers;* that was what a legion of statesmen asserted in their discussions of the new state and national constitutions. There might, to be sure, be some room for maneuver, but not enough to provide any basis for hope for revolutionary change.

Sometime in the eighteenth century a new theory emerged—one which we can, with some propriety, designate "American," perhaps the *first* American principle. We can call it, for convenience, the theory of environmentalism, or of change, or even of progress. It was this: man was not really depraved or virtuous, but a creature of circumstances—a point of view which found support in the philosophy of "the Great Mr. Locke," and which seemed, besides, the common sense of the matter. Depravity, corruption, crime, vice, superstition, ignorance, folly—all these were products not of nature but of history, that is they were man-made, not God-made. Granted that in the Old World man appeared corrupt and ignorant, was that not because for centuries he had been weighed down by the tyranny of rulers, the might of soldiers, the superstition of priests; because for centuries he had been ground down in poverty, misery, and ignorance? Was it not because in the Old World man had never really been vouchsafed a chance to use those talents with which God and nature had endowed him?

But in the New World all this might be changed. For it was *really* a New World—it took a long time for that to sink in. Here, for perhaps the first time in modern history, man could escape the tyranny of the past, the tyranny of power, superstition, poverty, and ignorance. Here, for perhaps the first time, he could stand on his own feet, a free man exercising all his God-given faculties. Here there would be no tyranny of state, for he was the state; no tyranny of church, for he made the church; no tyranny of the military and of war, for there was no military, and the New World was to be free of those wars so long the curse of the Old. And there would be no tyranny of want, for no people in history had ever enjoyed such abundance—room enough, as Jefferson said, for our descendants to the thousandth and thousandth generation, and all enjoying the rich bounty of nature. All this promised to take care of a good part of the problem of depravity.

It did not, however, take care of the problems of ignorance and of folly. Those problems were to be taken care of by education. No wonder education so quickly became the American religion; no wonder all the Founding Fathers were educators—Franklin, Washington, John Adams, John Dickinson, Noah Webster, and, above all, Thomas Jefferson. Education was to be the instrument of change, change of nature (science was to make that possible) and of human nature. Education was to be what religion had been in a less secular age—the chief instrument for the regeneration of the human race.

It is superfluous to rehearse what is so familiar: the interest, the zeal, the passion for education which animated the generation of the Founding Fathers. All will remember how John Adams wrote provisions for education, and for the support of Harvard College, into his Constitution. All will recall how Franklin and Dickinson and Benjamin Rush founded learned societies and colleges and libraries in that Pennsylvania which was the eighteenth-century utopia. All are familiar with the story of Jefferson's educational interests. How appropriate that the greatest of American democrats should also be the greatest of American educators! And how touching was that provision written into the Northwest Ordinance: "Religion, morality, and knowledge being necessary to good government and the happiness of mankind, schools and the means of education shall forever be encouraged." Less familiar perhaps are some of the rapt poetic tributes to the role of education in the New World: Joel Barlow's *Vision of Columbus*, for example:

> In no blest land has science rear'd her fame
> And fixed so firm her wide extended reign;
> Each rustic here that turns the furrow'd soil,
> The maid, the youth, that ply mechanic toil,
> In freedom nurs'd, in useful arts inured,
> Know their just claims and see their rights secured.

Note that reference to the useful arts.

There is that other Connecticut wit, Timothy Dwight:

> How bless'd this heaven distinguished land,
> Where schools in every hamlet stand:
> Far spread the beams of learning bright,
> And every child enjoys the light,
> At school, beneath a faithful guide,
> In teaching skill'd, of morals tried. . . .
> For on this microscopic plan
> If form'd the wise, the useful man,
> Let him a taste for books inspire,

While you to nurse the young desire
A social library procure
And open knowledge to the poor.

How interesting that everyone, in Europe and America alike, agreed that the American people were the most generally enlightened on the globe, that here in these little American settlements a larger proportion of the people were educated, a larger proportion read their Bible, and almanacs, and newspapers than elsewhere on the globe. How remarkable that this uprooted and transplanted people, scattered along a far-flung frontier, should have created nine colleges before independence, and seven during the years of war and postwar confusion. How extraordinary that Jefferson's principle that self-government depended on an educated electorate should have been vindicated with such unprecedented promptness: the constituency was enlightened, and self-government did work. How impressive the level of public discussion of great political questions such as independence, or the state and Federal Constitutions, in town meetings, the state conventions, the Constitutional Convention, the press. Imagine publishing *The Federalist Papers* in our newspapers today.

II

Obviously an education which was required not merely to fit into some preexisting scheme of things, continue tradition, support the *status quo*, but to regenerate man and remake society, would have to be new and different. From the beginning American education was rooted in Old World experience; how could it be otherwise? But from the beginning, too, it departed from that experience, and the divergence grew sharper with the passing years. To this day Americans expect their schools to do a very different job from that which Old World schools perform; to this day they expect schools to do almost everything, which is one reason that they are continually disappointed in them.

In a broad sense the schools were to be the chief instruments for change in the New World, change in man and change in society. They were to be the chief instruments for the growth of democracy, equality, and freedom, and of morality as well. In many quarters they are still regarded in this light; that is one reason it seems to be assumed that if there are no prayers in school, prayer is at an end, that if God is banished from the school, then God is leaving us.

American schools were, and are, required to do a hundred and one things not expected of European schools: this is an old story, and a current one. Imagine a French *lycée* teaching driver training; imagine a German *gymnasium* teaching social dancing; imagine a Swedish high school teaching basketball, or cheerleadership!

The contrast between Old World and New grows sharper the higher we go on the educational ladder. So much was expected of the colleges and universities that they came in time not to be merely an American version of a familiar European institution, but a new kind of institution: a multiversity, not a university (I know I am using the terms wrongly but so did Clark Kerr), an institution whose business it is to supply all the needs of society and to provide training in all the skills which society thinks it needs, from mastery of atomic physics to mastery of hotel operations, from knowledge of Greek literature to knowledge of advertising copy, from training for medicine or law to training for athletic directorships. How appropriate it was that one of the greatest of American educational statesmen, Andrew D. White, should undertake to create a university where any person could study any subject. To the European, with his traditional standards of what constituted the domain of the university, much of this was absurd; to the American, impatient with traditional restrictions, the American policies were the common sense of the matter. It is not irrelevant to add that European universities today (like European schools) are adapting themselves, increasingly, to the American model rather than the other way around.

What Americans recognized, almost by instinct, and what Europe is only slowly coming to recognize, is the immense range and variety of abilities necessary for the efficient functioning of modern society, and the potential role of schools and universities in providing these abilities. During most of the eighteenth and nineteenth centuries Europeans persisted in using their schools for the re-creation of traditional skills and the perpetuation of inherited values. In the nineteenth century the Germans added research but even this was to be confined to orthodox subjects. The university was, in very fact, the citadel of tradition, its function to preserve the past and to train the young along familiar lines. Americans, most of whom (after 1640) came from groups unfamiliar with classical academic patterns, and whose society and economy demanded very different patterns, had no misgivings about using their schools and universities to do the things they wanted done, no misgivings and no embarrassments. How illuminating that almost from the beginning American colleges were more concerned to attract a wide cross section of society than to preserve religious orthodoxy, and that even colonial colleges, like the College of New Jersey (Princeton) and Rhode Island (Brown), provided in their charters for representation from various religious dominations. Contrast this to Oxford and Cambridge Universities where dissenters were rigorously excluded from student body and faculty until the last quarter of the nineteenth century. How illuminating, too, that so many of the early American educators, like Franklin and Benjamin Rush, should have opposed the classical pattern of education and championed, even at this stage, education for commerce and business, while Oxford and Cambridge did not give up their Latin requirements until the 1950s.

There is, to be sure, a sobering qualification to all these generalizations, one which gives us pause in our animadversions of Old-World and our celebration of New-World education. It is this: the Old World had, after all, any number of institutions to do the various tasks and supply the various skills required by its society, and did not have to rely wholly on schools and universities. The Old World could allow the Academy to continue in its ancient ways, and mostly did so, until the middle of the nineteenth century or later; it could permit the four faculties largely to monopolize university education; ignore much of modern science and almost all of modern technology; indulge the extravagance of academic resources concentrated, or wasted, on a very small segment of a social elite. After all the Court, the aristocracy, the Church, the Army, the Navy, the Temples and Inns of Court, the museums, the libraries, the technical institutes, the highly structured society, and—in other areas— the merchant guilds, the great Companies (who founded their own schools), the apprenticeship system, even—in ways not wholly duplicated in America—the family, with its traditions of authority and its close-knit social and business interrelationships—all these stood ready to prepare each new generation for its familiar functions and duties. If there was no education, excepting the everlasting discipline of drudgery, for farmers and laborers, there was general agreement that these classes had nothing to contribute and had no place in the educational scheme of things.

The situation in the New World was the opposite of this in almost every respect. Here there were few of those familiar institutions prepared to carry on the social arrangements of the past and scarcely even communities, in the Old World sense of the term. Inevitably the schools were called on to do almost all the things that a score of institutions did abroad, and we have been calling on them for these services ever since. And here, too, in this new society there were a great many more things to be done, in a rather simple way, practical and material things, as well as intellectual, scientific, and even moral things. Once again much of the burden for seeing that they were done was put on the schools and, a bit later, on colleges and universities. And here, finally, were no class distinctions, none that mattered anyway, except those of color, and the whole of the white population was supposed to be involved and absorbed in the educational enterprise.

All this is familiar. In America the school was called on to teach the most elementary things, things which every European school would take for granted—a single language, for example. It was called on to teach those social habits and practices taught mostly by family and society in the Old World. It was called on to create or foment a sense of nationalism; that was familiar enough, in an overt way, in countries like France and Germany in the nineteenth century, but the American task was at once broader and more delicate. It was called on to teach morals, a subject which the Church and the family took care of in Europe. In many communities, particularly those with a substantial immigrant population, it was called on to teach, vicariously, the parents.

For these reasons, and others, American schools at almost every level early developed into general-purpose institutions. How interesting that the term "general education" should have caught the fancy of Americans, and how interesting, too, that in this country it should harbor some of the ambiguities that Americans read into the word "university." Schools, and universities too, were called on to prepare the young for everything in general: for the professions, for industry, for farming, for business, for nursing, for the stock market, for marriage, for citizenship, for society, even for life. No other educational system on the globe is required to be quite this eclectic or this ambitious. The wonder is not that American schools so often fail, but that they so often succeed in these miscellaneous aims.

This eclectic program had important by-products. One of them, very much in the American grain, was that it did in fact raise the general level of education, and even of culture, if we may use that ambiguous word, with most unexpected consequences. Unexpected? That most perspicacious of observers, De Tocqueville, in *Democracy in America*, foresaw what would happen, and rejoiced in it.

When I survey this countless multitude of beings, shaped in each other's likeness, amid whom nothing rises and nothing falls, the sight of such universal uniformity saddens and chills me, and I am tempted to regret that state of society which has ceased to be. When the world was full of men of great importance and extreme insignificance, of great wealth and extreme poverty, of great learning and extreme ignorance, I turned aside from the latter to fix my observation on the former alone, who gratified my sympathies. But I admit that this gratification arose from my own weakness; it is because I am unable to see at once all that is around me that I am allowed thus to select and separate the objects of my predilection from among so many others. Such is not the case with that Almighty and Eternal Being whose gaze necessarily includes the whole of created things and who surveys distinctly, though all at once, mankind and man.

We may naturally believe that it is not the singular prosperity of the few, but the greater well-being of all that is most pleasing in the sight of the Creator and Preserver of men. What appears to me to be man's decline is, to His eye, advancement; what afflicts me is acceptable to Him. A state of equality is perhaps less elevated, but it is more just: and its justice constitutes its greatness and its beauty. I would strive, then, to raise myself to this point of the divine contemplation and thence to view and to judge the concerns of men.[1]

Even now, more than a century after De Tocqueville wrote, this point of view is not everywhere adopted, or taken for granted, and there are still those who fail to see either justice or beauty in the American attempt to lift the general level of culture by universal education just as there will be those who will fail to see either justice or beauty in the proposals to expand education beyond its present boundaries and to extend it to millions still denied or deprived of its potentialities.

Another product, or by-product, of universal education was that it did help discover talent among the "mute inglorious Miltons," and did encourage the most varied kinds of creativity.

To this day many Europeans, and particularly many English, cling to the notion that education—certainly "higher education"—should indeed be limited to a natural aristocracy, and that that natural aristocracy is, almost by definition, small. There are persuasive practical reasons why the English are reluctant to expand higher education, but behind and controlling these is the widespread conviction that there are not many young people who are capable of taking advantage of it. They are persuaded that their elitist educational system has worked well, and, though less confidently, that it will continue to work well; they look with grave misgivings on the American experiments in mass education and admonish each other to avoid the error of American ways. This is not the place to deal with the English view, but it is relevant to note that the United States was the first to challenge it. The American theory is that gold is where you find it—in short, that talent is evenly distributed throughout the whole population, and that it is, on the whole, generously distributed. The American position is that talent is not something given, and fixed, but something that can be discovered, encouraged, and developed.

Of all educational philosophers it was the American Lester Ward who argued most persuasively this principle of the ubiquity and universality of talent, and the role of education and of the state in discovering and

---

[1] Alexis de Tocqueville, *Democracy in America* (New York: Vintage Books, Random House, Inc., 1961), vol. II, chap. VII, pp. 350–351.

encouraging such talent. He was, you will remember, characteristically American in his own universality and his ambition. A poor boy who grew up on the Illinois and Iowa frontier, he had little formal education, and most of that bad, but it did not occur to him that this mischance should exclude him from the ranks of the learned, and he became in time perhaps the most deeply and variously learned man in America—botanist, geologist, paleontologist, and founder and leader of American sociology. He was at the same time one of the most original and profound of all our educational philosophers, and takes rank here with such giants as Jefferson, Horace Mann, Jane Addams, and John Dewey. His philosophy, set forth first in *Dynamic Sociology* (1883), more elaborately in *The Psychic Factors of Civilization* a decade later, and then in *Applied Sociology* (1906) is by now orthodox enough, at least in the United States. All progress, Ward insisted, comes through art, not nature—here we are back with the Founding Fathers and their rejection of fixed laws. Nature is wasteful, slow, and indifferent; man is economical: he speeds up the natural processes, and is himself inextricably involved in the process. Man has survived, and created civilization, by triumphing over nature. Indeed, civilization *is* the triumph of art over nature; it is, precisely, artificial. All civilization comes from the deliberate intervention by man in the processes of nature. Now what directs this intervention, and what assurance is there that it will be benevolent rather than malign? The answer is simple and unambiguous. Government directs the intervention—government is indeed organized intervention—and government is therefore the most important of man's instruments for creating civilization. And as for the assurance that intervention will be benevolent, that must come from education. The function of education is to achieve and prosper civilization. It is a function of any society, for on it depends survival and progress.

What this meant, as Ward never ceased to point out, was that society could not afford to waste any of its intellectual or psychic talents. Heretofore it had always done so, and one reason that progress had not advanced more rapidly was this waste. Ward was convinced, and on scientific grounds, that talent was to be found everywhere, and everywhere, too, in equal abundance—among the poor as among the rich, among Negroes as among whites, among the perishing and dangerous classes as among the respectable. Certainly it was to be found as richly among women as among men, indeed rather more among women than men; Ward's law of gynecocracy, or the natural superiority of the female over the male sex, took care of that! Ward rejected *in toto*, then, an elitist philosophy of education, as he rejected *in toto* the notion that government should play a merely passive role in civilization.

These are the principles on which most Americans acted, almost instinctively, from the beginning, and on which they still act, though with less confidence than in the past. A new society, one without the historic institutions of older societies, needs to find varied and disparate talents to do the most miscellaneous jobs. That means that it must look everywhere for talent. The responsibility is social, that is to say governmental. If the talent can be found, and utilized, there is some ground for hope that it may suffice to prosper civilization; if it cannot, the prospect is bleak.

Of course, the country paid a price for this enterprise of educating almost everybody in almost everything, for using the educational establishment for broad social purposes, for rejecting Old World concepts of culture and of an intellectual elite.

What specifically were some of the costs of this approach to education? First, it meant that almost all education was to be the same, and the tendency was (there were exceptions) to level down rather than to level up. Second, this often meant low standards or no perceptible standards in secondary or higher education. There is no better illustration of this than the legal requirement which still obtains in a good many states—Ohio and Missouri, for example—that institutions of "higher" learning admit any graduate of a state high school. Third, it meant that "formal" education was less important than informal. The business of the high school and even of college was almost incidentally to train the mind. It was, very much, to "adapt" the young to their society, or to provide common social experiences, or to train for jobs, or to serve as a marriage mart. We may think this is a thing of the past, but only this year a *New York Times* survey discovered that over 50 per cent of students planning to go on to college placed the social advantages of education first in the hierarchy of values to be derived from college, and a substantial number placed the academic last. Fourth, it encouraged the notion that schools exist in large part for the benefit of the parents, and of the immediate community, rather than for the benefit of the students. Thus at almost every level schools were expected to adapt the young to their society; the prospect of confronting young people with ideas alien to society has commonly filled parents with alarm. Society has acquired the habit of "using" the schools to teach whatever society happens to be interested in: to teach "values," to teach citizenship, to teach the dangers of communism, to teach laudable things like world history or world literature, to teach science when the Russians are ahead, and private enterprise when the welfare-staters threaten us, and Christianity when the Supreme Court goes wrong. Fifth, the notion that education is a quantitative experience, consists of so many years, or so many courses, rather than of an ascertainable body of skills or of knowledge, persists, and this, too, has made its way into "higher" education. Only American colleges are organized around courses, attendance, majors and minors, grades, and other quantitative factors rather than around tests of professional competence.

All this is explicable in the light of the past.

But all of it really belongs to the past.

III

We are all prisoners of that past, perhaps more so collectively than individually, and perhaps more in the realm of ideas than in the realm of the practical. It is easier to change the social attitudes of an individual student, for example, than of a fraternity, and while every professor rejoices in radical thoughts about the curriculum, the faculty, collectively, almost always has sober second thoughts. American education, at all levels, is still conditioned by the body of beliefs and practices which emerged at independence to meet the special needs of this special society and to adapt to the special circumstances of the New World. Both those needs and those circumstances have changed, profoundly. Educational principles and practices have not changed to meet the new circumstances. A new nation was growing, higgedly-piggedly, a nation made up of the most diverse elements, a nation called on to conquer immense new territories, to create a new body politic and a new society, to raise standards of living, to vindicate democracy and equality and religious freedom—that nation could not be too exacting or too scrupulous in the means it used. It took what was at hand, used what it had, wastefully and even recklessly, in education as in other natural resources. It used the schools, used them for purposes not really educational. Yet on the whole this worked, and because it worked we have tended to go on pretty much the same way, using the schools for whatever comes to hand, using them wastefully and recklessly.

It is in the light of this history that we are called on to consider the proposal of an additional two years of schooling for all. This proposal comes at a time when everything seems to point to the necessity of additional training to equip the young for the kind of society and economy in which they will live. It comes, too, at a time when the demands on the time and energies of the young are heavier than in the past, and when there is, therefore, strong pressure for saving time, for condensing rather than expanding what has been the normal educational experience.

In the eighteenth century young men completed their formal education at eighteen or nineteen, read law or medicine for two years or so in some office, and were prepared to take their place in the life of the community in their early twenties. Now, what with the prolongation of youth, the increasing demands of society on the services of the young—military, for instance—the requirements of professional and scientific training, and the continuous and cumulative increase in knowledge, young men (and now women) are rarely prepared to begin their careers before their late twenties. We have prolonged life by a decade or more, but it is doubtful whether those who survive into manhood do in fact have any more years of service to their society than did their forebears in the eighteenth century.

Preparation for effective service in the kind of society we are forming will, then, make ever greater demands on the young. At just this time we indulge most of them in a kind of mass frittering away of their time and talents, a frittering away which neither they nor society can afford.

There is now every reason to believe that we will need—and require—an additional two years of schooling for most of our young men and women. A high school education is now what a grade school education was a generation ago; a college education is little better than a high school education was then. Even now those with only a high school education are at a desperate disadvantage in the marketplace; that disadvantage will grow. It is unnecessary to spell out other familiar considerations: the technological revolution which will manage with a relatively smaller labor force; the probability that organized labor will prefer to eliminate competition of both the young and the old; the growing complexity of the economy which will require ever greater expertise.

But if we are to add two years to the present academic offering, or requirement, to what should we devote those two years? Should we consider the two years as essentially an extension of high school? Should we consider them as preparatory to senior college? Should we devote the two years to new—or old-new—forms of education, vocational, for example? In short, should the additional years be assimilated to secondary or to higher education or to something quite new?

The American instinct is for a quantitative solution to most problems, even educational problems. We tend to add on school years, as we have in the past, without giving much thought to the nature of the experience.

But if it is merely two more years of schooling that we need, we can get it in the twelve years that we now consign to elementary and high school. The majority of junior and senior high schools fritter away two or three of the six years which they devote to education. Graduates of European schools—English, French, German, Swiss, Scandinavian—learn by the age of eighteen what few of our students learn until they reach the third year of college. This does not apply to the products of our exceptional schools, the Bronx High School of Science, for example, or the New Trier school; nor am I considering what might be called nonacademic education—the kind of thing which American youngsters learn (sometimes) on the playing fields or in student government, or student newspapers or orchestras, but it does apply pretty generally.

What is the explanation of this?

We sometimes overlook the obvious. We ascribe to tradition, or to a high standard of selectivity, or perhaps even to talent, what has a much simpler explanation. One reason, perhaps the chief reason, why the graduate of the English Public School, the French *lycée,* the German *gymnasium,* is well ahead of his American cousin is that, by the age of eighteen he has had two or three more years of actual schooling. The European high school student customarily attends school until five o'clock each day, five and one-half days a week, and for ten or ten and one-half months a year. Add all that up and you quickly get your two years.

There are doubtless other considerations that should be kept in mind: European schools concentrate on the intellectual and academic job far more than do most American schools; on the whole, European secondary schools teach a privileged group—those from middle- and upper-class families with some cultural background; competition is sharper abroad than here, competition for grades, and for entrance into the university.

These things, rather than native ability, account for the relative backwardness of American secondary education, account for it—and determine it.

There are, of course, extenuations and even justifications for the American practices and malpractices. These are for the most part rooted in history and we are the prisoners of history. But this history is no longer particularly valid. The school day, week, and year were originally adapted to the needs of a rural society where children were expected to go home and do the chores and to help put in and get out the crops; they are no longer expected to do this, but the school year has not changed perceptibly. The habit of prolonging youth was originally rooted in a revolt against Old World habits of child labor and an indulgence in a pleasanter image of childhood than was possible abroad: it is no longer necessary to indulge or pamper the young. Relatively easy standards of education were rooted in the interesting fact that in America alone it could be taken for granted that each new generation was better educated and smarter than the last. This meant that the young held the whip hand, as it were, set their own standards, which could always be counted on to be somewhat higher than those of the past but never too exacting. This is no longer true. The habit of putting social interests first and academic interests second was rooted in those historical functions of the school which we have already considered: the schools are no longer the sole or the chief agencies for fulfilling these functions, and can now devote themselves to academic and intellectual pursuits.

We can, if we will, incorporate the equivalent of two additional years of schooling into the present twelve years of school, not for all students perhaps, but for a large proportion of them. We must avoid the temptation to make these two additional years which we are now planning merely an extension of high school, academically or socially. To do this would continue that waste of resources and of talents in which we have so long indulged ourselves, and this just at a time when everything urges us to speed up our educational processes. To do this would be not only academically but psychologically pernicious, confining men and women of nineteen or twenty to high school activities.

It is probable that the additional two years should be not only a different but a separate educational experience. Two-year colleges, or academies—perhaps we will have to have a new name for them—should be assimilated to higher rather than to secondary education, as their students should be part of the adult rather than the adolescent world. In the making is the use of the two-year colleges for a great variety of educational purposes. Some may provide what the Danish Folk high schools so magnificently provided in the nineteenth century, education both cultural and technical. Some will doubtless be college preparatory, as are so many of the community colleges in the California state system, and if they can and do function well in this arena they may relieve the universities of the burden of teaching elementary subjects and permit them to begin where almost all British and European universities begin— with what is generally our third year of college. This, in turn, may enable some of our universities to build on the state colleges, and devote themselves exclusively to graduate and professional work. Still others of the two-year colleges will, let us hope, fill one of the notorious gaps in our educational enterprise by training the young to technical and semiprofessional careers. They can supply us with nurses, electricians, automobile mechanics, accountants, skilled farmers, small-town and school librarians, playground and recreation directors, teachers of art and music in the schools and in adult education programs—for the thousand different vocations and semiprofessions that are now so badly served.

Frank P. Merlo writes, in "The Burgeoning Community College": [2]

[2] *Saturday Review,* December 19, 1964, pp. 51–52.

By 1975, at the latest, it is estimated that about one-half of the labor force will be employed in managerial, semi-professional, technical, and sales positions. Academic preparation for most of these positions will require education beyond high school but not the baccalaureate degree. The two-year college, then, is the logical institution to train this half of the labor force and it is expected that most of this manpower will be trained by the community colleges. . . .

If the United States is to keep abreast of the demands, both economic and social, as well as the developments resulting from increasing and accelerating technological change, provision must be made to offer more technical, health, and business programs. It is expected that the Higher Education Facilities Act of 1963, which provides over $50.6 million a year for two-year colleges, will help community colleges to construct, rehabilitate, or improve the more expensive technical facilities.

IV

The extension of schooling to the age of twenty is consistent with the American tradition, and with American faith in the sovereign effect of education in our kind of society. It is, too, consistent with the demands of the new economy and technology which the next generation will have to confront. Because we are, inevitably, creatures of the past, our tendency is to use each additional year of schooling as a mere quantitative extension of previous years, and to fit our schools into existing and familiar patterns. That habit was not unjustified in the nineteenth century, but the justification for it has disappeared. We are confronted, in planning for the next generation, with a demand for more radical reforms. We are required to reconsider the functioning of our whole educational enterprise from, roughly, the age of twelve on; to look at it not so much in historical context as in the context of current and future requirements. Just as the problems of Western Europe are coming to be more and more like ours, so our situation is coming to be more and more like that of Western Europe. While they are developing a classless society and recognizing the necessity of an immense extension and expansion of their educational enterprise at all levels, we are coming to realize that we have a highly complex and sophisticated society, with many agencies for carrying on the large educational enterprise, and that we can at last afford to concentrate the formal resources of our schools on the academic and intellectual task, in order to prepare the next generation for a world far more exacting than the world of the nineteenth century.

Here are some of the implications of a program of fourteen years of education for all: (1) A tightening up and speeding up of education in grades seven to twelve. Every community should be expected to have some schools, or some divisions of comprehensive schools, which do substantially what the better schools of Western Europe have so long been doing. (2) An increasing concentration on the academic job and a gradual sloughing off of nonacademic activities and inactivities now so familiar—athletic and social. This in turn will require (3) that the many other agencies in the community now looking for useful work will undertake some of the nonacademic jobs which have in the past been foisted off on the schools. Let the American Legion and the Rotary Club or insurance companies take on driver training; let the women's clubs teach social dancing; let the students run their own games and sports—perhaps all dads' clubs should be abolished, and all those pernicious community organizations dedicated to inspiring big-time football and basketball for the young. (4) The other side of this is that the two years which are to be added onto our current educational enterprise should provide a new educational experience, and should be used for other than high school purposes. The new colleges should emulate neither the high school nor the university but find their own character. What a pity if those who control them should suppose it necessary to copy the high schools in their athletic programs, or the colleges in their fraternity and sorority organizations. (5) This calls for something neither original nor surprising: experimentation. We have already a good body of experience, American and European, to fall back on. In all likelihood we will now need statewide, and perhaps even national, planning to assure that we do get a variety of experiments. Such planning should not make for uniformity; quite the contrary. Uniformity comes voluntarily in our country—De Tocqueville saw that back in the 1830s—as communities ape one another. Perhaps only centralized planning can assure that experimentation so essential to the prosperity of this new enterprise.

There is no doubt that the national government will find itself involved in this enterprise, both on the academic and the financial levels. The pattern here may well be the familiar one of our agricultural experiment stations, first launched in 1887. There are now some fifty of these, largely supported by Federal funds, working on a wide variety of agricultural experiments and programs under both state and national supervision. Another pattern is in process of being worked out by the Health, Education and Welfare Department—support of the most miscellaneous kinds of scientific investigation in colleges and universities, and proposed experimentation in the teaching of language, history, geography, and economics. We can learn something, too, from British and European experience: from the teacher training and technical colleges of Britain, from the trade and technological schools of Germany, from the Folk high schools, now vastly changed, of Denmark. The principle of universal education is rooted in history, but the application of that principle, in the past, was vastly experimental, and the application of that principle, for the future, should be no less bold and imaginative than in the past.

Daniel Burnham, the master planner of the world's Columbian Exposition, and of the plans for Chicago and for Washington, used to say "make no little plans." If we are to extend universal education by two years, let us be sure that we make no little plans. Let us not permit the potentialities of this immense forward leap to go by default.

State Systems of Higher Education

THOMAS R. McCONNELL, Chairman,
Center for the Study of Higher Education,
University of California, Berkeley

During his campaign, President Lyndon Johnson declared that every qualified student should have the opportunity for education beyond the high school. We may assume that the limiting adjective "qualified" will be interpreted very broadly. Writing on "The Enlargement of Opportunity in Higher Education," Tickton said recently that the people of the United States now expect that virtually all youth will enter some kind of collegiate institution. This, he continued, clearly implements every major policy statement on higher education from that of the Truman Commission of 1947 to President Kennedy's statement on education in 1963. Now we have President Johnson's intention to make education available for every young person to his highest level of ability and accomplishment.[1]

When President Truman's Commission declared in 1947 that "The time has come to make education through the 14th grade available in the same way that high school education is now available," many critics charged that the Commission was more interested in quantity than quality, that its proposal threatened the colleges with "a tide of mediocrity," and that the

[1] S. G. Tickton, "The Enlargement of Opportunity in Higher Education," *Educational Record,* vol. 45, no. 1, Winter, 1964, pp. 86–87.

Commission would swell the number of incompetents in American colleges and justify it under the slogan of "equality of opportunity." [2] Actually the Committee hedged its proposal for making formal education beyond high school available to all by stating that "At least 49 per cent of our population has the mental ability to complete 14 years of schooling with a curriculum of general and vocational studies that should lead either to gainful employment or to further study at a more advanced level." The Commission asserted that by 1960 a minimum of 4,600,000 young people should be enrolled beyond the twelfth grade. To the charge that any such enrollment would weaken educational standards all along the line, other critics added the assertion that any such enrollment prediction was fantastically improbable. The figure was, in fact, not reached by 1960, but by the fall of 1964 the Commission's estimate was exceeded.

HIGHER EDUCATION FOR ALL

In 1964 the Educational Policies Commission was unequivocal in recommending education beyond the high school for everyone. "Unless opportunity for education beyond the high school can be made available to all, while at the same time increasing the effectiveness of the elementary and secondary schools," the Commission said, "then the American promise of individual dignity and freedom cannot be extended to all." The Commission reiterated the Truman Commission's recommendation that the thirteenth and fourteenth years of education in public colleges should be free of cost to the student. "Not only must there be no tuition charges," said the Commission, "but if there is to be equal educational opportunity for youth, the student who has no public college close by must be provided with transportation to and from the nearest one, or with the means of living away from home." The Educational Policies Commission also repeated the other Commission's assertion that education at this level must be accessible to all, regardless of sex, racial, religious, cultural, or economic barriers, and concluded its report with the following paragraph:

The goal of universal education beyond the high school is no more Utopian than the goal of full citizenship for all Americans, for the first is becoming prerequisite to the second. If a person is adjudged incapable of growth toward a free mind today, he has been adjudged incapable of the dignity of

[2] T. R. McConnell, "A Reply to the Critics," *Journal of Educational Sociology*, vol. 22, April, 1949, pp. 533–550.

full citizenship in a free society. That is a judgment which no American conscious of his ideals and traditions can likely make.[3]

Inexorable social, economic, and cultural forces are making higher levels of education mandatory. The classification of manpower by major occupational groups has been changing rapidly and the redistribution will continue. The occupational structure within broad categories is also changing rapidly, even in the highest professions. It has been estimated that more than 2 million jobs will be eliminated over the next decade in this country as a result of technological advance and improved productivity.[4] In the meantime technological development will call for higher and higher levels of education. This demand has been expressed as follows:

> The evidence is that in the decades ahead the rate of economic growth will be increasingly dependent on the rate of technological development. And since the rate of technological advance depends on the availability of technical personnel, the education of people in the professional, technical and skilled occupations becomes a prime factor in increasing the growth rate of the national enterprise.[5]

The lack of employment for youth of late high school and junior college age, the desire of employers for more mature workers, and the necessity for different kinds and higher levels of education and training will keep more young people in school for longer periods of time. Social as well as economic pressures for access to higher education will increase, a phenomenon which will be even more apparent in countries where educational opportunity at the late secondary and postsecondary stages has been much more restricted than in the United States. This pressure, for example, will be especially noticeable in England. Sir Peter Venables, the Principal of the College of Advanced Technology in Birmingham, has observed that:

> "Appetite grows by what it feeds on"—increasing schooling has always been followed by increasing demands for further and higher education; first generation graduates and certificate holders see to it that their children have the advantage of a more prolonged education; graduates themselves prolong

[3] Educational Policies Commission, *Universal Opportunity for Education Beyond the High School* (Washington: National Education Association, 1964).
[4] Panel of Consultants on Vocational Education, *Education for a Changing World of Work* (Office of Education, U.S. Department of Health, Education and Welfare, 1963), p. 14.
[5] Grant Venn, *Man, Education and Work: Post-secondary, Vocational, and Technical Education* (Washington: American Council on Education, 1964), p. 21.

their own education; and firms managed by the professionally qualified expect more from the next generation and provide more for them.[6]

Among the inevitable results of the pressure of numbers, changes in the occupational structure, the prolongation of the period of education, and the expansion of adult education, is the shift of specialized education upward in the educational system. When junior college education becomes as common as high school graduation, the four-year institution may then become the people's college. A state university president recently proposed that the standard undergraduate curriculum should be lengthened to five years for the baccalaureate degree.[7] The master's degree may soon become as common as the baccalaureate degree is today and the number of postdoctoral students is increasing apace. This progression, which characterizes both general and specialized education, has been illustrated as follows:

> Now, technology has advanced many occupations on the technical, skilled, and semi-professional levels to a point where they require higher levels of specialization and related knowledge that are best learned and taught within educational frameworks. Manifestations of this upward push are to be found, for example, in engineering, where the two-year engineering technology curricula of today compare in rigor and breadth with the four-year engineering curricula of twenty-five years ago. As engineering continues to become more complex and specialization is delayed, graduate study will become a must for the engineer, and, by the same token, it is probable that within the present decade the bachelor's degree will become a must for many technical occupations. Similarly, the skilled crafts are now making their appearance on the junior college level.[8]

Keeping youth in school longer and postponing specialized education create serious problems of motivation, perceived relevance of education to life and career, and coordination between general and specialized, theoretical and applied, and in-school and out-of-school educational experiences.

NEED FOR A DIVERSIFIED EDUCATIONAL SYSTEM

Everything we know about human variability, not only in aptitude and achievement but also in interests, motivations, attitudes, values, and in-

[6] Sir P. F. R. Venables, "Technical Education—New Dimensions" (Manchester, England: Union of Lancashire and Cheshire Institutes, 1963), p. 3.
[7] F. H. Horn, "Five Years for College?" *NEA Journal*, vol. 53, November 1964, pp. 40–41.
[8] Venn, *op. cit.*, p. 17.

tellectual dispositions, emphasizes the need for a highly diversified educational system. Likewise, the more we learn about the highly differentiated manpower required by a complicated industrial, technological society, the more we appreciate the importance of differential educational opportunities. Furthermore, our growing perception of the almost infinite nuances of human sensibilities dictates a preference for variety rather than uniformity in educational arrangements. The need for diversity of educational resources, as Bowles has shown, pervades the whole of higher and secondary education. As he pointed out,

> Any concept of national manpower utilization postulates the fullest possible employment of all individuals according to their abilities. It assumes, therefore, the existence of a secondary school enrollment which eventually will provide teachers at all levels, trained technicians, and recruits for the professions, for management, and for the upper levels of government service. This concept of the full use of human resources is in direct opposition to that implied by the selection process now used by most higher educational systems.[9]

The fuller use of human resources has not only made higher institutions larger and more numerous, but very much more complex in organization. To illustrate this growing complexity, Bowles quoted the following section on Canadian Universities from the 1961 *Commonwealth Universities Yearbook:*

> Even while the center of gravity of the arts course moved steadily away from the ancient humanities towards the social sciences and the pure sciences, the needs of a whole regiment of new professions became recognized, under pressure, as requiring advanced training, preferably under university auspices. Such were agriculture, architecture, dentistry, pharmacy, forestry, library science, engineering, social work, veterinary science, pedagogy, music, home economics, fine arts, fisheries, journalism, public administration, and a flock of others, each demanding a separate faculty, institute, or "school."[10]

It should be noted that many of the professions in this list can be studied at various levels and with differing emphasis on theory and practice or on science and technology. Furthermore, associated with several of these professions are technical or semiprofessional occupations such as those of dental and electronic technicians. At the other end of the educational spectrum these professions reach into research and scholarship of a high order. In the colleges and universities of the United States higher

[9] Frank Bowles, *Access to Higher Education,* vol. I (New York: Columbia University Press, 1963), p. 55.

[10] *Ibid.,* p. 142.

education has probably attained the widest scope and has included the greatest number of degrees of altitude.

In any system of education covering so many levels and so many kinds of education, a reasonable division of labor among higher institutions would seem to be imperative. The most comprehensive effort to lay out a differentiated and coordinated system of public higher education produced the California Master Plan encompassing a tripartite system composed of junior colleges, state colleges, and the University of California. The Master Plan assigned both common and differential functions to these three groups of institutions. It provided that the primary function of the state colleges should be to offer instruction for undergraduate and graduate students through the master's degree in the liberal arts and sciences, in applied fields, and in certain professions including teaching. The Plan specified that the University of California should be the primary state-supported academic agency for research. The University was given exclusive jurisdiction in certain fields of professional education and was accorded the sole authority to award the doctoral degree in all fields of learning, except that it might agree with the state colleges to award joint doctoral degrees in selected fields.

THE TENDENCY TOWARD UNIFORMITY RATHER THAN DIVERSITY

The Master Plan was the third attempt to differentiate the functions of public higher institutions in California. This has proved to be a formidable task and the effort has been only partially successful. Since 1948, when the first of the three reports was issued,[11] state college and university systems have steadily become more similar, at least in organization and in implicit, if not avowed, purposes. Some of this convergence was undoubtedly necessary. It is not as easy as it once was to divide educational programs among institutions. It was once reasonably sensible to emphasize the biological sciences at a land-grant college and physical sciences at the state university. Today these fields are so interdependent that it is impossible to study the biological sciences without recourse to the physical sciences, and new subjects, such as biochemistry and biophysics, have joined once-separate disciplines. Professional and other forms of applied education require a firm foundation in underlying disci-

[11] M. E. Deutsch, A. A. Douglas, and G. D. Strayer, *A Report of a Survey of the Needs of California in Higher Education* (Berkeley, Calif.: University of California Press, 1948).

plines. Nevertheless, it would seem to be axiomatic that no state now possesses or will acquire resources that would justify the unnecessary duplication of costly forms of advanced and specialized education. I can only conclude that there should be some differentiation of responsibilities among public higher institutions and a distribution or allocation of programs relevant to these functions. I think it is self-evident that the unnecessary duplication of educational programs will defeat the attainment of educational excellence. Unfortunately, many institutions would prefer being a pale reflection of a prestigious university rather than a more limited institution of quality. Consequently, instead of finding their appropriate places in a diversified system of higher education, colleges and universities tend to converge rather than to diverge, to become more similar rather than more distinctive. By striving to be as much like one another as possible, institutions will fail to provide the diversity of educational opportunity that our economy, culture, and polity require.

The seemingly natural tendency toward similarity rather than diversity is not limited to the United States. It may be found in Great Britain also, and no doubt in other countries as well. In Britain, in accordance with a recommendation by the Robbins Committee on Higher Education, the ten colleges of advanced technology established after 1956 to offer university-level courses in applied science and technology are to be transformed into technological universities. The colleges of advanced technology developed differently, for the most part, from the technological divisions of the universities. The former responded much more sympathetically and directly to industry, both in teaching and research. Their particular educational innovation is the sandwich course—alternate periods in industry and in the college. But now that the colleges of advanced technology are to become universities, there is already evidence that they may abandon their distinctiveness and attempt to outdo the universities at their own game. There are rumors, for example, that some of the new technological universities plan to give up their sandwich courses for more conventional curricula.

The Robbins Report also proposed that certain regional technical colleges should have the opportunity to become parts of universities or universities in their own right. Some of the curricula in the regional colleges had already been approved for the award of the Diploma in Technology, the substitute for degrees (which are awarded only by universities) invented for university-level courses in the colleges of advanced technology. Although the regional colleges had transferred most of their lower-level courses to local or area technical colleges, they had continued an extensive offering for both full-time and part-time students at the intermediate or technical level. After the Robbins Report dangled university status in front of them, many of the regional colleges began to vie with each other to become universities or to become federated with universities. Many leaders in technical education believe that this will lead the regional colleges to underemphasize or to abandon much of the work that should be done in technical education in favor of what is considered to be of university nature and level. Thus, the colleges may discontinue many of the services which are essential to the education of a sufficiently large body of technicians for the staffing and revitalization of British industry.

The pressures toward conformity rather than distinctiveness seem to operate in any society and in any educational system. The problem of finding social supports for institutions of different types in a differentiated system has yet to be solved.

Perhaps there is time for one more example of the tendency of institutions to imitate prestigious models. I have in mind the probability that, as junior colleges or community colleges are recognized as belonging to systems of higher education—as they now are in California and other states as well—rather than as extensions of secondary education, some of the values of the comprehensive institution may become increasingly precarious. Investigations at the Center for the Study of Higher Education at Berkeley have shown that junior college teachers who previously taught in high schools and those who were recruited from four-year colleges or directly from university graduate schools tended to differ in their attitudes toward some of the functions or programs of the comprehensive community college. Those who came from the high schools were more favorably inclined toward unselective admission, remedial education, terminal curricula, and educational and vocational counseling.[12] There is a movement in the California community colleges to select faculty members with higher academic qualifications and to secure them directly from the graduate schools. It is no longer necessary in California to take professional courses in education to secure at least a temporary junior college teaching credential. Without a background of professional courses on junior college education, new junior college teachers may have a narrower conception of the purposes of the institution and may be less receptive to the *comprehensive* principle.

These factors, coupled with the virtual incorporation of the two-year institutions into the California system of public higher education, have already had their influence on organizational structure. Responding to faculty pressure, the California State Board of Education has made the

[12] L. L. Medsker, *The Junior College: Progress and Prospect* (New York: McGraw-Hill Book Company, 1960), pp. 171–204.

organization of an academic senate mandatory in the public community colleges where the faculties wish it. Faculty members are pressing for more participation in formulating educational policy and in administrative operation. They are also pressing for academic rank. All these innovations reflect the characteristics of four-year academic institutions and the attitudes of faculties with more academic status. As these attitudes are consolidated in junior college faculties, they will be subtly communicated to students, parents, and other elements of the community. We may predict that as a consequence, terminal curricula will be held in even lower esteem, that it will be increasingly difficult to attract students to these courses, and that these colleges may become essentially institutions to prepare students to transfer to four-year colleges and universities. We also may expect faculty pressure to establish admission standards that will screen out students considered unfit for an academic program. I should not be surprised if many two-year community colleges abandoned their open-door policy and their comprehensive functions and programs, and turned themselves into preparatory institutions.

NEW INSTITUTIONS REQUIRED

If this transformation occurs, it is almost certain that other institutions will be established to provide educational programs for students who do not transfer to four-year colleges or universities. Technical institutes of various sorts may become more numerous, for example. Industrial firms may establish or expand their own educational activities. (There is already more technical education of this kind in the United States than many educators realize, and some English firms have extensive internal educational programs.) Entirely new educational ventures or institutions may emerge under the auspices of governmental agencies other than the usual educational authorities. (The new programs of the Federal government are cases in point.)

As a matter of fact, even if community colleges continue to profess, and to some degree to serve, comprehensive functions, they may fail to adapt their programs effectively to the characteristics and needs of many young people. It is increasingly apparent that work-study or study-work programs should be greatly expanded for youth of junior college age. England has developed a system of part-time technical education from which we could learn a great deal. That country depends too heavily on part-time education after age fifteen or sixteen, and a vast increase in full-time technical study has been called for.[13] Furthermore, the system is

[13] Venables, *op. cit.*, p. 4.

based too heavily on the firm—employers may release workers for study at a technical college on a day-release or a block-release scheme. The chance for part-time education depends too greatly on getting employment in industries (such as those in electricity, gas, and water) which release large percentages of employees for college work, or in firms, most of them relatively large, which offer the opportunity for part-time schooling. Financial support from Parliament is now available to encourage firms to establish or expand release plans, and recommendations have been made for the expansion and improvement of "work-based" part-time trade and technical education.[14] These measures may be insufficient to stimulate further education of a sufficient percentage of youth, but there is widespread belief in England in the efficacy of part-time education, partially because relating work and study is an effective means of motivation.

We could profitably give much more consideration in the United States to the combination of work and schooling, both for general and vocational education. This country should not rely so heavily on part-time formal education as does England, and work-study programs should probably be more often "school-based" than "firm-based." Nevertheless, this kind of education should be enormously expanded. If community colleges cannot gear themselves to do it, new institutions should be created, or new programs should be established in other institutions, such, perhaps, as area postsecondary vocational schools, preferably under educational authorities. For example, reforestation is badly needed in many parts of the United States. Youth might be recruited for this work at reasonable rates of pay, and relevant education in forestry and the natural sciences could be correlated with it. If present educational institutions and authorities are unable to adapt quickly to such needs and opportunities, other agencies will assume educational functions. Institutional lines frequently become rigid, and programs become conservative or even obsolete; the time may come, therefore, when new institutions must be invented. In any event, statewide coordination and articulation of institutions and programs will be essential, as will coordination with Federal plans, operations, and financing.

STUDENT CHOICE AND DISTRIBUTION

Let us assume for the moment that a state has devised a diversified system of higher education which offers a wide range of educational

[14] Department of Education and Science, *Day Release* (London: Her Majesty's Stationery Office, 1964).

opportunities making different demands on students' aptitudes, abilities, interests, and personality structures. The problem then becomes one of aiding students to distribute themselves appropriately among the institutions and/or programs which comprise the system. Bowles has pointed out that a relatively narrow system of higher education tends to control student entrance by examination or a series of examinations. The other method of controlling student entrance—the one appropriate to a wider range of educational opportunities and specializations—is "through advice based on student performance, judgments of student abilities, and expressions of student preference—in short, control through orientation or guidance. . . . The barriers must be rebuilt into gateways through which students may move with assurance that their preparation is appropriate to their choices, and that their opportunities are commensurate to their abilities." [15]

Before the method of guidance can be effectively employed, however, we need to know far more than we now do about the total flow of students through diversified systems of institutions and curricula. The ultimate purpose, of course, should be to enable the student to find the best place for him in the system; however, at this point we know relatively little about differential recruitment, either to institutions, or systems, or programs within them.

Most is known, of course, about distribution in accordance with academic aptitude and previous academic achievement. Darley has made the most extensive study of the compatibility of students and institutions. He reported the distribution of academic aptitude among entering students in a national sample of institutions stratified by type of control, region, and level of program. He also provided extensive data on the distribution of aptitude and ability of freshmen among the colleges and universities in Minnesota and Wisconsin. I shall not summarize these data here, since they are of the sort with which everyone is familiar.

Darley also analyzed differential recruitment with respect to socioeconomic background as reflected in the father's occupation. He found a significant relation between the father's occupation and type of institution entered. Without summarizing the data I shall quote Darley's comments on what he found:

> Throughout the state, stratification of educational opportunity in terms of parental resources was clearly evident. If the quality and scope of educational offerings are comparable throughout several institutions, society's needs are well served by such stratification. But if the quality and scope are markedly divergent among the types of institutions, then societal and

[15] Bowles, *op. cit.*, p. 168.

individual needs may not be well served. The day has passed when a person can rise above a poor educational environment to realize his full academic potential by struggling upward through several layers of differing educational quality . . . Society's manpower needs are such that we cannot safely maintain an educational system built on a two-way break, if, as we have reason to suspect, the good student in the poor institution therefore fails to attain his own optimal development or if the poor student in the good institution fails in tasks not coordinate with his potentials.[16]

Darley's data show clearly that there is limited rationality in the distribution of students among institutions, and he presented considerable evidence of incongruity between students' abilities and backgrounds and the educational programs they chose. He underlined the necessity, first, of making educational opportunities actually available to students who should embrace them and, second, of aiding students to choose wisely among them.

We do not have comprehensive information concerning the flow of students into and through the California tripartite system, but I shall briefly mention three studies that throw some light on the congruence of student attributes and institutional characteristics.

Farwell studied the characteristics of students in two demonstrably different programs of agricultural education, those at the California State Polytechnic College and the University of California at Davis. The State Polytechnic College emphasized agricultural production and learning by doing through individual projects. At Davis, on the other hand, the faculty emphasized theoretical and scientific training. Davis required students to take half of their work in applied agriculture, while Cal Poly required only a quarter. On the other hand, Davis required that students spend a third of their time on the supporting sciences, while the Polytechnic College required students to spend only a fifth of their time in the basic disciplines.

Farwell found that the two student bodies differed in general scholastic aptitude, since the requirements for admission to Davis are considerably higher than at the other institution. A greater percentage of Davis freshmen also had high scores on the scientific keys of the Strong Vocational Interest Blank but the differences, although statistically significant, were small. However, other differences on the Strong were not in the direction that would have been predicted if the differential objectives of the two institutions were functionally effective in attracting students. It was Davis

[16] J. G. Darley, *Promise and Performance: A Study of Ability and Achievement in Higher Education* (Berkeley, Calif.: Center for the Study of Higher Education, University of California, 1962), pp. 63–64.

rather than the Polytechnic College which had a higher percentage of students with interest patterns in technical and business fields. One would have expected the difference to be in the other direction.

If the institutions and student bodies were relevantly paired, the Davis students presumably should have been significantly higher on measures of complexity of outlook, originality, and interest in abstract ideas, characteristics which the Center for the Study of Higher Education has found to be associated with a theoretical and scientific orientation. Surprisingly, the two student bodies were not significantly different in these attributes. One must conclude, as Farwell did, that prospective students failed to perceive the differences in objectives and educational programs and were perhaps unaware of their own psychological characteristics, or else that students' choices were more influenced by such factors as geographical proximity than by the nature of the institutions they chose.[17]

Dustan studied the characteristics of students in nursing education in four institutions in San Jose, namely, the public junior college, San Jose State College, and two hospital schools of nursing. The junior college, the state college, and the hospital schools professed different objectives and their curricula differed substantially. Dustan's hypothesis was that the four-year baccalaureate program would attract students with the highest average scholastic aptitude, with more pronounced scientific interests, and with a more theoretical disposition than the students who attended the junior college and the hospital schools. Such, however, was not the case. The junior college nursing students had the highest mean scholastic aptitude score and possessed scientific and theoretical interests which equalled those of students in the four-year program at the state college. A substantial number of the junior college nursing students expressed the desire to complete a baccalaureate degree and some of them aspired to a master's degree. Nevertheless, they were engaged in a terminal program with very little transfer value. Dustan concluded that the junior college students were not appropriately placed, but were in a program which would not adequately capitalize their interests and abilities.[18]

Tillery has recently studied the choice of college by the California public high school graduates of 1961 who were eligible to enter the University of California—a group which comprised 14.8 per cent of a 10 per cent sample of high school graduates. Although the University-eligible

[17] T. R. McConnell, *A General Pattern for American Public Higher Education* (New York, McGraw-Hill Book Company, 1962), pp. 71–73.

[18] L. C. Dustan, "Characteristics of Students in Three Types of Nursing Programs," unpublished doctoral dissertation, University of California, Berkeley, 1963.

students were supposedly fairly homogeneous in high school achievement, Tillery assumed that there might be significant differences among them in academic aptitude, motivation, social maturity, attitudes toward college, cultural background, and so on. He wished to know how students who chose different colleges differed in these regards. He especially compared the University-eligible students who in fact attended the University with those who entered junior colleges.

The mean Scholastic Aptitude Test score of those who went to the University was about 120 points higher than the mean of those who attended junior colleges. He secured the scores of both groups of students on certain scales of the Omnibus Personality Inventory (OPI), which was developed for research purposes at the Center for the Study of Higher Education. He was especially interested in the scales which purport to measure interest in reflective and abstract thought, theoretical orientation, aesthetic values, and complexity of outlook. In the sample he was studying, the correlation between scores on these measures and scores on the Scholastic Aptitude Test was not high. He devised a means of combining the four OPI scales into a rough measure of intellectuality and divided students into high, average, and low groups on the composite score. He discovered that 31 per cent of the University of California entrants were in the high group as compared with 18 per cent of the junior college students. Sixteen per cent of the University of California group were in the low category, but 25 per cent of the junior college sample were at that level.

Tillery also had scores on the social maturity scale of the OPI. This is a complex scale which is not very well described by its title. Harold Webster has characterized the high-scoring student on this scale as follows:

> He is flexible and realistic in his relationships with others; unromantic but at the same time uncynical; kind and impunitive in general, but capable of aggression when it is appropriate; tolerant and undogmatic, but not merely in accordance with some uncritical policy or ideology; and personally free, without requiring rules and rituals for managing social relationships.

About 40 per cent of the University students had high social maturity scores, and just 7 per cent had low scores. However, only 20 per cent of the junior college students were in the high group, and three times as many of them had low scores as University of California students. There were also differences in cultural background and educational aspiration between the students who attended the junior colleges and those who went to the University of California.

Tillery discovered that University of California students were not all of the same cloth, either. For example, 45 per cent of the Berkeley women had high intellectuality scores but only 35 per cent of those at UCLA were in the same category. Only 4 per cent of the Berkeley women were in the low group, but 22 per cent of those at UCLA were at that level. Also, 47 per cent of the Berkeley students ranked high in social maturity, and less than 5 per cent low. At UCLA the corresponding figures were 33 per cent and 12 per cent. How wisely these students had decided where to go to college one cannot, of course, say. Tillery thinks a considerable number were probably misplaced. One could determine this only by complex studies of student development in relation to original status, and of differences in development of comparable students in different college environments.[19]

The California Coordinating Council for Higher Education has begun to make studies of the admission and progress of students in the three segments of public higher education, as well as problems of student transfer from institution to institution and from system to system. Effective guidance, sound admission policies, and appropriate choice among available educational opportunities all depend on such a program of investigation.

There are still more complicated problems of student choice and distribution. Consider for a moment differential recruitment to the professions and to different specializations within a single profession. Wolfle has published distributions of students' intelligence test scores by fields of specialization. His data showed variations in mean score from field to field. For example, the average Army General Classification Test scores of students in business administration and dentistry were strikingly lower than those in engineering and medicine. The data also showed considerable variability within each field.[20]

In spite of the fact that there is wide variability in the scholastic aptitude test scores of students entering any one of the professions, we have tended, nevertheless, to assume that a profession is essentially a unitary occupation. Such, of course, is not the case. But only recently have we begun to chart the variation in intellective and nonintellective characteristics of students who choose different specialties in a broad professional field. We need to know far more than we do about the

[19] Harry Dale Tillery, "Differential Characteristics of Entering Freshmen at the University of California and Their Peers at California Junior Colleges," unpublished doctoral dissertation, University of California, Berkeley, 1964.

[20] Dael Wolfle, *America's Resources of Specialized Talent* (New York: Harper & Row, Publishers, Incorporated, 1954), pp. 199–203.

demands which these specialties make on human abilities, interests, and dispositions, and about the profile of characteristics of people who are successful in the practice of their specialties.

We now know that the medical specialties recruit students who vary greatly in Medical College Aptitude Test scores. Gee has summarized some of the data as follows:

> Only about one-quarter of present-day medical college graduates expect to become general practitioners. The average ability levels of those who do, and the majority who expect to specialize, produce a distinct intellectual hierarchy of medical disciplines—a hierarchy, incidentally, that bears no relation whatever to the students'—or faculty's—views of the prestige level of the disciplines.
>
> Students planning to enter general practice have the lowest mean scores ... and those planning to enter psychiatry have unexpectedly high mean MCAT scores. Approximately one full standard deviation of MCAT score units separates these two groups, which rank respectively 11th and 12th among medical disciplines in rated prestige. In casual conversation among medical faculties and administrators, internists are considered the intellectual leaders of the medical community, but in terms of measured abilities, the average present-day aspirant to this field ranks distinctly below the average aspirant to a career in psychiatry.[21]

Differences in the personality test scores of medical school students planning to go into different specialties are even more interesting. Gee has reported that

> The Theoretical value mean score (on the Allport-Vernon-Lindzey Scale of Values) remains highest for all subgroups, but with respect to other values, both mean scores and hierarchies of values differ. Certain regularities again appear. Although relationships are not evident at all levels, Religious and Economic values vary inversely with the intellectual ability level of the specialty group, and Aesthetic and Theoretical values vary directly with intellectual ability level.[21a]

Gee also discovered that the hierarchy of values of students planning to go into research and teaching was identical with that of students in the Harvard Medical School, which produces a very large number of teachers and researchers for other medical colleges. The combination of high theoretical and high aesthetic values has been found by MacKinnon and

[21] H. H. Gee, "Differential Characteristics of Student Bodies—Implications for the Study of Medical Education," in T. R. McConnell (ed.), *Selection and Educational Differentiation* (Berkeley, Calif.: Field Service Center and Center for the Study of Higher Education, 1960), p. 132.

[21a] *Ibid.,* p. 141.

his associates at the Institute for Personality Assessment and Research to be characteristic of creative individuals in a large number of professions and specializations.

There is a great deal of variability among medical schools in the number of students who possess this pattern of high theoretical and high aesthetic values. This fact raises two questions: Should not students choose medical schools with full knowledge of the dominant characteristics of their student bodies? How can a particular medical school—for example, one whose students vary widely in scholastic aptitude and in intellectual disposition—stimulate each student to realize his potentialities?

"Pairing" students and educational programs is a highly complicated process and I have only touched its complexities. I have not mentioned, for example, the possibility that the "fit" between student and program might be too "good" under certain circumstances. For example, a student with highly authoritarian attitudes might find an institution or a curriculum which would confirm rather than challenge these attitudes, and I should think it would be better for this student to land in a place which might make him less rigid and more flexible, less dependent and more able to stand on his own feet. We need many more studies of the effects of varying degrees of congruity and incongruity between student characteristics and environmental sanctions and demands.

THE STUDENT AND THE SYSTEM

I have said elsewhere that

> implicit in the policy of differentiating the roles of public colleges and universities is the assumption that a democratic system of higher education need not accord all students the privilege of attending the same kinds of institutions, any more than it need permit all to pursue the same curricula.[22]

I have also contended that

> Although even in a democracy it is not necessary for every student to have access to every kind of institution, he should not encounter unreasonable barriers to transfer from one kind or level of institution to another. No ultimate educational or professional opportunity should be closed to a student at an early point in his schooling. A flexible educational system must include a succession of choice points at which a student may go in one of two or more directions—at which, for example, he may choose among dif-

[22] McConnell, *A General Pattern for American Public Higher Education*, p. 83.

ferent institutions or specialties, or transfer from one college or university to another.[23]

The implicit assumption in the last two statements is that students should be helped to choose appropriate gateways through which to enter the system of higher education and through which they may fan out into the labyrinth within. A second implicit assumption is that we do not yet know enough about careers, student characteristics, and the character and impact of college environments to establish a tidy array of differentiated institutions and to enable students to distribute themselves among them according to their individual traits. Neither do we know enough at this stage to pair students and specialized curricula with any precision. It seems to me that these assumptions lead to the inescapable conclusion that students should be able to change their route without excessive penalties as they, and the institutions they attend, learn more about each other's characteristics, and as students arrive at sound educational and vocational choices.

If this conclusion is sound, it follows that it is indefensible to permit something like the 11-plus examination in England to determine, with relatively few exceptions, a student's educational and vocational destiny. It also follows, I think, that lateral movement within institutions and systems should be possible without undue cost to the student in the completion of an educational program. Sir Douglas Logan, Principal of the University of London, pointed out to me last summer that if a student transferred to one of the constituent colleges of the University of London after one year at another British university, he would get no "credit" for his previous university work but would, so to speak, have to start all over again.

It is known that many students, including those of high ability, change their educational and vocational goals, not only during high school or between high school and college, but also after entering higher institutions. The Center for the Study of Higher Education at Berkeley has found, for example, that 40 per cent of the winners and runners-up in the 1956 National Merit Scholarship Corporation competition changed their intended fields of specialization between the summer before college entrance and the end of the sophomore year.[24] The University of Keele, which is unique among the English universities in requiring a four-year program for the baccalaureate degree in which the first year is given over

[23] *Ibid.*, p. 170.
[24] J. R. Warren, "Self Concept, Occupational Role Expectation, and Change in College Major," *Journal of Counseling Psychology*, vol. 8, no. 2, Summer, 1961, pp. 164–169.

primarily to a broad program of exploratory and general education, has also discovered that about 40 per cent of its students change their plans for specialization by the end of the basic year.

So complicated are the problems of selection, admission, placement, and educational and vocational choice that we will not be able to solve the problem of prediction of academic achievement, or, even more significantly, the prediction of optimal individual development, for a long time to come. In the meantime many students will make false starts and find it necessary to change directions. Therefore, as I have said before, "within the present limits of our knowledge about the 'fit' between students and institutions it would be indefensible, even in a coordinated and differentiated system, to assign a student once and for all to a particular institution or a specific curriculum." [25] Any system of higher education, to perform adequately, must remain reasonably open and flexible.

NECESSITY OF COORDINATION

I have referred several times in this paper to the need for a differentiated and coordinated system of higher education. A basic plan for educational development will propose constructive methods of *mobilizing* and *coordinating* a state's resources for higher education. To many people the term coordination has mainly negative connotations. Too often it is identified primarily with measures to avoid duplication of educational goals and programs and with other forms of restraint and control. I think it is abundantly clear that, although effective coordination sometimes undeniably requires restraint, its results will be unfortunate if they are mainly negative. One of the most important purposes of a coordinating agency is to define new educational needs and stimulate present institutions—or, if necessary, new institutions—to meet them. A coordinating board must engage in purposeful planning. It must also encourage individuality and innovation within broad purposes.

I have long been an advocate of the voluntary coordination of higher education. [26] At the meeting of the American Council on Education in 1964, I recanted this position. I have come to the conclusion that purely voluntary methods are almost certain to be ineffective in the long run. First of all, they are unlikely to produce the continuing and impartial planning on which a comprehensive and diversified system of higher

---

[25] McConnell, *A General Pattern for American Public Higher Education*, p. 190.
[26] *Ibid.*, pp. 136–169.

education must be built. Second, they are unlikely to produce the efficient allocation of resources for educational expenditures and capital outlay that an adequately financed system of higher education requires.

I have come to these conclusions as the result both of periodic studies of the coordination of British universities and of the assessment of the results of coordination in some of our states. Let me first comment briefly on the effectiveness of coordination by the British University Grants Committee.

The University Grants Committee has brought about some concerted movement, but the amount of positive planning and coordination has been, in my view, minimal. The result is a system of higher education far short of the nation's needs. It is my judgment that, even if the Robbins Committee's recommendations are fully adopted, the system will still fall far short of what is required for the economic growth and industrial efficiency necessary to enable Britain to compete in the increasingly technological marketplace. Whether the government would have financially underwritten a bolder or more adequate national system of higher education is admittedly doubtful, but, in any event, neither the University Grants Committee nor a voluntary association of the universities themselves has ever come forth with any such plan. During my conversations in Britain last summer, I found little conception that there will have to be, first, comprehensive planning of the system of higher education; second, prudent allocation of resources in relation both to the number of youth qualified for higher education and the needs of the economy and polity for specialized manpower; and third, extensive and continuing research as the basis for planning and allocation. The day of intuitive improvisation in university affairs is over if higher education is to give Britain the leadership and specialized manpower she needs to restore her falling fortunes.

The failures of intuitive improvisation are equally if not more apparent in some of our own states. The failure of the purely voluntary Coordinating Council for Higher Education in Michigan to plan and monitor the orderly development of postsecondary education in that state is a case in point. Increasingly, however, our states are moving to some type of formal coordination, although the nature and powers of coordinating agencies vary from place to place.[27] Examples of recently established coordinating bodies may be found in Illinois and Ohio.

It is not possible here to make an extensive analysis of the responsibili-

[27] L. A. Glenny, "State Systems and Plans for Higher Education," in *Autonomy and Interdependence: Emerging Systems in Higher Education* (Washington: American Council on Education, 1964), pp. 24–42.

ties and powers which a coordinating agency should exercise. Let me say simply that in my judgment the statutory powers of the new Ohio Board of Regents represent the minimum authority which such an agency should exercise. The statute provides that the Ohio Board of Regents shall make studies of state policy in the field of higher education and formulate a master plan for higher education for the state; report annually to the governor and the general assembly on the findings from its studies and the master plan; approve or disapprove the establishment of new branches or academic centers of state colleges and universities; approve or disapprove the establishment of state technical institutes or any other state institution of higher education; recommend the nature of the programs (undergraduate, graduate, professional), state-financed research, and public services which should be offered by the state colleges, universities, and other state-assisted institutions of higher education; recommend to the institutions programs which could be eliminated and others which should be added; make recommendations to the governor and general assembly concerning the development of state-financed capital plans for higher education; review the appropriation requests of the public community colleges and the state colleges and universities and submit to executive departments and legislative committees its recommendations in regard to appropriations; approve or disapprove all new degrees and new degree programs at the institutions.

Most students of higher education believe in the greatest possible degree of institutional autonomy. Furthermore, they consider it essential to leave room for imagination, innovation, and improvement of the educational process all along the line. Nevertheless, many scholars are convinced that the essential outlines of the development of public institutions and public systems of higher education must be subject to the sanction of a coordinating body and responsive to an agency charged with planning a comprehensive statewide educational program sufficiently varied to accommodate the characteristics and needs of a diverse student body and of an incredibly complicated society.

Implications for Education and for Adjustment of Curricula to Individual Students

NEVITT SANFORD, Director, Institute for Study of Human Problems, Stanford University

In approaching this topic I shall put the emphasis on those of our high school graduates who are not now entering our colleges. I assume that in the years immediately ahead higher and higher proportions of these young people will be receiving some kind of education beyond the high school. I assume further that these young people as a group are hardly to be distinguished psychologically from many who are now entering junior colleges or community colleges in some parts of the country, or, for that matter, from many young people who do not finish high school.

The topic is one that appeals to me very much, for it offers an opportunity to discuss education for individual development without having to deal with the objections of educators who are primarily concerned with other goals. When I entered the field of higher education the 1947 report of President Truman's Commission on Higher Education was a prominent if somewhat controversial statement of educational purposes, and it suited me fine. Let me quote from that document.

The first goal in education for democracy is the full, rounded, and continuing development of the person.... To liberate and perfect the intrinsic powers of every citizen is the central purpose of democracy, and its furtherance of individual self-realization is its greatest glory.

It is well to recall that this was not only pre-*Sputnik* but pre-McCarthy. We organized our research at Vassar College with the Commission's report very much in mind and, of course, could not change our direction every time a crisis in our society brought a different emphasis in education. Nor did we have any desire to change. It seems to me now, as we contemplate offering more education to more and more of our citizens, that our best general guide is the ideal of the "full, rounded, and continuing development of the person."

In the recent past, stress on this ideal has encountered the opposition of educators who are mainly interested in specialized excellence, or in building strong departments, or in teaching subjects instead of students, or in preparing as many students as possible for graduate school. One may hope that in focusing on a new group of students, those who are not now entering the four-year colleges or any college at all, we may avoid this somewhat tiresome controversy, for college and university people cannot object to education for individual development as long as we are talking about students they do not want. We have in the present situation an unparalleled opportunity to plan totally new kinds of institutions for developing persons. As Frank Bowles has said, we are in a revolutionary situation; it calls, I think, for radical actions.

One source of new models might well be the work that is now going on, or is about to be undertaken, in the interest of those large numbers of our children and young people who have been culturally deprived. When one observes, for example, the work that Martin Deutsch and his group are doing for poor children in New York City his natural reaction is to wish that his own young children could have something as good. This reminds me of the boarding schools in the Soviet Union. Planned in the first instance for children who for one reason or another could not live at home, these schools were so attractive and successful that soon the elite of the country were demanding that their children be admitted—and this indeed was done. Dr. McConnell has mentioned the camps that are being planned for boys in the college-age range who have had less, often much less, than a high school education. I have been much interested in the program of the Office of Economic Opportunity that calls for the establishment of residential centers for girls in the sixteen to twenty-one age range who have grown up in poverty. These centers, it seems, have to be institutions for developing the person. Everything needs to be done for these girls, and it seems clear that they cannot be taught very much in the way of basic skills until their self-conceptions have been changed and they have been induced to orient themselves toward the future. The imagination that is going into planning of these new kinds of institutions is of a higher order than that usually to be found in contemporary planning for institutions of higher learning. This may have to do with the fact that the planners, in the first case, represent many professions in addition to education; at least they are not bound by the assumptions and habits of thought that entrap many of us who have spent long years in educational institutions. It would not be at all surprising if in time some of these new institutions and programs for the culturally deprived began to suggest to ordinary citizens that something of the kind ought to be done for *their* young people. Indeed, it is conceivable that institutions planned with a view to developing the person might come in time to stand as a counterforce to the tendency toward conformity found among our institutions of learning. The new institutions might begin to attract people of the kind who now enter colleges; this would make for at least some diversity, for there would certainly be no competition between the new institutions and those that devote themselves to specialized excellence.

Not all the culturally deprived are to be found among school dropouts; they may also be found among people now in college and people who have been to college. Not infrequently individuals of these latter groups are encountered in mental hygiene clinics and psychiatric hospitals. Recently I heard presented the case of a young woman who suffered from a morbid fear of eating in public places. It was possible without much difficulty to formulate her case in psychoanalytic terms, but as the history unfolded it became clear that probably her greatest difficulty was a lack of those resources that we ordinarily expect to come from education. Although she had come from a home which, purely in economic terms, would have to be described as upper-middle-class and had gone to college for a year she had never learned to read with enjoyment, or to do anything that might enhance self-respect or offer self-fulfillment. Her personality seemed to have been formed through watching TV programs and reading advertisements which instructed her in how to be "feminine" in the narrowest sense of that word. Now the wife of an airman and living on a base, without marketable skills and so far without children, she had no notion of what to do with herself. It could be presumed that having a baby would help her—but then one would have to start worrying about the future of that baby. Psychotherapy could without doubt remove her major symptom, but she could be given the full course of psychotherapy without alteration in the cause of her difficulty. She would still have to be educated. Indeed it could be argued that if she were properly educated, starting now when she is aged twenty-two, she would not need psychotherapy.

Supporting this same general point was the experience that some of us psychologists had when working in the County Mental Hygiene Clinic during the period of our research at Vassar College. Many of the patients that we saw in that Clinic were the wives of Ph.D.'s who worked at the local electronics laboratory. These young women who, typically, had dropped out of college to get married and now had two or three children, brought us all kinds of interesting "symptoms," but it dawned on us in time that their real trouble was that they needed someone to talk with. Here it was the husbands who had been culturally deprived. All they could talk about was "shop" and sports; their education had neglected the area of humane feeling; their boredom and insensitivity when it came to such questions as what might be a good life for the children left their wives in despair. There was not much that we could do.

Our state mental institutions are largely filled with people for whom life in our complex society is too difficult. A generation ago many of them would have led more or less untroubled lives working at simple jobs in human communities. Today they display a wide range of psychiatric symptoms, but what many of them have in common is a kind of incompetence. What skills they may have learned have become valueless and they lack the resources for coping with the ordinary demands of life. They represent failures in education, and their future well-being will depend heavily on such education as they are given from now on.

It is, of course, unimaginable that schools as they are now constituted can do all that needs to be done for the people to whom I have been referring. How often, when the issue of character education or education for personal development has been discussed in educational circles, have we heard the objection, "These things should be left to other institutions of our society." But the point is that for vast numbers of our children and young people there are no such institutions—not any more. A society that cares for its own has no alternative to creating such institutions; and for us the time is now.

This should be our major philosophic emphasis as we approach the challenges of universal higher education: the poor, the culturally deprived, the stupid are *our own;* our public agencies must have for them the same kind of concern that we have for children in our own families. The fact that a child or a young person has low intelligence or is "unmotivated" is not a reason why he should not be educated—up to the level of his potential, which is usually unknown.

A model for us as a society might be what the British aristocracy of a century ago did as a class. As I understand it, stupidity was no bar to a university education—not when the parents of the stupid young man controlled the universities and regarded their prime function to be doing something for their young people. Every young aristocrat was to be taught something that was useful to him, in the sense that it enabled him to enjoy life and to participate as a full member of his class. If he could not be taught to enjoy books then he could be taught riding; in any case he could be taught how to speak, and what to say on most occasions, and thus to take his place in his society.

In a truly democratic society every individual is to be regarded as an aristocrat, in the sense just described. Given our present affluence and our promise for the future we can take quite seriously the prospect of realizing what the Truman Commission called democracy's "greatest glory," that is, the fullest possible development of each individual's potential.

It must not be supposed, however, that once we have given the individual his education he has now built into him the means for functioning as a totally independent, self-starting, self-determining individual—a sort of entrepreneur who will now sell his labor in the most favorable market. Thomas Jefferson was right, as Professor Commager has pointed out, in saying that we ought to give every person a chance to develop himself as an individual and that he would do so, given a decent environment. But Jefferson never imagined the sort of environment that our less privileged citizens live in today. It is not possible to imagine a program of education or a course of study that will enable these citizens to fulfill themselves or to be fully human unless their environment can be made more supportive than it is at present, and unless arrangements can be made for continuing education. The British aristocrats of the last century, after all, not only gave their young people such education as they could absorb but they initiated them into a society that continued to support and to shape them.

I am arguing that in our present situation we have to go beyond the idea of equal opportunity, that what we do for our young people should be guided less by considerations of merit than by considerations of welfare. We have to take our young people as they are. It is clear that large numbers of them are not "qualified," owing largely to deprivations of the past, to enter existing programs of education, that they are not in a good position to "benefit" from those programs. It is our task, then, to create programs and institutions that they *can* benefit from. Education in our society today is a right. It is a human right, like the right of children to grow up in a stable home. To deny it is to say that some people have no right to survive and to maintain themselves as individuals.

This is not to deny those rights that are earned by dint of hard work in school, or even those "rights" that are enjoyed by virtue of inheritance or privilege, for in the foreseeable future there will be ample rewards for those who achieve the most or compete most effectively. Thus what I am urging is not to be taken as a threat to existing institutions of higher learning. I am talking about different students, and different kinds of institutions which are to be operated by different kinds of personnel. The present system of merits will continue. By and large, the ablest will continue to be given the best opportunities and will receive the best rewards for their efforts. As long as we are a free society the able will find ways to look after their interests, and if we move in a totalitarian direction, with talent becoming increasingly organized in the national interest, the most able will be even better rewarded than at present.

I can envision only a mixed or pluralistic system, part meritocracy, part welfare state or "aristocracy" in the sense indicated above. In such a system, interestingly enough, the education of leaders will have much in common with the education of the least privileged. In both cases education will have to be outside the merit system, outside the system for training specialists and technicians. The young person who is to become a leader, like the untalented individual, must have a basis for self-respect other than his achievements and a basis for satisfaction other than external rewards; of neither of these groups of people do we ask contributions to society that are commensurate with what they have received. If a person is to lead, his inclination to look after the interests of others, and eventually the interests of all, must come spontaneously from within himself; it cannot be the final product of a scramble up the ladder of success; it is rather the natural product of a humane upbringing and a humanistic education which assures that the impulse to give comes from a sense of fullness.

At the same time, however, it must be assumed that those who make their contributions through achievement in various specialties, and are appropriately rewarded for it, are made aware of their responsibilities to society. It can hardly be just every man for himself in the world of technical and professional training. Indeed, this idea is staunchly resisted by many young people now on our college and university campuses. The general philosophy I am advocating can serve these young people by suggesting a social purpose that is worthy of them; it may offer an answer to the old question: specialized education for what?

Now let us come back to the young people on whom I said my discussion would be focused, that is, those who are graduating from high school but not entering four-year colleges. Although the general philosophy I have outlined holds for education in general, and although, as we shall see, all education should be guided by the same general theory of individual development, different kinds of programs are appropriate for people of different levels of advantage and disadvantage. I now want to consider what sort of program might be most suitable for the great mass of our young people, those whom we expect, provided there are no radical changes in our social fabric, to hold jobs, raise families, and participate fully in all the rights and duties of citizenship.

One way to approach a conception of educational goals for this group, or, as I should prefer to say, to appreciate the importance of individual development as the supreme goal, is to consider the requirements of life in our society of today. I am thinking particularly of the advanced stage of our technology and industrialization, and also, of course, of the shrinking world in which we live. My general point is that anyone who is going to live in this world, who is going to produce and be a real person in it, has got to develop rather well as an individual.

Let me call attention first to the world of work, in which automation goes on apace. Role requirements are changing rapidly in the whole occupational world. Jobs for which one prepares in school disappear almost as soon as one graduates. We have vast programs for retraining people, and as soon as they are retrained, the requirements of their new specialty have been radically altered. Production is becoming more and more highly organized, and the requirements of a particular position in an organization change when some more efficient way of running the whole organization is discovered. Or a new machine is invented. Jobs at the technical level disappear most rapidly. We can expect momentarily that the role of typist, for example, will no longer be with us. Consider how many people are leaving the farms each year. The dean of a school of agriculture told me recently that it had been years since he had occupied himself with the techniques of agricultural production. His concern is with how to help people adjust when they leave the farms. This is a rather different kind of role for agricultural specialists.

Change is taking place at the highest professional levels and not merely at the technical levels. If you inquire of people who are leading in the professions today, it will soon be discovered that relatively few of them are actually working at jobs for which they were trained, and that those who have moved along and are now most productive are those who have somehow been able to go on learning on the job. The specialties develop so rapidly that techniques or "know-how" learned in graduate school are no longer relevant. The implication is that we must offer education that develops general capacities, and particularly the capacity to go on learning; these will serve the individual in a great diversity of work situations.

We must consider also the increasing determination of people's behavior by their occupational roles. As work becomes more and more highly organized, more and more of our lives are determined by our place within the productive organization. Our great organizations, which take over more and more of the productive work of the country, penetrate even into the private lives of the individuals who work in them; there are role requirements even in the life outside the factory or office. So highly organized is the productive activity that the individual who doesn't fit precisely the requirements of his role is like a monkey wrench in the works. Any individuality—any personality, one might say—that is expressed in such a situation is like "noise" in a communication system. Even Ph.D.'s in vast research-producing organizations are virtually "programmed," much like the high-speed computers with which they are supposed to work.

We must have an education that will give the individual other sources of values than the norms of the organization for which he works. He will have to have something inside himself that will support his values, despite the demands made on him by his contemporary situation. Somehow or other he must acquire, in school or college, an orientation to values that will stay with him despite opposing pressures that he will most certainly encounter in his work situation. More than that, if he is to remain an individual, he must be able to see himself in his situation; to be himself, he must see himself existing independently of the organized structure within which he works. In our society today the demands of production are such that people tend to get processed earlier and earlier in their lives so that they will fit the different kinds of productive roles that have been determined by industrial processes. Segregation according to age, sex, and even personality is determined by the requirements of the work that people are going to do.

So great has been the success of our industry that overproduction is chronic. The result is not only that we always have unemployment with us, but the whole meaning of work is changing. There are people spending their time on jobs that have had to be "made" for them. How can a man in these circumstances teach his son the traditional values with respect to work? Or how can he find in his work any basis for his own self-respect?

I don't see how we can meet this situation except by new kinds of education: education for consumption and education for new kinds of production. People must learn to do more kinds of things that cannot be duplicated by machines. They must be educated for creativity in all forms of art and for all kinds of services to other people. If, however, people are to spend more time producing creatively, then we must educate people who can appreciate these new kinds of creations. An example of what I mean is the hi-fi phenomenon of today. Here virtually a new industry was created because more and more people were educated to a place where they were able to consume a product of art. This suggests the direction in which we must go. As the standard of living goes up, people have to become more complicated in order to participate fully in what our affluent society has to offer. And as they do become more complicated, through education, they will sustain the creative aspects of life through their consumption of the new creations of our more talented people. If the level of taste in our culture is to be maintained, education must produce increasing numbers of sensitive and discriminating people.

As a result of the increasing complexity of our society, there are more and more kinds of roles—outside the work situation—that people can take. We have known for quite a long time that it was impossible to educate women for any particular social role. It has been obvious that women actually were called upon to do such a diversity of things that to speak of educating them for this or that particular activity has made no sense. The situation is rapidly becoming much the same for men. A man can no longer define himself as just a breadwinner or just in terms of his vocational role. A man is also a father, an educator, a committee man, a citizen, and probably—if he is in the middle class—an all-around do-it-yourself man. The requirement, then, is for general education, something over and above training for any particular kind of social role. Particularly is it required that a man be able to conceive of himself in terms other than just those of vocational identity. He must be flexible enough in his self-conception, must have a self-conception based on enough familiarity with the different aspects of himself, that he can take these different roles comfortably without feeling that his masculinity is somehow being impaired.

What this adds up to, it seems to me, is an argument that the only kind of education that will produce a person who can perform well and be a real person in our society today must be general education. The more specialized a person's skills, the more likely is the demand for them to disappear in this changing world. Education, then, must develop skills that are basic, durable, and general so that they will serve the individual in a great variety of work-role and life-role demands. He must be able to analyze and to synthesize, to handle data, to see relationships, to see meanings, to judge evidence, to generalize, and so on. These are the kinds of things that must somehow be taught more and more generally, even to people whose work requirements are not going to be on a very high level.

More than that, education must produce a kind of flexibility in the person, an adaptability that permits him to go on learning and to change rapidly from one social role to another without feeling that he has lost his sense of himself. Further, there must be a value-orientation that is truly durable. Such an orientation can be arrived at only through thought and understanding, so that it is felt by the individual to be part of himself. When this is so he can resist pressures to act according to the norms of a particular social group. A person who has developed this capacity is prepared to take part in decisions affecting the whole community, and thus to be a responsible citizen.

Again, there is the requirement for a kind of self-awareness that permits the individual to participate fully in all that is human. With the world shrinking as it is, tribalism no longer has any place. A person who regards himself as categorically different from other human beings lives in the past and is a threat to civic harmony. Fundamentally, the individual who can't feel any solidarity with people of different countries, or of different ethnic or social groups, is one who can't admit into his consciousness some of his own dispositions. Whatever in himself he cannot recognize is likely to be attributed to other people who are then regarded with suspicion and hostility. This state of affairs is overcome in proportion as the individual develops as a personality, develops in the direction of the integration of the personality, so that all of its parts become a conscious totality.

Finally, a person who would realize himself in the world of today must be sufficiently complicated so that he can respond to many different aspects of our culture.

Let it be noted again that we are talking about qualities of the person: skills, flexibility, social responsibility, self-conception, values, openness to experience. These qualities cannot be described in terms of knowledge that has been acquired. They are features of the person which continue to exist after the content of his academic courses has been forgotten. Such qualities do not exist at birth, and for that matter, they exist in only rudimentary form in college freshmen. They must, therefore, be developed.

Happily there is evidence today that this kind of personal development does take place in some colleges. This, indeed, was the major finding of our work at Vassar College, and I am glad to know from Dr. McConnell that our findings are being confirmed elsewhere.

It is interesting to note that despite such evidence students do not as a rule expect to change in college, nor do they understand that this is what they are supposed to do. Last year in my course in the psychology of personality I used some material from our Vassar studies in describing some of the conditions and processes of personality change in college. Students who got the point were amazed. For some who spoke to me individually the idea that they were not stuck with the same old personality, one about which they were not too happy, was absolutely sensational. They took to reading like mad, mainly in the works of the philosophical psychologists, for if they could change, then perhaps they could have a hand in determining what they would become, and if this was so, then they must lose no time in deciding what they should become. Why should the idea of change seem new to students? Perhaps because it is so rarely mentioned in contemporary discussions of education; perhaps because the notion from dynamic psychology that the personality is formed in childhood has taken deep root in our culture.

If we are to educate for individual development we must be guided by a theory of personality and its development under the impact of the social environment. There must be conceptions of the highly developed person, of what makes for developmental change, and of the course of treatment. This is not the place to attempt to work out a general theory, but I would like to offer several ideas that should have place within it.

The human individual is all of a piece. He functions as a unit, and his diverse features develop in interaction one with another. Intelligence, feeling, emotion, and action can be separated conceptually—as they are in psychological experimentation—but in actual life no one of them functions independently of the others. A student's behavior in relation to his social group and to student culture, his relationships with his teachers, his behavior in the classroom, and his reactions to the content of courses, all are closely related; they are related in the sense that all express and are in part determined by the same organization of underlying processes in the personality.

Consider an example. Recently I was told at a southern college that the students were on the whole very bright but afraid to think. They were afraid that thinking would lead to their alienation from their culture. The same kind of thing may be observed among students at our leading colleges and universities; they have a clear conception of a rewarding life after graduation which will be theirs as long as they do not kick over the traces or permit themselves to be influenced by their teachers. The point is of enormous significance, for—such is the wholeness of personality—when people are afraid to think particular thoughts, or to entertain particular ideas, all thinking is impaired. It seems obvious that fear of thinking cannot be overcome merely by exposure to a set of academic courses; it can yield only to educational procedures that aim at stirring up the students' emotional relationships and orientation to value. On the other hand, we need not suppose that improvement in thinking must always await some kind of restructuring of the personality. The cognitive and the emotional-motivational are mutually related. Sometimes an intellectual insight can ramify throughout the whole personality and initiate changes in fundamental structures. Teachers who do not want to upset their students but only to train them in some specialty must be aware of the fact that they are living dangerously, for ideas implanted at times when there is special readiness for them—perhaps when the student has a positive emotional attitude toward his teacher—can have far-reaching effects.

The implication of this last is that the new institutions we create must be something like colleges. However much we might emphasize work, or social organization, or variety of experience, we must remember that exercises of a more or less intellectual nature are still the best means for promoting development of the total personality. Development after the age of about two, after the acquisition of language, is in considerable part a cognitive—one might even say "intellectual"—matter. It involves in a crucial way the use of symbols—words, images, thoughts. Development is largely a matter of expanding the range of things—images, concepts, ideas—that can be appreciated, and the range of responses—largely involving the use of symbols—that can be made. Books, with their gift of boundless vicariousness, are a great benefit to parents or teachers who would develop personalities. It is through utilizing the symbols of his culture, in the life of the imagination, that the individual may most appropriately, and most joyfully, express his deepest impulses and feelings. It is through solving problems with the use of his intelligence—typically in the manipulation of symbols—and through being held to the requirement of seeking, and being guided by, the truth, that the individual develops, through exercise, the functions that enable him to control himself, in accord with the demands of reality. And it is largely through confrontation by a wide range of value systems and ethical dilemmas that conscience becomes enlightened and therefore stabilized.

Development of the personality is in the direction of greater *differentiation,* that is, an increasing number of different parts or features having different and specialized functions, and *integration,* a state of affairs in which there is enough communication among parts so that different parts may, without losing their essential identity, become organized into larger wholes in order to serve the larger purposes of the person. In the highly developed person there is a rich and varied impulse life—feelings and emotions have become differentiated and civilized; conscience has been broadened and refined, and it is enlightened and individualized, operating in accord with the individual's best thought and judgment; the processes by which the person judges events and manages actions are strong and flexible, being adaptively responsive to the multitudinous aspects of the environment, and at the same time in close enough touch with the deeper sources of emotion and will so that there is freedom of imagination and an enduring capacity to be fully alive.

Developmental change can occur at any time of life. All of us, at whatever age, have potentialities that have not yet been led forth. What actually happens depends on conditions—conditions that can, to some extent at least, be controlled. Developmental change takes place when there is a challenge—of such a nature or intensity that the individual cannot manage by behaving just as he did before but must evolve new ways of responding. The challenge must not, however, be too severe—beyond the adaptive capacities of the individual—for in that case there will be a falling back upon primitive modes of adaptation. This is not uncommon in the selective colleges of today, where the pressure of meaningless work is so great that students are driven to use all sorts of manipulative devices for getting by and are prevented from doing work in which they are genuinely involved.

Individual development is progressive. There is some order to the succession of developmental changes. The essential idea is that certain things must happen before other events become possible. The child must walk before he can run. The earlier happening contributes to a state of readiness for change, but it does not make the later happening inevitable; an outside stimulus of the right kind is still necessary. The meaning of events depends on the context in which they occur. Marriage, or vocational commitment taking place too early, say at seventeen or eighteen, is in our culture likely to result in a foreclosure of the personality; the individual may be so taken up with the requirements of his role that he is prevented from having experiences that could develop him.

In our culture, as in most no doubt, there are times when it is considered appropriate to introduce people to the major experiences of life. There are times for going outside to play with other children, for going to school, for leaving home, for going to work, and so on. Probably it is not appropriate to ask high school students to be searchingly critical of themselves and of their society. But it is appropriate to ask this of college students; indeed, they must be set to this task if they are to achieve the clear perceptions necessary to responsible citizenship.

Cultures differ, of course, with respect to the speed with which the events of life are permitted to succeed one another. We, who can afford it, tend to favor as the ideal a long period in which the child and the youth are encouraged to develop before adult responsibilities are taken up. There is wisdom in this, for it is a reasonable assumption that, within limits, the longer this period of preparation the richer and more productive the adult life will be.

Actually, we know far too little about how much time should be allowed for various developmental attainments or about the implications, for later stages, of time spent in earlier ones. Harold Nicolson has argued in defense of shyness that a man who is not shy until he is forty will be a bore after that.

It is a natural consequence of the progressive nature of development that much education has to be remedial. Such is the continuity of events that failures at early stages lead to distortions in all later ones. If a boy has not learned to read and write by the time he enters college, there is nothing else to do but to go back and straighten him out. By the same token, a college freshman who did not have in high school the experience of totally merging himself with a group of his peers, of uncritically accepting the group's goals, and throwing himself into the effort toward their achievement, should be permitted to have the experience now so that he can get it out of his system and move on to a more reasoned and independent participation in organized activities. A graduating senior who has not been through a phase of ethical relativism must sooner or later have this educational experience, for otherwise it is hard to see how his values can be genuinely his own.

Several reasons why everyone should have education beyond the high school have been offered by others. Another argument for such education is implicit in what has been said about the progressive nature of development. Some things that every citizen needs to develop in himself cannot be brought forth in high school because the necessary readiness which is linked to age and general experience of life cannot have been built up at that time. If education were merely a matter of filling the individual with academic content it would be appropriate to begin as early as possible and to speed the process by all possible means—perhaps compressing the present twelve grades of school into ten and the present four years of college into three. It seems, indeed, that this is being tried, and this may explain why it is that some students entering graduate schools of psychology today seem to know everything—except what it is all about. Education for individual development cannot be hurried in such fashion; it must be suited to the developmental stage of the individual, with due attention to individual differences in rates of development. If people of high school age are not ready for certain kinds of educational experiences, then how about college students, or new college graduates? It seems likely that certain lessons cannot be learned until after the individual has had some of the major experiences of life, such as leaving home—psychologically as well as physically, getting married, or holding down a full-time job. The implication of this is not that young people should have these experiences earlier (when they would lack meaning and contribute little to development); it is rather that education for individual development should be continuous.

Once we have decided on individual development as the major educational goal we have to think about what kind of institutional environment might best favor the attainment of this goal. What is taught, how it is taught, the social organization of the student community, the roles and behavior of administrative personnel, and other policies and practices all have to be considered with attention to how they might promote developmental objectives.

There seem to be two major ways in which the study and planning of educational environments might be approached. One is to take some quality of the person, such as those mentioned above, to ask what in general terms are the conditions and processes of developmental change in that quality, and then to inquire how various factors in the educational environment might effectively be brought to bear. The other approach is that suggested above: to take the various substructures of the institution, one at a time, its procedures, programs, instrumentalities—for example, the curriculum, the residential arrangements, the conduct of the office of the dean—and ask how far and in what ways they provide stimuli for development. I should like to illustrate these approaches.

Let us, by way of exemplifying the first approach, consider social responsibility, a requirement of citizenship and an almost universally agreed educational desideratum. Assuming that the child is already a social being in the sense that he has formed attachments to other people and has some disposition to control his behavior in accord with the norms of the larger society, what can a school do to build up in the individual a dependable sense of responsibility for the well-being of the group he belongs to and a willingness to work for the group's goals even when this involves some sacrifice of his private interests? Most schools do, of course, afford a child the experience of being a member of a group, so that he learns something of the rewards of participating in group purposes and of the punishments that might follow neglect of the group's interests. Adolescence, perhaps the high school years as a whole, is the great time for unqualified group loyalty. The young person, unless he has problems that make him hang back, spontaneously seeks to merge himself with the group and to throw himself into the effort to achieve its goals. The harder the task, the greater the demands upon him, the better he likes it, so long as he can see that he is making a contribution and that this is recognized by others.

Feelings and attitudes of these kinds, which are nourished and brought to the fore in face-to-face groups, are easily transferred to the whole school and to the state and nation. Indeed, this kind of social reponsibility is highly valuable to the nation, perhaps necessary to its larger purposes; but, let it be noted, it serves tribes and dictatorships as well as it serves democracies. This is social responsibility below the neck, one might say. Nations can always use this sort of unquestioning loyalty, but they also have need of people who can help decide what is worthy of such devotion. And from the point of view of individual development this kind of adolescent social responsibility leaves much to be desired. If the individual is to become mature he must become capable of criticizing the group's, the nation's, goals, and of working to attain them even though he realizes that they are not the best that might be conceived. In the ideal case he finds in social purposes channels for the expression of his individual needs, and values that are genuinely his own because they have been arrived at through his best thought and judgment and are integrated in his personality. If he never becomes capable of criticizing the purposes of the group he remains, as it were, its plaything—easily exploited by it, easily led in any direction, in danger of being left at sea should the group dissolve.

Here is additional argument for that staging of educational experience that I mentioned earlier. The high school period, or at least the early high school period, is not a good time for teaching social criticism because this would be likely to interfere with the development of group loyalty or primary social responsibility. The high school period, by this same reasoning, would be the best time to teach history in a way that stimulates the imagination, offers conceptions of greatness, and gives a sense of participation in a cultural tradition. The argument from developmental theory is that primary social responsibility, which is to be encouraged and cultivated in high school, is a necessary ingredient of mature social responsibility. It can be argued, further, that because a stage of unquestioning loyalty to the group is a natural part of growing up in a society like ours, it cannot be omitted without disrupting to some extent the whole course of development; if it is not lived through at the appropriate time some need for it will remain—and be a source of susceptibility to totalitarian appeals later on.

It must be admitted that a great many of our young people, particularly those who are early singled out for scholarly careers, are denied the experience of group identification in high school. Our culture today tends to separate categorically the scholars from the athletes and the "regular fellows." A young man is supposed to go directly from being "mama's boy" to "success" at our leading institutions of higher learning. Small wonder that our intellectuals often feel alienated from their society, and that our society, for its part, does not always accord them a high measure of respect.

If we are to have intelligent leaders in our society then our most gifted young people must somehow learn to be at home among men. For this the experience of cooperating in the work of a group is essential; and if this is not offered in school, then it must be offered in college. This means, of course, that the college must break down the false dichotomy of "the intellectual" on the one hand and everything else about the person on the other.

There are other ways in which the college, or new institution beyond the high school, may proceed with the business of developing mature social responsibility. Although its first task in this general area is, as I have said, to shake up the blind loyalties that have been generated earlier it must bear in mind that intellectual analysis by itself is not enough; other loyalties—of a more flexible and differentiated sort, we may hope —must take the place of those that are to be given up. Indeed, a college cannot effectively challenge values that are supported by family, group, or community loyalties unless it can set in opposition to them loyalty to itself and its purposes. More than this, critical analysis of society, leading to the discovery that our most imposing institutions have faults and that highly placed individuals have weaknesses, can easily lead to cynicism, rebellion, or alienation from society. To keep these tendencies within bounds the college must embody within itself some worthy social purposes, and must include among its faculty and administration some suitable models of mature social responsibility.

Perhaps most essentially, the college must be a community. Steps should be deliberately taken to ensure that students feel themselves to be a part of the whole undertaking, that if they do not share in making the rules they at least understand why these rules exist, that they are offered opportunities for contributing to the welfare of the whole. Authoritarian modes of controlling students won't do. Social responsibility cannot be legislated. Although students must learn to come to terms with authority, it is a serious mistake to suppose that they can acquire a sense of responsibility through being subjected to rigid discipline. Students must be governed, but they must also be trusted, even though it is known that the trust will not be justified in all cases. Rules that punish all for the transgressions, or the anticipated trangressions, of a few should be avoided as far as possible. Individual falls from grace must be handled with primary attention to the educational needs of the individual involved, and disciplinary crises involving groups of students should be made occasions for discussions about the responsibilities of membership in a community.

A true community is one in which the more advanced people feel some responsibility for helping other people. And a good way for students to learn something of the social and human purposes of intelligence is to create situations in which they can be helpful to others. It is rare in our educational institutions that intellectual endeavors are carried out by teams or accompanied by a team spirit. Research work does, of course, often have this aspect, but it is rare that undergraduates are able to take part in activity of this sort. Perhaps those who work on the school paper learn something of intellectual cooperation but, by and large, in hard academic work it is every man for himself. We should, in our new institutions, deliberately counter this state of affairs by such measures as setting the more advanced students to teaching the least advanced ones, or organizing projects, e.g., for study and action in the community, that require intellectual cooperation and in which the whole team and not just the star is rewarded.

We are far from having explored fully the psychology of social responsibility and from having exhausted the possibilities for developing this quality through educational procedures. My aim has been to suggest something of what is involved when we think of using an educational environment in order to do something for the individual student.

Now let us turn to the second general approach to study and planning: the examination of the different features of the educational environment in terms of what they might contribute to the development of the individual. Here I intend to illustrate the approach by offering some more or less concrete suggestions of what might be done.

The first point is that the extracurricular or nonacademic aspects of the institutional life should be integrated as closely as possible with the academic and intellectual aspects. It should go without saying that "student personnel workers" should teach and that teachers should take an interest in students and their affairs. What I want to stress is that activities in the nonacademic sphere should be organized and carried out in a way that will further intellectual understanding. There should be discussion with students of "why we do things in this way," and programs of work or action should always be accompanied by related formal instruction. Critical events in the life of the institution should be made occasions for teaching. If disciplinary crises are fine opportunities for teaching morals, so are crises involving academic or political freedom ideal occasions for instruction in this vital area. Instead of trying to hush up or smooth over disturbances on this front so that the institution "can go about its business" it should be recognized that instruction in the meaning and conditions of freedom *is* the business—the first business—of an academic institution in a democratic society. A crisis involving student or faculty freedom should be the subject of symposia in which all members of the community take part. Classroom teachers should happily allow themselves to be led "off the subject" for the day while deans and counselors organize special meetings and discussion groups. It seems likely that more can be learned about democracy during a week of such discussion and dialogue than during a year of untroubled formal course work.

The curriculum in our ideal institution would be regarded as the major instrument for developing the individual, rather than as a "body of knowledge" that must be imparted to the student or that must be offered because other institutions offer it.

Happily, it is possible to say that all the major subjects usually taught in colleges can be taught in ways that are developmental. This includes vocational subjects, which might provide the means for introducing students to valuable developmental experiences. But the great liberal arts subjects are the easiest to support on the ground of developmental theory. History is a great instrument for showing students, quickly and inexpensively, the joys of more or less independent inquiry; philosophy, and especially ethics, is probably still the stand-by for challenging unexamined belief systems and for giving the student his necessary introduction to relativism of values; and literature is the great means for acquainting the student with his own feelings—through showing him something of the variety and depth of what is humanly possible. Each teacher should ask himself just how his subject, as he teaches it, contributes to the development of the individual.

If we take this view of the matter it will become possible to be somewhat relaxed in our consideration of how much material is to be covered. Colleges are constantly seeking new arrangements that will make it possible for the student to get to know the teacher as a person, and these arrangements usually involve *additional* demands on the teacher's time. The college that truly values individual development and understands its conditions and processes will arrange for teachers to *substitute,* in suitable proportions, informal activities with students for classroom teaching.

Another suggestion in this general area is that we aim to educate for wisdom rather than with a view to teaching facts or preparing for specialized advanced training. This would mean that we offer students some means for anticipating the problems of life they are soon to be facing or are facing already. It has struck me as quite remarkable that seniors in one of our best women's colleges don't know how to think about sexual morality. They are still governed in this sphere by beliefs and attitudes taken over quite automatically from parents or peers. They have never made any connection between what they were offered in courses and the real problems with which they have to deal. The fact that in a school of this kind a majority of the senior women could still believe in a double standard of sexual morality suggests to me either that they are not being offered a liberal education or that what they are taught about ethics has not been getting through to them. Again, consider the students at a men's college that sends over 70 per cent of its students to graduate schools. I was told there recently that a student committee for revising the parietal rules had got nowhere because the individuals on it had not learned how to function as committee members. This is relevant to what Professor Commager said about inviting students to do more for themselves. If we take up every moment of the student's time in a program of specialized education designed to get him ready for graduate school, how is the student going to have any experience as a member of a committee? More than this, it was not really possible to induce the students of whom I am speaking to think of themselves as members of a community. They regarded any rules as direct assaults on their freedom. Their education had not suggested to them that after all they will be living, as they do now, in a society, that they will be required to have some responsibility, and that there is much more to life than getting good grades in biochemistry and thus being admitted to a first-rate graduate school. In the new institution we are talking about there will be plenty of time for relating education to life, plenty of time for talk about sex and morality, civil and human rights, government on the campus, and the responsibilities of citizenship. The great issues that concern us all, but which academic men rarely let creep into their courses, will become the major focus in the curriculum in this institution. This, I insist, is not unintellectual. It is merely unacademic. Any of these problems can be used as a basis for the most deep-going kind of intellectual discussion.

The curriculum would also give particular accent to society's problems, and to the human problems that exist in the community where these young people live—problems such as those having to do with civil rights, war and peace, unemployment and the uses of leisure, sex-role differentiation, alcohol, delinquency, the proper role of the police, and so on. Since these problems exist "off campus" as well as on, students should not be discouraged from going off campus to look into them or even to engage in actions affecting them. It would be the task of the faculty to supply the intellectual context and meaning for what was observed or engaged in. The teacher would regard such off-campus activity as fieldwork for a course that was being given, or if some type of off-campus activity seemed particularly interesting or important the teacher would develop a course to take advantage of it.

Far from being unintellectual or unscientific these problems make the greatest demands on the intellect and on any science that attempts to understand human behavior as it is found in nature. If one approaches a human or social problem with a view to doing something about it he will soon discover that this problem exists in a context of processes, that to understand it he has to become familiar with multiple complex determinants, and that to take action affecting it he has to consider a range of possible consequences. This means not only that relevant scientific theories will have to be more comprehensive than those we are being offered today, but that we must abandon the pretense that science can be detached from value. The kind of psychological and social science that abstracts part-processes from life with a view to studying them intensively in the laboratory, the kind of science that resists translation into terms that are relevant to action but which is sometimes, unhappily, imposed on life—this kind of science, as everybody knows, has its place; it is enthroned in the universities. Our folk institutions will need trouble themselves but little with it.

Our new institutions would allow for easy access in and out. Students could study part-time, or they could go off for a time to work or have some other kind of experience with the understanding that readmission would be easy. The expectation would be that all students who "finished" such an institution would understand that in any case he had to go on learning, and that some of this learning might be accomplished back at his old school. Or his old school might go to him. There are a great many people working on the kinds of problems mentioned above who would benefit from what can be offered by teachers in our institutions of higher learning. Let the teacher go to them. Instead of asking, say, parole officers, to go back to school to take a course in company with miscellaneous undergraduates, let the professor of social science meet with these professionals as a group to consider their problems in the light of what he knows.

The institution will have many relationships with agencies, associations, and individuals in its community, and will draw them into its work of teaching. Sometimes individuals from the community will come to the school to teach, and sometimes students will obtain practical experience under the guidance of community agencies or professionals. If agencies or associations of the right kind do not exist they can be created. An example would be our work with the Junior League of San Francisco. This League had a Committee on Alcoholism. Some of us on the staff of the Cooperative Commission on the Study of Alcoholism (working at the Institute for the Study of Human Problems at Stanford University) had the idea that some of these ladies might help us with some of our work. We also had an interest in the continuing education of women college graduates and could think of no better way in which such women might further develop themselves than through helping a university group plan and carry out a research project. So members of the Committee met in seminars with some of our staff to plan a study of drinking among teenagers and their parents. All members of the seminar took part in designing an interview schedule, considering what might be significant questions and how they might best be phrased. (This meant that all hands had to do a certain amount of sorting out of his or her own attitudes respecting his own drinking and that of his children—an educational experience in its own right.) Then came the rounding up of a suitable sample, the interviewing itself, the talking over of experiences, the analysis of the data, discussion of what to do next. So was accomplished one of the very few studies of teenage drinking that we have—perhaps the only one that reaches any depth. But this was perhaps not the major accomplishment of this little project. The ladies had no sooner begun their interviewing than they discovered, as they said, that they were social successes. Whenever the conversation lagged at dinner parties, they could always bring up the subject of their research. They thus began to get the subject of alcohol out from under the rug, and to raise the level on which it is usually discussed. Moreover, it wasn't long before they had a real sense of what goes on among teenagers; they were much put out to see the persistence of wrong stereotypes in the news media and, as we should expect, they were getting prepared, and getting their husbands prepared, for action, action which we might hope will become the subject of more research.

It became obvious to us that there was virtually no limit to the number of such groups that could be organized in the San Francisco Bay Area. Notable also was the fact that the enterprise took little staff time; there were two meetings involving several members of the staff at the Institute, and then Mervin Freedman held perhaps a dozen meetings with the group throughout a year while spending some time arranging for interviews with young people at a local "Y." It would be easy to establish a large aggregate of such work groups or task forces in metropolitan centers across the country. There are plenty of women with some time to give, or be paid for, and, of course, there is no shortage of problems. The key to the success of such an enterprise is research; it is the interest of the problem rather than its social importance that holds the lay investigator to the task, for interest deepens as inquiry proceeds; but action follows naturally upon inquiry, for as soon as intelligent women acquire a sense of familiarity with the facts about a social problem they think in quite concrete terms about what should be done. It seeemed to us that the young women with whom we worked were on the road to becoming community leaders.

In offering this example I have two things in mind. One is that we have here a model that might well be followed in our people's institutions, a model in which inquiry into genuine problems, with action in view, becomes a means for involving the student, for teaching him facts and procedures, and for developing his personality. The other point is that we have here, as a product of our own innovation, a community "agency" with which our new institution might interact. Our ladies of the League are quite ready now to take on undergraduates as assistants or apprentices and to teach them what they themselves have learned. It would be possible to accent the educating function of such community groups as this, and it would not be difficult to develop them on a large scale. Indeed, we may imagine a time when faculty members of educational centers spend relatively little of their time in classroom teaching and much of their time generating ideas and organizing activities in which people of different ages and different walks of life educate each other.

The present situation offers unparalleled opportunities for educational experimentation—a point that has been made by others. There is plenty of room for imagination both in the design of new kinds of institutions and in the trying out of different ways of doing things in the same kinds of institutions.

If such experimentation is not to be hit or miss it must be guided by theory. One may hope that the developmental theory broached above, but not spelled out, will be of service here. There is critical need for knowledge of how people in the age range we are talking about may develop. What kinds of changes in what areas of the person may now be induced and through what kinds of experiences? This is a sadly neglected area of psychological and social research. Much could be learned from careful observation of what happens as the result of different practices in the institutions that now exist and are yet to be created.

It is not to be expected, however, that this experimentation can go forward in accord with the model that is usually employed in laboratory research. People who undertake new educational ventures rarely do so in an objective spirit or merely out of curiosity; rather, they have a passionate concern with what they are doing and much faith in its effectiveness. Thus the question of "what works better" will have to be answered by researchers who have the opportunity to observe two or more institutions or practices at the same time, with due attention to numerous necessary "controls." This kind of research is very difficult to carry out, and it rarely yields satisfactory answers. The crucial point here is that an educational experiment is in reality a venture in social change. If it "succeeds" it is mainly because it fits in with and finds support from the community within which it takes place; and in this case it persists far beyond the time when it would be appropriate to call it an experiment. Another index of the success of such an enterprise would be the degree to which it influenced or was imitated by or became a model for others. Interestingly enough one or the other, or both, of these outcomes may become apparent before the results of any scientific evaluation become available.

It follows from this that the benefits of educational experimentation may lie not so much in what can be found out from it as in the effects that it has on those who take part in it. Almost always an educational experiment interests and challenges the students who are its objects—they are touched by these signs of interest in them—and they respond by performing well and showing various signs of desirable change. And so with teachers who carry out experimental programs. Their desire to see these programs succeed leads to extra effort on their part and, most important, to a fresh interest in students; this makes them better teachers, and the students respond by behaving as the designers of the experiment predicted. Thus it is that processes which make scientific work in this field extraordinarily difficult are the very ones that lead to immediate educational gains.

The final question is, Who is going to do all these things? As Professor Commager said, we are extraordinarily unprepared to think about universal higher education. College faculties by and large are not likely to be interested in the problem. Our graduate schools have not put in their curricula any courses or professional programs designed to prepare people to run institutions of the kind we need. Psychologists by and large tend to specialize in narrow areas on the frontiers of knowledge and are not so interested in large problems such as how people develop and how they might develop better. One would think that the teachers in the community colleges might be good candidates for work in this field but we are told that many of them want to be like the professors in the prestigeful institutions. The fact remains, however, that these colleges do have a group of teachers who want to teach students and who are not concerned about being researchers.

I believe that we must develop a new profession, a profession in which generally educated people become specialists in individual development and in the operation of institutions designed for this purpose. In the meanwhile where do we find, immediately, people who can run these institutions? For one thing we might use all the people who are now engaged in counseling, student affairs, and so on, in the best universities and colleges. They are the kinds of people, I think, who at the moment seem best qualified and if they were all taken out of the places where they now are, and where they are not much appreciated, their places would have to be filled by members of the faculty; if this should happen those members of the faculty would become better teachers. All the people who are now doing individual psychotherapy are prospects for this kind of work, and since individual psychotherapy becomes less often the treatment of choice it might not be too difficult to recruit these specialists. Returning Peace Corpsmen might also be well suited to this work. Some 10,000 will be returning to this country in a couple of years, and it seems that the kind of experience they are having would make excellent preparation for what we have in mind.

Another great resource that we have is the educated women who have some time to devote to worthy enterprises. To set them to work in our folk institutions would help to solve another big problem we have, and that is what should be done about the continuing education of women. One of the best ways to continue their education would be to take part in educating other people.

The Impact on Manpower Development and Employment of Youth

DANIEL PATRICK MOYNIHAN,
Assistant Secretary of Labor

A point is reached in the development of any major social standard when the ability to conceive must be succeeded by the capacity to measure. That point is clearly at hand with regard to the question of universal opportunity for higher education.

American society has been working toward this standard for some generations now; in a sense, from the outset. The average level of education has steadily advanced; we have in the past two decades reached the point where a very large number of persons go on from secondary to higher education. With the resulting advantage both to the nation and to the individuals firmly established in terms of productivity, life income expectations, and the like, the comparative disadvantage of those who do not go on has become equally evident, whereupon the dynamics of a democratic and to some degree egalitarian society take hold and produce the demand that these opportunities be available to all.

The 1964 Democratic Party platform marks, in the 124-year sequence, the transition from merely encouraging higher education to, in effect, insisting on it. The preceding platform had declared the belief "that America can meet its educational obligations" but had not really defined what those obligations might be. Rather, the 1960 document called for a series of specific categories of Federal assistance, leaving it for the future to determine just how much money and how many people would be involved. The 1964 platform, in contrast, said little about forms of assistance, but was explicit as to the objectives to be attained thereby.

> Our task is to make the national purpose serve the human purpose: *that every person shall have the opportunity to become all that he or she is capable of becoming.*
> We believe that knowledge is essential to individual freedom and to the conduct of a free society. We believe that education is the surest and most profitable investment a nation can make.
> *Regardless of family financial status, therefore, education should be open to every boy or girl in America up to the highest level which he or she is able to master.*

Having committed ourselves to that standard—as I know the administration is committed, and feel the nation is approaching—the next principle question (and in some ways the most difficult one) is instantly posed: What are the highest levels of education which various groups in the population are able to master, and what are our resources for providing them?

Until now—that is, for better than a century—we have been able to put off this decision as we have moved toward the goal. Clearly, everyone needs and can benefit from an elementary education. If that is not quite so clear about universal secondary education, most doubts can be resolved in favor of keeping young persons out of the labor market, and so on. But at the point of reaching universal opportunity for higher education, we reach the point of harder decisions. Unless we are utterly to debase the standards of higher education, and in effect issue fraudulent certificates to many persons, it becomes necessary to exclude a large number of persons from higher education on the grounds that they are not able to master it.

That is not an easy thing to do. Those of us who have given our personal commitment to the long and honored quest for social justice in the liberal tradition of Western democracy have perhaps not given enough thought to the cruelties that must follow the final triumph of our ideals, a triumph which cannot, I think, be very far away. It is a harsh thing to turn a young man away from a university because he is too poor to pay. As a product of the City College of New York and the GI Bill, I lived close enough to that possibility to understand its rancor. But I fear it may be no less harsh a thing to turn a young man away because he is too dumb. Society's injustice is succeeded by nature's. Could it be that at the end of all our long struggles lies a super-Calvinist society in which the gulf between the elect and the damned is all the more inexorable for the statistical refinement with which it is determined? This is not, I hope, an altogether irrelevant aside. If that is so, I suspect we are likely to pull back in time. This would have considerable implications for the calculations that follow: It may be that institutions will have to be developed that will permit everyone to attend a thirteenth and fourteenth year of schooling. But for the moment it makes the most sense simply to try to measure the requirements based on the current and more or less traditional levels of performance and ability required to enter college.

COLLEGE ATTENDANCE
IN RELATION TO COLLEGE POTENTIAL

Any estimate of the number of young persons who possess the level of ability required for success in post–high school education depends on the kinds and levels of educational institutions involved. The number of persons capable of completing junior college is greater than the number who might be expected to succeed in a normal four-year college course, and only a fraction of the latter group have the capacities needed for postgraduate professional study. The term "college potential" will be used here to refer to the number of persons possessing the level of intelligence and aptitude required for successful performance of each of these three levels of college education.

(This concept of college potential does not, to repeat, include all persons who might benefit by some kind of post–high school education or training. Some who do not meet the requirements for college success have specific aptitudes or talents that might be utilized by the creation of *new types* of educational opportunities, both within and beyond the high school, which are not presently available to any large number of potential students.)

Amount of College Potential at Various Levels

The tests most commonly used in predicting future success at various levels of the educational system (at elementary, high school, or various college levels) are tests of "general intelligence" or "academic aptitude" which generally measure verbal, mathematical, and spatial aptitudes, with considerable emphasis on verbal items which show a good correlation with progress in school. *Any intelligence test is only in part a measure of innate ability;* test scores inevitably reflect also the extent to which environment, past training, and opportunity have permitted this ability to be translated into capacity to perform. Some studies have shown that "more than three-fourths of all items in the most widely used intelligence tests of today sharply differentiate middle-class from lower-class children," and that many of the latter "do possess abilities that suggest potentialities for further education if the schools had broad enough goals to utilize talents of these kinds."

Such tests, therefore, do not fully reflect the innate capacities of many individuals from economically, socially, or culturally deprived environments; they do, however, provide a fairly valid basis for predicting probable success in educational institutions as they are.

A useful estimate of the distribution of various levels of "college potential" among the total working population can be derived from the norms for *G* (general intelligence) developed in connection with the General Aptitude Test Battery used by the United States Employment Service.

On the basis of these norms, 50 per cent of the population have at least the capacity to complete two years of junior college (many of these, of course, have capacity for more than this amount of college). About 31 per cent have the capacity for a normal four-year college course, and 16 per cent have the capacity for an advanced postgraduate degree. (The *G* scores required at each level are indicated in Table 1.) [1]

These norms, it should be noted, do not represent the average *G* score of persons who enter or graduate from each of the three levels of college education, but the minimum required for a reasonable prospect of succeeding at each level. In practice, as we all know, college entrance requirements are not based entirely, or even primarily, on intelligence test scores, but take into account other factors such as high school grades and various tests of performance or academic aptitude. Moreover, the same individual may achieve somewhat higher or lower scores at different times, or on different tests, and the IQ can change with age. Thus, there will be some individuals who score below a given norm, but actually can succeed at a given level of college education (and vice versa). But for the

[1] Some caution is in order here: there are ethnic groups in the American population, whose members range across the social classes, which manage to send a much higher proportion of their young persons to college than the "normal" distribution of talent would warrant. A study by Alfred Jospe of B'nai B'rith (1963) indicated that between 70 and 82 per cent of Jewish youth attend college. The 1960 Census revealed that Americans of Japanese and Chinese ancestry were attending college in proportions twice that of "whites."

TABLE 1. Relationships between College Potential (Persons with the Required Mental Ability) and Actual Educational Attainment, at Three Levels of College

Level of education	G score (level of intelligence) required *	Per cent of population		Actual (column 3) as per cent of potential (column 2)
		With required level of intelligence *	Who have completed at least specified amount of college †	
Total population:				
All levels	—	100.0	100.0	—
Junior college:				
Total	100	50.0	23.1 ‡	46.2
Male	100	50.0	27.4 ‡	54.8
Female	100	50.0	18.9 ‡	37.8
Four-year college:				
Total	110	31.0	11.0	35.5
Male	110	31.0	14.4	46.5
Female	110	31.0	7.8	25.2
Postgraduate college:				
Total	120	16.0	3.8	23.7
Male	120	16.0	6.0	37.5
Female	120	16.0	1.6	10.0

* U.S. Department of Labor, Bureau of Employment Security, *Guide to the Use of General Aptitude Test Battery*, Section II = norms, October, 1962.
† U.S. Bureau of the Census, *Census of Population: 1960, Final Report PC(2)-5B*.
‡ Data refer to persons who completed one to three years of college.

population as a whole, the norms do indicate the approximate percentage of youth with a given level of capacity.

Amount of Unused College Potential

By comparing the estimates of college potential with the number of persons who actually complete various amounts of education at the college level, we obtain some measure of the extent to which American youth, in the recent past, have failed to achieve the level of higher education for which they are "eligible" in terms of intelligence or aptitude.

Table 2 presents such a comparison, based on the educational attainment of persons from twenty-five to twenty-nine years of age in 1960. This is the youngest age group, old enough to have substantially completed its formal education, for which data are available. (The eventual educational attainment of persons now of college or high school age will be significantly higher, if assumed goals—discussed below—are confirmed.) The 1960 data show that:

For both sexes combined, 50 per cent had the capacity required for success in junior college or some higher level, but only 23 per cent of the age group had completed one or more years of college. About 55 per cent of the men, but only 38 per cent of the women with the necessary capacity actually completed a year or more of college.

At higher levels of college education, the gap between "potential" and actual completion of college education widens. While 31 per cent had the capacity for a four-year college degree, only 11 per cent had obtained one —including about 46 per cent of the young men but only 25 per cent of the women with the required capacity.

Persons with the exceptional level of talent needed for success in a postgraduate professional school make up 16 per cent of the population, but less than a quarter of them had actually completed a year or more of graduate work. At this level, the difference between the sexes is particularly great: Nearly two-fifths of the men, but only one-tenth of the women with the capacity for a postgraduate degree had actually completed a year or more of graduate study.

If the relative loss of college potential is greatest at the four-year and postgraduate levels, the absolute loss—measured by the number of individuals who fail to obtain a college education consistent with their capacity—is represented by persons with college-level intelligence who fail to complete even a single year of college. Table 2 presents rough estimates, based on the norms and census data used above, which show that among persons from twenty-five to twenty-nine years of age in 1960:

There were more than 2.9 million persons capable of at least a junior college education, who had not completed even one year of college. These represent more than a quarter of *all* persons in the age group, slightly less than a quarter of the males, and nearly a third of the women.

The average annual loss of college potential, during the period when these college eligibles might have obtained a college education but failed to do so, was about 585,000 persons, including about 240,000 young men and 345,000 young women who might have benefited from college, but ended up with no college education. Currently, the annual loss is larger because of the larger number of persons at college entrance-age levels.

This loss includes not only persons barely qualified for junior college, but also many who have the ability for four-year college or postgraduate study, but fail to complete any college education.

A similar analysis for persons with potential capacity for a four-year (or higher) degree shows that, among persons from twenty-five to twenty-nine years of age in 1960:

Nearly 2.2 million persons with capacity for a four-year college education, and more than 1.3 million with a capacity for postgraduate professional study, had failed to attain the level of education for which they were qualified.

The annual loss of four-year college eligibles who failed to attain that level of education was about 435,000, including more than 175,000 potential male college graduates and nearly 260,000 young women.

For the same age group, the annual loss of potential professional school graduates was about 265,000, including about 110,000 males.

A failure of this magnitude to make full use of our human resources raises two basic questions: What accounts for the failure of youth with

TABLE 2. Approximate Number of Persons with College Potential at Various Levels, Number with Unused Potential, and Annual Loss of College Potential

(Based on data for persons from twenty-five to twenty-nine years of age, 1960 Census)

Level of education and sex	Number of persons (thousands)				
	With required level of intelligence *	Who completed at least specified amount of college †	Who failed to complete specified amount of college		
			Total age 25–29 in 1960	Per cent of age group	Annual equivalent
Junior college:					
Total	5,437	2,511 ‡	2,926	26.9	585
Male		1,463 ‡	1,207	22.6	240
Female		1,048 ‡	1,722	31.1	345
Four-year college:					
Total	3,376	1,201	2,175	20.0	435
Male		771	886	16.6	175
Female		430	1,285	23.2	265
Postgraduate college:					
Total	1,739	412	1,327	12.2	265
Male		323	539	10.0	110
Female		89	797	14.4	155

* U.S. Department of Labor, Bureau of Employment Security, *Guide to the Use of General Aptitude Test Battery*, Section II = norms, October, 1962.
† U.S. Bureau of the Census, *Census of Population: 1960, Final Report PC(2)–5B.*
‡ Data refer to persons who completed one to three years of college.

college potential to receive postsecondary education? And what can be done to eliminate these barriers to college attendance?

In general, taking the educational system as it is, it is possible to predict with fairly high accuracy the success of individuals at the high school and college levels, to identify those who are likely to drop out at various points, and to identify "superior" students at a fairly early age. Nevertheless, the "ability" to profit from education is increasingly recognized as something which is not fixed at birth, but reflects "complex processes through which potential qualities are transformed into recognized and educated performances of many different kinds." The abilities that might be liberated and used by more effective programs of education are not limited primarily by genetic factors (though these, of course, exist); the actual limits, for practical purposes, are determined by the economic, social, and educational environment of the individual.

Because youth with below-average IQ's are more likely to drop out before completing high school, persons with at least junior college "potential" make up considerably more than half of all high school graduates. The estimates made by the Commission on Human Resources and Advanced Training (1954) indicate that more than 65 per cent of all high school graduates have IQ's of 100 or more. Among graduates in the top two-thirds of the Project Talent scores for academic aptitude, nearly two-fifths had not entered college within a year after leaving high school.

Factors Related to College Entrance and Success

Ability is only one of the factors that determine whether a high school graduate will go on to college. Also essential are (1) motivation, (2) suitable preparation during high school and adequate school grades, (3) availability of suitable opportunities to enter a college-level institution, and (4) the necessary finances. All these factors are to a considerable extent interrelated; a high school student's motivation and interest are partly determined by his family's social and economic characteristics, by his (or his parents') ability to pay for college, and by his school record and the attitudes of his teachers and fellow students.

Studies of the college plans and actual college attendance of boys and girls who graduated from high school in 1960 show that college attendance is very definitely influenced by family income, the education and occupation of parents, and the types of curriculum chosen in high school. Data from Project Talent indicate, for example, that at any given level of academic aptitude, college attendance tends to be lowest for students from poor families, and to increase with annual family income.

Even a fully developed system of community colleges, providing a "universal opportunity" for two years of free public education beyond the high school, will not wholly eliminate the barriers to full utilization of the full college potentials of our youth. Some low-income families will be reluctant or unable to bear the direct costs of supporting children through two more years of schooling. More important, a considerable number of persons with the *capacity* for a four-year or postgraduate degree will fail to go beyond the "junior college" level unless financial barriers to further education (often away from home) are removed.

In an ideal society, we might well set our sights, eventually, on eliminating or greatly reducing the financial barriers to education beyond the first two postsecondary years. The possibilities for Federal action that might be considered, assuming such a policy decision, would include (1) a broad system of loans, available to *all* students meeting specified conditions—these might be direct loans by the Federal government, or private loans guaranteed by the government as in the case of FHA and VA housing loans; and (2) a more limited system of direct grants, to cover subsistence and tuition, and possibly some part of the financial responsibilities of students with dependents. Eligibility for such grants would have to be restricted on some basis, certainly with relatively high academic ability as one factor considered. Other possible eligibility conditions might include service in the Armed Forces, family income level, or marital status of the potential students.

An ideal society might well consider also some way of reducing the financial barriers to completing even the first two post–high school years, perhaps by special tax credits to parents who have children enrolled in higher educational institutions, or by direct "educational allowances" to low-income families.

IMPACT ON THE ECONOMY

Impact on Labor Force, Employment, and Unemployment

The impact on labor force, employment, and unemployment of added years of education and training for our youth depends, of course, not only on the size of the increase in school enrollment, the type of education provided, and educational levels achieved, but also on the additional employment created by the necessary construction, operation, and maintenance of additional facilities, as well as the increased teaching and other personnel required.

It depends also on the length of time it will take to arrive at established goals. If we could provide by 1970 a universal opportunity for free public education for two years beyond the high school and sufficient aid to eliminate the economic deterrents for those with the ability and desire to continue their education beyond this level, we might at that time have a million more students enrolled in the various postsecondary and higher education institutions than are now projected for that year. This increase in school enrollment is based on a rise in postsecondary enrollments to 50 per cent of the school-age population (eighteen to twenty-one). Currently we fall short of this level by almost 1.4 million but the difference over the next decade to 1975 would average about a million a year. A higher proportion of these additional 1 million students would be enrolled in either two-year institutions or in the first two years of four-year colleges. Assuming some rise in the proportion of the two-year students in total college enrollments, up to 350,000 [2] of the million additional students might be enrolled in the last two years of college or university. If the rise in baccalaureate degrees were proportionate to the rise in enrollments in these years, between 23 and 24 per cent of our twenty-one-year-old population might finish college as compared with a proportion between 20 and 21 per cent projected for 1970.

Provided that the education received were tailored to the abilities of the students and to manpower needs, we would materially improve the work prospects of the additional students not only for any employment but for employment in better jobs than they would otherwise have. Such upgrading of this part of the labor force would make room for the less well trained in the lower-level jobs they would vacate. At the same time the program would help meet anticipated manpower needs for better-educated and trained workers.

Approximately 85 per cent or 850,000 of these additional students would normally be in the labor force if not in school; but if the additional students had the same propensity to work as those who now attend college, 40 per cent or 400,000 would be both in school and in the labor force. Thus, the labor force would be reduced by some 450,000. Adjusting the number for the proportion who would have been unemployed, we

[2] This estimate is based on an adjustment of the distribution of enrollments to take into account the third of the twenty-to-twenty-one-year-old population in 1970 with ability to finish college and the markedly lower college enrollment rates of married men and women in this age group. Twenty-six per cent of the men in this age group are married and fifty-two per cent of the women; only seven per cent of the married men and two per cent of the married women are enrolled in college. Over time, with economic assistance available to them, a higher proportion might be enrolled.

might expect to release an average [3] of 400,000 jobs annually over the decade which could be occupied by other unemployed in the labor force. The number of jobs thus released would be about sufficient to offset the number of unemployed youth in the same age group. Such an offset would occur, of course, only if unemployed youth in the same age group were, in fact, hired to fill the vacated jobs. Though a complete offset is unlikely, a considerable part of the offset is quite possible owing to the nature of the jobs left vacant by youth who continue in school. While some slight expansion of the labor force under these circumstances is not unlikely, it would probably be balanced by the 400,000 students remaining in the labor force who would become part-time workers rather than full-time workers.

In addition to the jobs vacated by increased student enrollment, the number of additional jobs which would be created by the construction, maintenance, and operation of needed facilities, and the additional teaching and nonteaching personnel is estimated at about 300,000. Half of these jobs would represent additional personnel needed on a continuing basis for the maintenance, operation, and instructional services required for the additional schools rather than the construction phase of the program.

Impact on the National Product

Estimates of the monetary value which the additional education of this group might contribute to the national product are beset with many pitfalls. Dr. Edward F. Denison's efforts to measure education as a source of economic growth have made a major contribution in this field. He concludes that education represents one of the largest sources of prospective economic growth, and calculates, roughly, that if it were possible over the twenty-year period, 1960–1980, for 40 per cent of the labor force to receive one year more of education than they otherwise would, the national product could be increased by 1.4 per cent. He estimates further that this would represent an increase in the growth rate over that period of 0.07 per cent. Over the long run, a period sufficiently long to assure an additional year of schooling for the entire labor force, the average annual economic growth rate could be raised by 0.10 percentage points.[4]

In the near term, with only a small percentage of the labor force obtaining additional education, the effect would be negative because of

[3] Based on an assumption of an overall unemployment rate of 4 per cent.
[4] Edward F. Denison, *The Sources of Economic Growth in the United States*, Supplementary Paper, no. 13, C.E.D., January, 1962, pp. 74–75.

the attendant loss of labor involved. One might reason that some of this loss could be absorbed or replaced by employment of the unemployed in the labor force. Over the first decade, if 15 per cent of the labor force obtained a year of additional education and the quality of the labor force were raised by 1.1 per cent (using his computation) and most of the loss (computed at 1.3 per cent) balanced by putting unemployed persons to work, the improved quality might represent an addition to the national product. Further, to the extent that the education achieved a better matching of workers and requirements, and thus reduced the structural unemployment problem, it would provide an added stimulus to economic growth.

Effect on Lifetime Earnings and Working Life

While the effect on the gross national product of an increase in the proportion of the labor force with an education beyond the high school cannot be forecast with any precision, it is clear that workers who have completed two or four years of postsecondary education will (if their training is properly keyed to manpower needs) be more productive than they would be with only a high school education. This is suggested by comparisons of the lifetime and annual incomes of men who have completed various amounts of education. Table 3 based on 1961 incomes and appropriate tables of working life, shows that men with from one to three years of college education could anticipate a lifetime income of over $273,000, or 22 per cent above the lifetime income of high school graduates with no further education. Men with four or more years of college could look forward to a lifetime income of more than $360,000, or 61 per cent above the income of high school graduates.

The data for men with one to three years of college education, as shown in this comparison, may somewhat understate the possible effects of universal opportunity for two years of college education. Those who had completed one to three years of college in 1961 were presumably, in large part, people who had aimed at a four-year college degree but for some reason had dropped out without reaching that goal. Most of them presumably did not obtain solid preparation for employment. A much larger proportion of the future graduates of two-year postsecondary institutions will, if all goes well, have completed an occupation-centered curriculum that prepares them adequately for a technical or subprofessional field of work, and the impact of their college training on their future incomes may be greater than for past college dropouts.

The rise in income and productivity will, of course, be partly offset by the cost of providing the extra two or more years of education, and by the loss of potential earnings (or production) while the student is in college. This loss of income, if it is taken as twice the average annual earnings of a male high school graduate, would be something over $12,000 (in 1961 dollars) as compared with a gain of about $50,000 in lifetime earnings for the two-year college graduates, and about $136,000 for those who complete four years or more of college.

TABLE 3.   Lifetime and Mean Annual Incomes of Males 25–64 Years Old, by Years of School Completed, 1961

| Years of schooling | Lifetime income | | Mean annual income | Years of working life |
	Amount	Per cent of income of high school graduates		
Elementary:				
Less than eight years	$124,930	56.0	$3,483	35.9
Eight years	168,810	75.0	4,750	35.5
High school:				
One to three years	193,082	87.0	5,305	36.4
Four years	224,407	100.0	6,102	36.8
College:				
One to three years	273,049	122.0	7,392	36.9
Four years or more	360,604	161.0	9,530	37.8

SOURCE: Based on U.S. Bureau of the Census, *Statistical Abstract of the United States, 1963*, p. 122.

The two "lost years," moreover, are not a permanent loss because college-trained workers are more likely to remain in the labor force in their later years; their total "working life" is slightly longer than that of the high school graduate. And those who obtain a four-year or postgraduate degree will, on the average, add five extra years of work to their working lives, making their average lifetime employment nearly thirty-eight years, as compared with thirty-seven years for the high school graduate.

THE CHARACTERISTICS, EDUCATIONAL POTENTIALS, AND EDUCATIONAL GOALS OF THE ADDITIONAL COLLEGE STUDENTS

While the basic estimates presented above are admittedly a "model" rather than a prediction, they imply that the *percentage* of American youth who will enroll in some kind of postsecondary education in 1970 will be much higher than at present and that there will be also large increases in the percentage completing various levels of post–high school education.

The characteristics, capacities, and educational objectives of these additional students will differ in many ways from those of the present college population. They will be less heavily concentrated in the upper ranks of academic aptitude, will come from different socioeconomic backgrounds, and have different vocational goals. These differences, along with the changing occupational requirements of our economy, will have an important bearing on the kinds and amounts of education to be provided under the expanded program, especially during the first two years beyond the high school.

To reach the overall goal, we must assume that 50 per cent of all persons who reach age eighteen, and two-thirds or more of all high school graduates, will eventually enroll in some type of post–high school educational program if a universal opportunity is made available for two years of free education beyond the high school. (Some states, such as California, expect to go considerably further; other states, of course, will fall below the national average.) Currently, only about 38 per cent of our youth, and a little more than 50 per cent of our high school graduates, enter post–high school institutions.

Education for the "Middle Range"

The goal of providing some kind of college-level education for a much larger fraction of our youth cannot be achieved simply by increasing the *quantity* of education provided, with no change in the nature and goals of postsecondary education. The additional students at the junior college and more advanced college levels will be quite different in talents and interests from those who enter college under our existing programs, except in those few states and cities which already provide a universal (or nearly universal) opportunity for free public education beyond the high school.

Our decisions as to goals and structure of postsecondary education must therefore take into account not only the prospective demand for workers in occupations that require education beyond the high school, but also the characteristics and abilities of the people who make up the additional college-level population.

In large part, our present college entrants tend to be concentrated among the children of parents in the higher socioeconomic groups, the children of professional, managerial, white-collar, or skilled workers. Children from small families, whose parents have above-average incomes and education, are most likely to have the required traits.

Still, our society provides enough upward mobility so that bright children from other backgrounds also make it into college. But for any given level of academic ability, college entrance has tended to be much higher among the children of the better-educated, the better-off, and those with essentially "middle-class" goals and attitudes. In large part, our colleges and universities have been training institutions for professional, managerial, and administrative workers (or their wives).

The new, expanded college population will include some persons with goals and capacities similar to those of our present college students. Project Talent data show that nearly three-tenths (28 per cent) of the 1960 high school graduates whose academic aptitude scores were in the top 40 per cent of their class did not enter college within a year; more than one-third (34 per cent) of the girls in this upper group failed to enter college. This upper 40 per cent corresponds roughly with the group likely to have the capacity for a four-year college degree.[5] A larger proportion of the "new" students will come from lower levels of academic aptitude.

One big change will be that, where our colleges and junior colleges have been dealing mainly with persons who aim eventually to receive a four-year or postgraduate degree, our new post-high school institutions will have to meet the needs of a much less homogeneous group. Some will want the traditional types of higher education; but many will look on a year or two of post–high school training as the terminal goal of their educations—as the period in which they must acquire the knowledge and skills to enter an occupation that calls for more than a high school education, but less than a four-year college degree.

From various studies made by the Census Bureau, the Department of Labor, the U.S. Office of Education, and Project Talent, we know quite a bit about the characteristics of high school graduates who now enter college, those who do not, and those who enroll but drop out of college in the first year. What is said below about the characteristics, abilities, and needs of the prospective additions to our "college" population is mainly from these sources.

---

[5] Since about 70 per cent of the population graduate from high school, and 31 per cent of the population have the "capacity" for a four-year degree, those with the required capacity make up slightly more than two-fifths of all high school graduates. Most of these probably score in the top 40 per cent on academic aptitude.

Academic Aptitude of the Additional Students

Project Talent, a nationwide survey of high schools and high school students, provides us with our most detailed information on the characteristics of those high school graduates (in 1960) who did or did not enter college within a year after graduation. In that year, about 42 per cent of all graduates (46 per cent of the boys and 38 per cent of the girls) entered some college-level institution, with nearly four out of five of these attending a four-year institution.[6]

The proportion of high school graduates who enter college is closely, but by no means perfectly, related to academic aptitude as measured by a battery of Project Talent tests. About 97 per cent of those in the top 1 per cent in aptitude, and 93 per cent of those in the top 5 per cent, entered college within a year. Among the next 5 per cent (the 90 to 94th percentile), 86 per cent did so. With each successive decline in aptitude level, the percentage of college entrants decreases, dropping more sharply for girls than for boys, as the following examples show:

Rank in academic aptitude (percentile rank among all twelfth-grade students)	*Percentage entering college within one year*		
	Total	*Male*	*Female*
95–99 (top 5 per cent)	93.4	94.7	91.8
85–89	80.5	85.6	75.0
75–79	68.9	76.4	62.0
50–59	44.7	54.6	37.5
30–39	29.1	35.9	24.4
0–9 (lowest 10 per cent)	14.6	16.8	12.4

Using these data in a different way, we can determine the distribution, by academic aptitude, of those high school graduates who did not enter college, and compare them with those who did enter. The noncollege group gives us a fairly good picture of the aptitude levels of those "additional students" who may enter postsecondary education under a program providing universal opportunity for two years of free public education after high school.

[6] Some high school graduates who do not enter college immediately do so later; a study by the National Science Foundation found that this was true for 25 per cent of the boys and 6 per cent of the girls who do not enter immediately.

As Table 4 shows, these "additional students" will differ in several ways from the group who now enter college:

Relatively few (less than 17 per cent) of the potential new students are in the upper range of academic aptitude (the top 30 per cent). In contrast, nearly three-fifths of the high school graduates who now enter college are in this upper group.

TABLE 4. Distribution by Academic Aptitude of 1960 High School Graduates Who Entered College and of Those Who Did Not

Percentile rank on general academic aptitude test (Project Talent)	Graduates who entered college within one year	Graduates who did not enter college (potential new college students)		
		Total	Male	Female
Total:				
Number	416,200	406,000	157,300	248,700
Per cent	100.0	100.0	100.0	100.0
90–99	23.2	2.7	3.1	2.4
80–89	19.1	5.7	5.7	5.7
70–79	15.4	8.2	7.8	8.4
60–69	11.8	10.5	9.6	11.1
50–59	9.3	11.7	10.5	12.5
40–49	7.3	12.1	11.1	12.8
30–39	5.3	13.2	12.5	13.6
20–29	4.0	12.5	12.5	12.5
10–19	2.8	12.2	13.2	11.6
0– 9	1.9	11.2	14.2	9.3

SOURCE: Adapted from Project Talent, data on 1960 high school graduates responding to the 1961 Follow-up Questionnaire.

However, more than a quarter of the potential new students (27 per cent) are among the top 40 per cent in academic aptitude—a range which probably corresponds fairly well with the group with intellectual capacity for a four-year college degree. Assuming public policies which encourage such students to go beyond two years of college, many in this group will be candidates for "transfer programs" which prepare them for further college work after the second year.

Almost exactly half (over 49 per cent) of the potential new students will be between the 40th and 80th percentiles in academic aptitude (among present college entrants, only 26 per cent are in this range). This group, in large part, will correspond with those who have the ability to complete junior college, but who would have difficulty in a four-year college.

Finally, at the bottom of the aptitude scale (the lowest 20 per cent) will be nearly a quarter of the potential new students. Most of these are probably in the IQ range just below the level generally considered necessary for completion of junior college. Many, however, will have aptitudes or motivation that will lead them to enter postsecondary education, if admission is open to all persons with a high school diploma.

The Need for a Wide Variety of Postsecondary Education

The new entrants into postsecondary education, under a program offering universal opportunity to do so, will thus be much less homogeneous than those now in college. While the top quarter will be much like the present students in junior college transfer programs, many of them will no doubt desire job-centered programs which will prepare them for technical or subprofessional jobs in two years' time.

Those in the middle range will have a variety of objectives. Most of them will consider the fourteenth year (or less) as their terminal educational goal. Among these, some will want generalized academic training, as a sort of abbreviated "college career." Others will seek primarily to prepare themselves for work through occupationally centered curricula.

Those in the lowest quarter, if they enter postsecondary schools, will in many cases need education quite different from what is now presented in the typical junior college. While they are relatively low in academic aptitude, many of them will have aptitudes which might make them good candidates for craft or technical training which fits their mechanical or other abilities.

The question will no doubt arise in many of the new community programs whether the needs of some types of students can be met best by special curricula within a "junior college," or by separate technical institutes or other institutions offering occupation-centered training. The possible appeal of such schools is suggested by the surprisingly large number of persons (about 1.3 million) who in 1962 were enrolled in special schools—such as trade schools, business schools, schools of nursing and beauty culture, and the like. To the extent that institutions outside the "college" system are set up, basic issues will also arise as to how much stress should be put on specific occupational preparation versus general academic work. It seems likely that there is no simple "all-or-none" answer to this question.

A large number of other special arrangements may be called for in a system offering universal opportunity for education beyond the high school. Our population of high school graduates, for example, contains a large number of youth whose *actual* educational attainment is far below the high school graduate level. Data on persons rejected in the Armed Forces Qualification Tests, and on the actual average scores of twelfth-grade students in reading comprehension, English, and arithmetic (from Project Talent), make it clear that large numbers of high school graduates are actually below the ninth-grade, or even the eighth-grade level in performance. Postsecondary institutions can, of course, deal with such students merely by letting them enroll, and then flunking them out. But it might be in the public interest to provide special arrangements for accelerated "catch-up" education, in which these victims of poor high schools or poor environments can be brought to at least the high school level of performance.

Other situations in which special arrangements and imaginative approaches will be needed include:

Arrangements for part-time institutional instruction, at the postsecondary level, for persons whose occupational goals can be met best by apprentice or on-the-job training, in some combination with academic training.

Residential schools, beyond commuting distance from the student's home, for persons from sparsely settled areas where an easily accessible community college would be economically impracticable or too small to be efficient.

Reexamination of admission requirements and selection techniques to assure that Negroes and others from disadvantaged groups are not in effect excluded from postsecondary education, either by being "counseled out" before entering, or "flunked out" soon after entering.

Development of various combinations of vocational, on-the-job, and institutional training to meet the needs of special groups.

Sex Distribution

The potential additional students, as Table 4 shows, will include a considerably larger number of young women than young men. Three out of five high school graduates who do not enter college are girls (61 per cent) and, if they make proportionate use of the "universal opportunity," they will make up a larger part of the community college population than they do among current college students. This would call for greater emphasis on occupation-centered training in those occupational fields that are suitable for women. It is possible, of course, that earlier marriage among young women, including those possessing "college potential" will continue to limit their use of college-level opportunities for higher education.

Socioeconomic Background and Geographical Location

From Project Talent and various other studies of factors related to college attendance, it is possible to give a socioeconomic profile of the high school students who at present fail to enter college. It is clear that

The noncollege group includes a much higher proportion of children from relatively low-income families. In fact, at any given level of aptitude, the proportion of college-bound high school graduates is highest among families with the highest incomes, and declines as family income is lowered to the poverty level. Also, the proportion of students with above-average academic aptitude is highest in well-to-do families, and lowest among the poorest.

A significantly greater proportion of the additional enrollment will come from the families of manual workers, and from families in which the parents have relatively limited education. In fact, census data on college attendance show that it is more affected by the educational level of parents than by the level of family income.

The additional students will include a much larger proportion who (now at least) are in "general" or "vocational" curricula in high school. In fact, the decision to enter something other than a college-preparatory curriculum, often made several years before high school graduation, is one of the most decisive factors.

College Potential and Attendance as a Phenomenon Determined by Many Factors

From these and many other data, it is evident that both college aptitude and college attendance are influenced by many factors—economic, social, cultural, and motivational—which tend to be mutually reinforcing. Long before many high school students approach graduation, their attitudes and their mental development are influenced by their family setting and by the essentially middle-class goals and values of the educational system itself. Middle-class children are typically encouraged by their parents to do good school work. Their ideals and their value system tend to coincide with those of their teachers and of the schools. The opposite tends to be true of children from lower-class homes.

These built-in restraints on educational development are reinforced by economic barriers. The lower-class child is likely to have little hope that his parents will finance education beyond the high school, or that he can earn his own way. Nor, even if he is motivated toward college, is he as likely to meet the entrance requirements of the better colleges. Other barriers may be presented by early marriage, a need to help support his parents or his siblings, or (in the case of students from rural areas or from the South) lack of educational institutions near his home in which he could obtain a college education.

The two main obstacles to use of a "universal opportunity" appear to be lack of financial ability, and lack of motivation toward or expectation of education beyond the high school. The financial obstacles can be reduced, but not wholly eliminated, by a nationwide system of free community colleges. One problem here is that, geographically, a large part of our unused potential is located in areas (such as the South and Appalachia) which have been unable, or unwilling, to provide adequate elementary and secondary education. Federal aid is indispensable if these geographical differences in opportunity are to be leveled out. We must also find some means, through tax credits, educational allowances to poor families, or some other means, to assist the students of low-income families in meeting the direct expenses (apart from tuition) which may make it impossible for them to afford two years or more of extra education.

The problem of motivation has to be dealt with long before the time of high school graduation. Universal opportunity beyond the high school will help to increase the expectation of receiving postsecondary schooling, but much will depend on the value and effectiveness of the education provided in community colleges. The question of what kinds of education and training will contribute most to individual success—in terms of jobs and incomes—is discussed below.

KINDS OF EDUCATION NEEDED TO ENSURE
EMPLOYABILITY IN SOCIALLY USEFUL WORK

The Occupational Profile

For about two decades now, the Department of Labor has been studying employment trends and factors affecting manpower needs, and making employment projections for the various occupations and industries. In doing this we have to make certain assumptions regarding the rate of economic growth and general levels of employment over the long run and we have to bar from consideration abrupt changes in work patterns, in population trends, in our fundamental economic structure, or in major national policy or situations which would destroy continuity of past trends. Nonetheless, we have been able to anticipate and project future levels of demand for workers in broad occupational groups and in many more detailed occupations with a respectable degree of accuracy. More recently, we have also directed our attention to assessing the impact of technological advance on manpower requirements in the occupations and industries most likely to be affected. Currently we are developing a method of surveying job vacancies throughout the country to provide a measure and description of current manpower needs, another piece of information essential to better manpower planning.

Our specific projections of growth or decline in the major occupations are now widely publicized and need not be repeated. For emphasis, I shall point only to a few major changes which differing rates of growth will produce in the occupational distribution of our work force over the fifteen-year period, 1960–1975.

Occupation	Per cent distribution		Per cent change
	1960	1975	1960–1975
All occupations	100.00	100.0	31
Professional and technical	11.2	14.2	65
Managerial	10.6	10.7	32
Clerical and kindred	14.7	16.2	45
Sales	6.6	6.7	34
Craftsmen	12.8	12.8	30
Operatives	18.0	16.3	18
Service	12.5	14.3	51
Laborers	5.5	4.3	— (no change)
Farmers and farm workers	8.1	4.5	−28

The most dramatic change (not unexpected) is the rise of the professional and technical group from 11.2 per cent to 14.2 per cent of the work force in 1975, or about one in seven workers. Translated into absolute numbers, this means about 12.5 million professional and technical workers. They will be outnumbered only by the clerical group and the operatives, each representing about 14 million workers and each accounting for about one in every six workers. The operatives, however, are growing at a much slower rate (an anticipated 18 per cent increase, 1960–1975, as compared with 65 per cent for professional workers and 31 per cent for all occupations) and thus losing their relative rank. The clerical group is still gaining in relative importance, though not as rapidly as in the past, owing in part to the technological impact on many of the routine jobs in the group. Its expected increase is 45 per cent by 1975, about half again as high as the total of all occupations, taken together. Interestingly enough, by 1975 the professional group will be about the same size as the service group, also expected to reach 12.5 million. This group, second only to the professional group in rate of growth (51 per cent by 1975), may after 1975 be outnumbered by the professional and technical workers in this country. Within the latter group, the technician category, during the past decade, experienced a far greater increase than the average of nearly 50 per cent for the group as a whole. The number of medical and dental technicians, for example, rose by almost 80 per cent while the number of physicians and surgeons rose only by about 19 per cent, and the number of dentists by about 10 per cent. The number of electrical and electronic technicians experienced the largest percentage increase for any occupation during the past decade. Engineering and physical science technicians doubled their number during this period. The combined increase represented more than a quarter of a million workers and accounted for 10 per cent of the total growth in professional and technical employment during the decade. As additional ways of using subprofessional personnel to assist and support highly trained professional workers are likely to be found in the future, the number of technicians is expected to continue its higher-than-average growth, even among the rapidly growing professional and technical group. The implications of these shifts in our work force for educational preparation for work are unmistakable.

Educational Attainment in Professional and Technical Occupations

The shifts toward work requiring higher education or skill have been accompanied by rising educational levels even in the same occupations. Just what is happening to educational levels in specific occupations is evident from a comparison of younger and older workers in the same occupations.

Such a comparison of the educational attainment of younger adult experienced workers in the professional and technical occupations with the older experienced group shows not only the kind of competition our young people have on entering the labor force but also the impact on educational requirements in some fields where the demand for workers was strong. The median amount of schooling of the professional and technical group as a whole already exceeds four years of college.[7] The significance of this median level increases with the knowledge that the group includes not only the recognized professions but many semi- or subprofessional

[7] Based on data from U.S. Bureau of the Census, *Census of Population: 1960, Final Report PC(2)–5B,* Table 8, p. 136.

TABLE 5. Percentage Distribution of Younger and Older Workers in Selected Professions by Years of College Completed, Age Group, and Profession, 1960

Profession	Age groups							
	25–34				45–64			
	Total percentage	Less than four years	Four years	Five or more years	Total percentage	Less than four years	Four years	Five or more years
Architects	100	17.9	24.4	57.7	100	35.1	30.4	34.5
Chiropractors	100	15.8	50.3	33.9	100	40.7	38.4	20.9
Clergymen	100	21.4	12.0	66.6	100	35.3	12.5	52.2
College:								
Presidents and deans	100	10.3	22.2	67.5	100	3.4	6.4	90.2
Professors and instructors	100	4.0	11.3	84.7	100	3.6	5.3	91.1
Dentists	100	2.9	2.2	94.9	100	6.8	28.4	64.8
Engineers	100	34.2	43.9	21.9	100	56.7	29.5	13.8
Lawyers and judges	100	2.2	4.3	93.5	100	14.7	17.2	68.1
Librarians	100	31.0	28.9	40.1	100	39.6	19.8	40.6
Natural scientists:								
Biologists	100	11.0	33.9	55.1	100	17.9	24.2	57.9
Mathematicians	100	19.5	31.0	50.5	100	29.9	21.6	48.5
Physicists	100	11.6	25.9	62.5	100	18.3	17.1	64.6
Optometrists	100	6.1	16.8	77.1	100	35.1	32.7	32.2
Osteopaths	100	3.1	3.1	93.8	100	3.3	38.3	58.4
Physicians, surgeons	100	2.1	4.1	93.8	100	2.0	4.6	93.4
Psychologists	100	0.8	8.7	90.5	100	6.6	3.0	90.4
Teachers, secondary	100	8.5	45.4	46.1	100	9.0	30.2	60.8
Veterinarians	100	3.0	2.5	94.5	100	8.4	39.7	51.9

SOURCE: Based on data from U.S. Bureau of the Census, *Census of Population: 1960.*

workers, such as entertainers of all kinds, athletes, and the still relatively new technician group.

Within the group the level of education therefore varies greatly by occupation. In many of the recognized professions, at least half the younger experienced adult workers (twenty-five to thirty-four years old) had completed five or more years of college or university.[8] These include not only the lawyers, the college professors, the psychologists, and the medical doctors, practically all of whom fall into this class, but also the architects, the college presidents and deans, the clergymen, the biological scientists, the mathematicians, and the physicists. The change over the years shows up in the generally lower percentages of older workers (forty-five to sixty-four years of age) who have attained the same level of education. Whether this is occasioned by a change in the nature of the work requiring a higher degree of knowledge and skill, or is a consequence of the rising level of educational attainment which has provided employers with a supply of better-educated workers, is not known. Regardless of the causal relationships, the situation reflects stiffer competition for jobs for young people who do not achieve the prevailing levels of education. A few figures from Table 5 illustrate the changes taking place. In 1960 only 34.5 per cent of the older architects as compared with 57.7 per cent of the younger ones had completed five or more years of college education; 64.8 per cent of the older dentists as compared with 94.9; 68.1 per cent of the older lawyers and judges as compared with 93.5 of the younger group; 32.2 per cent of the older optometrists as compared with 77.1 of the younger group; 58.4 per cent of the older osteopaths as compared with 93.8 of the younger group; and 51.9 per cent of the older veterinarians as compared with 94.5 per cent of the younger group. Generally, the proportions of older and younger medical doctors, natural scientists, and mathematicians are about the same.

In some fields, however, a change in the opposite direction is reflected, indicating some adjustment of supply to strong demand, or provision of financial incentives to employed persons. This is especially true of the teaching field. For example, 60.8 per cent of the older secondary school teachers had completed five or more years of college or university as compared with 46.1 per cent of the younger group. Among college professors and instructors 91.1 per cent of the older group as compared with 84.7 per cent of the younger group had attained five or more years of higher education. This latter may in part reflect increased utilization of instructors.

This general upward movement in educational attainment, of course,

[8] See Table 5 appended.

was evident at all levels. For example, in the large group of technical engineers, two out of three younger engineers had at least finished college as compared with two out of five of the older ones. Similar differences between the two age groups existed in most branches of technical engineering though the proportions completing college within each age group differed somewhat among the branches. A much higher proportion (about four out of five) of chemical and mining engineers, for example, had finished college than of engineers in the other branches (about two out of three).

Comparison of Younger and Older Technical Engineers by Years of College Completed, 1960

| Engineers | Age groups | | | |
| | 25–34 | | 45–64 | |
	Four Years	Five years or more	Four Years	Five years or more
Total	43.9%	21.9%	29.5%	13.8%
Aeronautical	42.2	23.9	28.6	16.5
Chemical	51.9	37.4	42.8	33.7
Civil	43.7	19.5	33.6	13.2
Electrical	43.2	22.6	33.4	14.3
Industrial	41.1	15.9	19.6	10.2
Mechanical	45.8	22.0	25.0	10.8
Metallurgical	40.9	27.3	33.0	24.1
Mining	57.8	29.0	34.1	16.0
Sales	47.8	19.2	28.9	9.0
n.e.c.	37.7	20.7	27.5	16.6

The same trend is apparent also among technicians and some other subprofessional workers whose younger workers are increasingly obtaining at least one to three years of college. In this group an educational level of one to three years of college is apparently becoming more and more characteristic of the younger group. Among designers and medical and dental technicians, there is an indication of some upward movement beyond this. The median number of school years completed by technicians as reported by a study of the education and training of technicians in the experienced labor force in 1960 [9] was just over fourteen years. Those specializing in educational services were likely to have more. Two out of three had four-year degrees. The study also showed that the level of

[9] "Education and Training of Technicians," *Monthly Labor Review,* November, 1964.

education had some influence on the technician's type of work. Fifteen per cent of those in supervisory or research and development work had degrees as compared with 6 per cent of those in repairs and maintenance activities or functions.

Comparison of Younger and Older Technicians by Years of College Completed, 1960

Technicians	Age groups					
	25–34			45–64		
	One to three years	Four years	Five years or more	One to three years	Four years	Five years or more
Designers	34.5%	18.2%	12.7%	24.5%	12.3%	10.0%
Draftsmen	37.1	6.4	4.5	26.4	11.0	6.6
Surveyors	23.9	5.6	2.8	17.0	7.6	4.1
Technicians:						
Medical and dental	34.8	17.2	7.2	20.5	11.4	5.3
Electrical and electronic	35.2	3.4	1.5	18.9	3.6	2.1
Other engineering and scientific	31.1	8.3	5.6	18.4	7.1	3.9
n.e.c.	25.7	11.7	6.8	17.8	4.8	4.4

In a follow-up study of the group in 1962, about a third of those still employed as technicians reported various types of training as qualifying them for the jobs they held at that time; three out of five credited work experience or a combination of experience and training. Among these employed workers much of the training credited with qualifying them for their 1962 jobs was special training by the employer, but there were significant differences among them. The largest proportion crediting such training was among the medical and dental technicians—two out of five. On the other hand, only one out of five draftmen credited such training.

In all, many ways of obtaining supplementary training (exclusive of formal education) were reported, including the military services, apprenticeships, high school extension courses, U.S. Armed Forces Institutes, work-study programs, workshops, seminars, and on-the-job or other company training programs. The situation as described by the study indicates that much of the training needed for upgrading employed workers is done off the job. This underscores the importance of the schools' role in this area.

The Need for Improved Utilization of Manpower Resources

At a time when we probably need more highly educated and creative minds to ensure continued advancement of knowledge and economic growth, and when our existing knowledge and skills are likely to become obsolete within a few years, the further education or training of employed workers for upgrading takes on new significance. One aspect of this problem lies in a further reassignment or reallocation of tasks in professional positions to create more subprofessional, technical, assistant, or aid positions—call them what you will—to free the minds and the time of these professional workers for more productive work. This would also create more opportunities for the next level of workers to utilize their potential and increase their productivity while vacating positions requiring less skill, knowledge, or ability for those whose jobs are disappearing from our occupational structure.

The growing technician group, especially in the medical, scientific, and engineering fields, is evidence of a start in this direction. We are just beginning to develop such aides in teaching, social work, counseling, recreation, and some health professions. Through imaginative experimentation, more sophisticated occupational analysis, and a review of already existing teamwork arrangements, we can help free the professionally trained for more creative work and help break the "bottlenecks" of insufficient managerial and professional talent where they exist.

One of our most critical problems of manpower development and utilization is the loss of potential resources represented by Negro youth. This loss is especially heavy among the Negro youth of the South where, in the past, they have had relatively few opportunities for training for professional and technical occupations. Their major resource for training of this kind has been the predominantly Negro colleges. But this resource has been extremely limited. The predominantly Negro colleges are severely handicapped by the inadequate preparation of many of their entering students and by their meager financial, physical, and other resources. Most of their students prepare for the traditional fields of education and medicine; few receive training for the scientific and technical occupations or the business professions which are among the fastest-growing occupational groups.

In 1962 well over half the graduates of predominantly Negro institutions were education majors, over twice the proportion among all graduates in the nation. Fewer than 2 per cent of the graduates had studied engineering and fewer than 4 per cent business and commercial subjects.

For the nation as a whole, the corresponding proportions were nearly 9 per cent engineering majors and 13 per cent business majors. The picture is particularly sad for men who graduate from predominantly Negro colleges. In 1962, nearly four out of ten majored in education compared with one out of ten for the nation as a whole.

The problem of the Southern Negro college student is accentuated by the fact that he is typically older than his white counterpart, that he is likely to be facing great hardships in supporting himself through college, and he is therefore harder driven to achieve an immediately attainable goal. The major emphasis on academically oriented curricula in the predominantly Negro colleges has provided little incentive for the Negro student already beset with other difficulties to continue in school and has resulted in a very high dropout rate among Negro men.

Public postsecondary technical schools could greatly broaden the curriculum offerings available to them by a diversity of occupational courses tailored to the needs of the economy. Under these conditions, it is likely that the proportion of Negro youth who could be attracted to higher education and who might stay and benefit from it would greatly increase. In the final analysis, they would not only contribute to their own personal economic and social development in an important and meaningful way, but would make a real contribution to the sum total of appropriate manpower resources required by the country.

The Need For Further Manpower Research

To improve our planning, we still need additional information about many aspects of our manpower needs. Thus far we have inadequate information about the occupational mobility of workers. Projections of manpower requirements in the various occupations, therefore, take account of replacements due to deaths, retirements, and withdrawals from the labor force, but not of those due to transfers among the occupations. Even so, the effect of replacement needs on demand for workers in certain occupations is greater than that of net employment growth. For example, in the current decade annual replacement needs for professional and technical workers are expected to average more than 225,000; for managers and officials, another 200,000. As we work on the problem of upgrading, replacement needs will gain further importance in educational planning.

We need also to know how well the educational levels of our population match the educational requirements of jobs. We have just undertaken a project in the Department of Labor which will attempt to close partially this gap in our information. Information on the educational levels of workers in the various occupations was gathered in connection with the *Dictionary of Occupational Titles* and we plan to tabulate it for such comparison purposes.

Another aspect of the whole utilization problem, which has educational as well as employment implications, is the disparity between actual and hiring requirements for many positions. We know that this disparity exists, but we have not yet studied it with the view to assessing its impact on the utilization and productivity of our human resources. Another project now under way will serve as a starting point for a better understanding of this problem. We have information for thousands of jobs on the general level of educational development in terms of reasoning, mathematical, and language development, as well as on the level of specific vocational preparation required for satisfactory performance of the work. Some tabulations are currently being made for analysis purposes. These would permit, if the information proves sufficiently adequate, comparisons with the educational levels of workers in these occupations.

THE FEDERAL INTEREST IN EDUCATION

Obviously education lies at the heart of a national manpower policy concerned with full development and use of our human resources. The educational system is our main instrument for preparing youth for productive work, whether as professional, managerial, white-collar, or blue-collar workers. The quality and suitability of this preparation determines the overall productivity of our labor force, and has much to do with its adaptability to technological and occupational change. Investment in education is an important factor in our rate of economic growth.

Just as clearly, educational policy is a major element in social policy. Since it opens the door to economic opportunity (or closes it for those who receive too little education) the workings of the educational system determine, in large part, how close we come to providing really equal opportunity—for employment, human growth, and fulfillment of one's role as a citizen. Today we are very far from providing this kind of equal opportunity, and one goal of the educational changes we are appraising must be to bring us closer to that goal.

Federal Participation in Higher Education

While primary responsibility for education rests with the states and there has been no inclination (apart from the armed services academies) to operate federally controlled colleges, the Federal interest in education is not new. It dates back to George Washington's first annual address to Congress, in which he said:

> There is nothing more deserving your patronage than the promotion of science and literature.... Whether this desirable object will be best promoted by affording aids to seminaries of learning already established, by the institution of a national university, or by any other expedients will be well worthy of a place in the deliberations of the Legislature.

Our present nationwide system of public colleges and universities owes its existence, in large part, to Federal action—the land-grant college legislation of 1862. In the words of President Kennedy, "A century of experience with land-grant colleges has demonstrated that Federal financial participation can assist educational progress and growth without Federal control." While no meaningful dollar value can be assigned to the Federal land granted to these institutions, the program's impact is suggested by the fact that 774,000 students were enrolled in them in the fall of 1963— representing 27 per cent of *all* students enrolled in publicly controlled colleges, and about one-sixth of all enrollments in any college-level institution, public or private.[10]

The direct use of Federal funds for higher education was very limited before World War II, although part-time jobs under the NYA program made it possible for many thousands of students to enter or remain in college. After the war, education and training programs under the GI Bill of Rights brought a huge upsurge in the Federal contribution to education, especially in college-level institutions and in various forms of adult education. When this program was at its peak in April, 1947, 2,383,000 veterans were enrolled in some kind of school or training program at government expense.

Table 6 summarizes the trend in Federal funds used for grants supporting education, at various levels, for selected years from 1935 through 1964, and Table 7 provides added detail on grants supporting higher education.[11] From less than $59 million in 1945, grants for higher education rose to more than $1.4 billion in 1947, and to between $1.7 and $1.9 billion in each year from 1948 through 1950. Nearly all this represented grants for subsistence, tuition, or supplies to veterans enrolled in college-level institutions. Altogether, some 2,200,000 veterans of World War II

[10] U.S. Office of Education, *Digest of Educational Statistics,* 1964, Tables 50, 91.

[11] In both tables, the totals given *exclude* the value of Federal surplus property transferred to educational institutions, for which no breakdown by level of education is available. Also, the "values" assigned to such property are in some cases arbitrary or unrealistic.

TABLE 6. Federal Funds for Education by Level or Type of Education: Selected Years, 1935–1964

(in thousands of dollars)

Fiscal year	Federal grants total *	Elementary and secondary education †		Higher education ‡		Adult education ‡	
		Amount	Percentage of total	Amount	Percentage of total	Amount	Percentage of total
1935	126,667	69,228	54.7	37,939	30.0	19,500	15.4
1940	160,319	74,190	46.2	37,752	23.5	48,377	30.2
1945	168,153	48,210	28.7	58,798	35.0	61,145	36.3
1946	491,447	46,000	9.4	275,447	56.0	170,000	34.6
1947	2,428,556	49,000	2.0	1,426,756	58.7	952,800	39.2
1948	2,955,462	52,000	1.8	1,755,762	59.4	1,147,700	38.8
1949	3,165,467	60,000	1.9	1,878,667	59.3	1,226,800	38.8
1950	3,002,122	73,084	2.4	1,781,830	59.4	1,147,208	38.2
1951	2,283,667	89,288	3.9	1,334,905	58.5	859,474	37.6
1952	1,683,433	178,874	10.6	924,092	54.9	580,467	34.5
1953	1,116,178	302,027	27.1	512,390	45.9	301,761	27.0
1954	968,729	291,329	30.1	430,900	44.5	246,500	25.4

Fiscal year	Federal grants total *	Elementary and secondary education †		Higher education ‡		Adult education ‡	
		Amount	Percentage of total	Amount	Percentage of total	Amount	Percentage of total
1955	1,159,336	341,786	29.5	522,250	45.0	295,300	25.5
1956	1,245,083	313,300	25.2	595,483	47.8	336,300	27.0
1957	1,309,695	323,347	24.7	647,048	49.4	339,300	25.9
1958	1,344,065	356,902	26.6	678,963	50.5	308,200	22.9
1959	1,418,849	414,753	29.2	751,228	52.9	252,868	17.8
1960	1,413,432	507,170	35.9	732,579	51.8	173,683	12.3
1961	1,383,453	502,360	36.3	770,159	55.7	110,934	8.0
1962	1,524,649	554,412	36.4	884,731	58.0	85,506	5.6
1963	1,786,857	601,513	33.7	1,078,652	60.4	106,692	6.0
1964	2,276,441	679,050	29.8	1,404,780	61.7	192,611	8.5

* Excludes value of surplus property transferred to educational institutions (not classified by level).

† More than half of this total, in fiscal 1963 and 1964, was for School Assistance in Federally Affected Areas. Also included are grants under Titles III, V, and X of NDEA, Indian education, public lands revenue for schools, vocational education, and other minor items.

‡ For description of items included, see Table 8 and footnotes.

SOURCE: U.S. Office of Education, published and unpublished data.

TABLE 7. Federal Funds for Higher Education and for Adult Education, Classified by Type: Selected Years, 1935–1964
(In thousands of dollars)

Fiscal Year	Total for higher education and adult education	Higher education					Adult education	
		Basic research and research facilities*	Total except research	Veterans' education	Student assistance†	All other‡	Veterans' education	All other including vocational education, ARA, and MDTA
1935	37,939	5,897	32,042	—	—	32,042	—	5,125
1940	37,752	10,000	27,752	—	2,000	25,752	—	24,600
1945	65,940	12,000	46,798	10,712	5,028	13,058	7,142	53,500
1946	433,489	14,000	261,447	237,064	5,200	19,183	158,042	10,800
1947	2,365,756	14,267	1,412,489	1,387,000	5,800	19,689	939,000	10,800
1948	2,889,752	25,190	1,730,572	1,700,985	6,200	23,387	1,133,990	10,800
1949	3,092,821	32,200	1,846,467	1,821,229	7,000	18,238	1,214,154	10,564
1950	2,929,038	35,050	1,746,780	1,721,000	7,500	18,280	1,147,208	10,649
1951	2,182,905	35,167	1,299,738	1,272,129	10,500	17,109	848,000	10,674
1952	1,493,414	37,053	887,039	853,983	17,000	16,056	569,322	10,345
1953	803,104	35,664	476,726	436,072	25,000	15,654	290,714	10,147
1954	666,145	34,482	396,418	352,869	34,000	9,549	235,245	10,168

		Higher education					Adult education	
Fiscal Year	Total for higher education and adult education	Basic research and research facilities*	Total except research	Veterans' education	Student assistance†	All other‡	Veterans' education	All other including vocational education, ARA, and MDTA
1955	804,363	36,668	485,582	423,171	45,000	17,411	282,113	12,140
1956	917,496	45,004	550,479	483,021	48,000	19,458	322,013	13,272
1957	969,802	57,392	589,656	484,114	61,000	44,542	322,754	15,432
1958	968,767	126,030	552,933	434,706	76,000	42,227	289,804	16,355
1959	984,296	210,518	540,710	363,267	150,833	26,610	233,068	17,800
1960	884,715	249,732	482,847	248,635	198,220	35,992	152,136	19,100
1961	856,192	307,873	462,286	160,867	252,246	49,173	86,033	20,800
1962	934,677	420,762	463,969	102,948	302,319	58,702	49,946	27,704
1963	1,107,659	551,376	527,276	68,446	387,800	71,030	29,007	67,551
1964	1,429,862	810,930	593,850	52,732	436,892	104,226	25,082	154,114

* Includes some grants not for the purpose of supporting education, such as those for health research classified by USOE as "funds for higher education" because of the "integral relationship between research and training in educational institutions."

† Includes fellowships, training grants, and traineeships.

‡ Includes special institutional support, special training programs, and funds for training of state and local personnel.

SOURCE: U.S. Office of Education, published and unpublished data.

enrolled in colleges or universities. In the fall of 1947, as many as 1,150,000 veterans were attending college at government expense. They represented more than 71 per cent of all male college students in November, 1947, and more than 50 per cent of all persons attending college.

There was a similar upsurge in Federal grants for adult education, largely due to grants for such training under the GI Bill. From about $61 million in 1945, Federal grants for adult education rose to over $1.1 billion in each year from 1948 through 1950. Much of this represents postsecondary (but noncollege) education, either in the institutional on-farm training program, or in apprentice and other on-the-job training.

Grants for college level education under the GI Bill tapered off in the postwar years, but grants under a similar program for Korean veterans kept the total cost of veterans' programs quite high (around $400 million a year) until as late as 1959. Federal grants for higher education reached their postwar low in 1954. Since then, the decline in veterans' programs has been more than offset by two factors: (1) Grants for basic research and research facilities, which are counted as "funds for education" by the U.S. Office of Education; and (2) a steady growth in grants for student assistance (fellowships, training grants, and traineeships) under the NDEA and other programs. Student assistance programs for nonveterans tripled in size in the five years from 1959 to 1964.

Even so, Federal grants for student assistance are now only about one-third as much as they were at the height of the GI program; in constant dollars, they represent a much smaller fraction than that.

Federal spending for adult education, much of which represents postsecondary schooling for persons desiring something other than an academic curriculum, dropped from about $1.2 billion in 1949 to less than $100 million in 1962.

Federal spending on education during the peak years of the GI education and training program was almost entirely for higher education and adult education. In each year from 1947 through 1951, between 58 and 60 per cent of all Federal grants for education were for higher education, and between 37 and 40 per cent for adult education. The total cost of the GI program, through 1955, was nearly $14.5 billion. More than two-thirds of this total (nearly $10.1 billion) was for subsistence allowances to veterans and their dependents; about $3.9 billion was for tuition; and about $0.5 billion for supplies, equipment, and fees.

Trends in the magnitude and distribution of Federal grants for education during the 1950s reflected mainly the gradual decline and termination of programs under the GI Bill, partly offset by a similar but smaller program for Korean veterans. Grants for higher education dropped to about 45 per cent of the total in 1953–1955; their rise in relative importance since then (to about 60 per cent in 1963 and 1964) is largely because of increased Federal spending on "basic research and research facilities," much of which is only marginally related to general support of education.

Federal grants for adult education, which accounted for nearly two-fifths of all Federal grants for education in 1950, had dropped to about 12 per cent in 1960, and reached their low point in 1962–1963, at about 6 per cent of the total. Increases since then, mainly through expansion of programs under the ARA and MDTA, still leave adult education by far the least important field of Federal grants for education. In relation to its total contribution, the Federal government was giving less attention to this important area in 1961–1964 than in *any* year from 1935 to 1960.

The Limited Federal Role Today

While total Federal funds for higher education, as reported by the Office of Education, were about three-fourths as great in 1964 as at the height of the GI program, the overall total is deceptive. As Table 7 shows, about three-fifths of the total consists of grants for basic research and research facilities (affecting educational opportunities for only a relatively small number of advanced students in specific fields). Grants for assistance to individuals actually represent a far smaller amount of assistance than they did in the GI years, and there has been no significant overall rise in such grants (for veterans' programs and other student assistance combined) in the past several years.

The Federal role, in relation to total public expenditures for education, has in fact dropped back to about the prewar level. Table 8 shows this trend in two ways. Data in the first three columns, based on Census Bureau reports, compare the total expenditure on education by all governments (Federal, state, and local) with the total Federal expenditure for this purpose, including both direct expenditures and intergovernmental transfers from the Federal government to state or local governments. On this basis, Federal expenditures represented 36 per cent of all public spending on education in 1948 and nearly one-third of the total in 1950, but dropped steadily to a low of less than 8 per cent in 1962.

The second comparison, in the last two columns of the table, shows the relationship between Federal grants for education as reported by the Office of Education (*excluding* grants for basic research and facilities) and total public expenditures as reported by the Census Bureau. While the data

TABLE 8. Relationship between Federal Expenditures for Education and Total Public Expenditures for Education (Federal, State, and Local): Selected Years, 1940–1964

(In millions of dollars)

Calendar year or school year ending	Public expenditures on education *			Federal grants for education (except basic research and facilities) †	
	Total—all governments (Federal, state, and local)	Federal government (direct and intergovernment)		Amount	Per cent of total public expenditures (column 1)
		Amount	Per cent of total		
1940	2,827	343	12.1	150.3	5.7
1942	2,696	186	6.9	N.A.	
1944	2,805	205	7.3	N.A.	
1946	3,711	504	13.6	477.4	12.9
1948	7,721	2,760	35.7	2,930.3	38.0
1950	9,647	2,839	29.4	2,967.1	30.8
1952	9,598	1,716	17.9	1,646.4	17.2
1954	11,196	1,114	9.9	934.2	8.3
1956	14,161	1,475	10.4	1,200.1	8.5
1958	16,836	1,570	9.3	1,218.0	7.2
1960	19,404	1,635	8.4	1,163.7	6.0
1961	21,214	1,670	7.9	1,075.6	5.1
1962	22,814	1,767	7.7	1,103.8	4.8
1963 *	24,690	2,135	8.6	1,235.5	5.0

* For 1940–1962, data are from U.S. Bureau of the Census, *Census of Governments: 1962*, vol. VI, no. 4, *Historical Statistics on Government Finances and Employment*. Data for 1963, also from the Bureau of the Census, are preliminary and based on a sample survey of governments.
† U.S. Office of Education, *Federal Funds for Education* and comparable data assembled for earlier years.

from the two agencies are not strictly comparable, the trend between periods is quite similar, and even more pronounced, than that shown in the first ratio. The Federal share in public spending on education amounted to nearly two-fifths of the total (38 per cent) in 1948, but dropped to less than 10 per cent in the mid-1950s and to about 5 per cent in the early 1960s. In 1963, regardless of which ratio is used, the relative Federal role is smaller than in 1940.

The trend in the relative importance of Federal spending for higher education and adult education, if satisfactory data were available, would obviously be even more striking. Unfortunately, the Census Bureau data do not provide clear-cut totals for public spending on each of these levels of education. However, the available data do suggest that during the peak years of the GI program (1946 through 1952) Federal grants for higher education and adult education amounted to more than half of *all* public spending on postsecondary education, and in some years probably more than three-fourths of the total. Since then, the Federal share in financing such education has declined sharply, to about one-fifth of the total in the years from 1960 to 1963 if grants for research are included, and an even smaller fraction if they are excluded.

Thus the vast growth in postsecondary education, in the past decade, has been achieved almost entirely by the states and local governments, with only a very small contribution, in relative terms, by the Federal government.

Education and training under the GI Bill, while it did not provide a universal opportunity for postsecondary education, came close to doing so for most young men in the World War II generation, since something like 80 per cent of all males who were 15 to 25 years old when the war began served in the Armed Forces and were eligible for benefits.[12] The readiness of young men to improve their educational level, given suitable financial incentives, was shown by the fact that GI education benefits were used by well over half (60 per cent) of all veterans who were under twenty-five years of age when they reentered civilian life.[13]

The GI program unquestionably raised the educational level of that generation, and their long-run productivity as measured by occupational level and purchasing power. At the same time it reduced the volume of postwar unemployment, since most of the 2.2 million veterans who entered college (and many of the 5.6 million who took other types of GI training) withdrew from the labor force and left jobs available for others who might otherwise have been unemployed.[14] From 1946 to 1948, their absence may have reduced the number of unemployed by well over 2 million persons.[15]

[12] President's Commission on Veterans' Pensions, Staff Report IX-A, *Readjustment Benefits: General Survey and Appraisal,* 1956, p. 43.
[13] *Ibid.,* p. 82.
[14] President's Commission on Veterans' Pensions, Staff Report IX-B, *Readjustment Benefits: Educational and Training, and Employment and Unemployment,* 1956, p. 22.
[15] Staff Report IX-A, *Op. cit.,* p. 59.

Needed Changes in Purposes and Programs of Community Colleges

JAMES W. REYNOLDS, *Professor and Consultant in Junior College Education, University of Texas*

Junior colleges have existed in the United States for approximately three-quarters of a century. While they retain, currently, many of the variable characteristics which in their early days made for diversity among them, certain central tendencies may be seen to be emerging. One of these is embodied in the term "community college."

It might be interesting, at least academically, to discover whether the term "community college" was developed originally as a protest against the invidious implications of the term "junior college," or as an appropriately descriptive title for an educational concept. Regardless of the outcome of such a study, the fact remains that its use in the literature dates back probably no further than twenty or twenty-five years.

The first use of the term "community college" in a title of an article listed in *Education Index* occurred in 1946. The late Jesse P. Bogue's book, published in 1950, was called *The Community College*. The writer noted in his article on the "Junior College," published in the *Encyclopedia of Educational Research,* Third Edition, that in 1958 there were only twenty-five instances of the use of community college as part of the official title of a school.

Recently the term "community college" has become more popular. The Sixth Edition of *American Junior Colleges* lists sixty-eight such educational institutions using the term in their official titles.

Of even greater significance in the popularization of the term, however, are two other developments. Two of the more recent definitive statements on the two-year college are *The Community Junior College* by James W. Thornton, and *The Community College Movement* by Ralph R. Fields. This use of the term in the field of publications by two recognized authorities on the junior college is evidence of the acceptance of the title as the more appropriate for describing the educational concept.

The second significant development is found in the action of legislatures in several states, using the term "community college" in legal descriptions. This action was taken in line with recommendations of state surveys in which the term was deliberately recommended.

The probability, then, that the original choice of community college as a name for two-year colleges was in the nature of a protest against the use of "junior college" is no longer of any consequence. Developments of the past four or five years clearly indicate that the term is used more and more as being most accurately descriptive of the educational concept involved. What, then, is this concept?

In brief, it is one which accords recognition to local educational and professional disciplines. The curriculum of the community college, thus, is made up of two major parts. Appropriate standards are maintained in each part of the curriculum to assure a high quality of student performance. Although in practice in the overall community college curriculum it is possible to observe the existence of each of the two parts, and although the nature of performance standards varies from one part to the other, frequently both parts are integrated in a single course, or in a series of courses designated as leading to an academic or a vocational goal.

The term "community college," as it is applied to a concept defined in the preceding paragraph, is limited in its usage to two-year colleges. It must be acknowledged, however, that the two-part curriculum, identified as the distinguishing characteristic of the community college, will be found also in some four-year colleges and municipal universities. In spite of this fact, the term "community college" will here be used, arbitrarily, as applying to two-year colleges.

Community colleges invariably have two administrative characteristics: they are public educational institutions, and their controlling board is made up of members who live in the locality (local school district or junior college district) in which the community college is located. If these two characteristics are added to the characteristic of a two-part curriculum to comprise the criteria for defining such schools, it will be found that many of the 694 junior colleges existing in 1963–1964 will not qualify for the classification of community college.

The restriction immediately eliminates the 272 privately controlled junior colleges of the 694 listed in *The Junior College Directory, 1964,* or 39 per cent. Added to these are thirty-five institutions which are branches of public four-year colleges, and twenty-six junior colleges which are by their specialized nature inconsistent with the definition of community colleges, together amounting to another 9 per cent. This means that almost half (48 per cent) of the 694 junior colleges extant in 1963 are eliminated from consideration as community colleges. Thus, the concept with which we are dealing applies to only 361 two-year colleges currently in existence.

Thus far, community colleges have been seen as educational institutions whose program comprises a dual orientation: (1) the cosmopolitanism of the traditional academic disciplines, and (2) the provincialism of serving educational needs which are peculiar to the community in which the college is located.

It might appear that where this type of two-year college is provided free of charge to prospective students, it would be favorably situated to accommodate the needs of American youth. Unfortunately, this conclusion is only partly valid. It ignores a factor long recognized as significant in providing the accommodation sought—the factor of the proximity of the community college to the residence of those students whom it serves.

The validity of the proximity factor in increasing the service function of community colleges to the educational needs of American youth is demonstrable through two types of evidence. In the first place, studies have shown that the establishment of such educational institutions in geographical areas where previously there were none increases the incidence of high school graduates continuing their formal education in college. Obviously, the previously existing circumstance of low-tuition or no-tuition junior colleges did not provide sufficient inducement for college attendance for all potential students when the college was a material distance from the high school from which the students were graduated.

A second type of evidence substantiating the validity of the proximity factor may be observed in the policy of the states of California and Florida. In California, the number of educational institutions of the community college type has long been large. Despite the fact that no tuition charges are imposed, the state has honored the proximity factor in continually opening new community colleges in sections of the state not previously served.

The state of Florida entered on the expansion of its junior college system at a much later date than did California. In the last seven years twenty-four of the twenty-nine colleges of the community classification in that state were established. It is obvious in both situations that state policy was developed consistent with observing the significance of the proximity factor. Thus it may be seen that the mere provision of free public education through the fourteenth year in community colleges must be accompanied with an observance of the proximity factor if the needs of American youth are to be served effectively.

Currently, there are many states in which strong deterrents exist to the development of a system of free community colleges. Among these deterrents are lack of public support for such an idea, financial limitations which make such a development seem unfeasible, and lack of competent leadership for such an undertaking. There is, however, an additional deterrent the nature of which indicates a complete absence of understanding of the basic mission of community colleges. This deterrent exists in the policy followed in some states of refusing to permit the establishment of such an educational institution in the same city in which there is either a private or public college or university, or within a specified number of miles of such colleges or universities.

From the standpoint of institutional stability, which appears in many instances to be the deciding factor, competition with existing colleges or universities afforded by community colleges is prevented. From the standpoint of providing appropriate educational services for potential students, however, a point which appears to receive little consideration, an erroneous assumption is often made. The policy assumes that the program of the existing institution is appropriate for the educational needs of all youth in the immediate vicinity of the existing collegiate institution, an assumption which is all too often groundless.

Evidence of the error this assumption frequently makes may be found again in the state of California. In several instances, publicly supported community colleges may be observed in the same city as publicly supported state colleges. Illustrations of this are found in such cities as Fresno, Sacramento, and San Jose, where both types of institutions are thriving, and it is recognized that they serve different clienteles.

Any consideration of needed changes in the purposes and programs of community colleges must, sooner or later, make a direct confrontation of the question of how many of these educational institutions will be needed. Similarly, the question of what the relationship should be between these community colleges and existing educational institutions at the lower levels must have an answer.

These two questions, it will be observed, are intimately interrelated.

The actual number of new community colleges will depend on the extent to which existing educational facilities are utilized to accommodate the needs of youth.

On the basis of this consideration, four-year colleges and universities may be eliminated as possibilities for providing the needed services. This rejection is based on the principle that since they are not controlled by local boards, there is no assurance they will satisfy the criterion of a broad program serving local needs. One notable exception to this, previously acknowledged, is that of municipal universities and four-year colleges. On these same grounds, the expansion of the idea of university extension centers, exemplified in Indiana, Pennsylvania, and Wisconsin, will also be unsatisfactory.

Public school systems, currently extending through the twelfth year, may be extended further to include the thirteenth and fourteenth years. This pattern is fairly common in the Middle West, and once was common in such states as California and Texas. In these two states, however, there has been a shift to the district type of community college in which control is maintained at the local (district) level, but in an organization completely detached from the existing public school system. The decision as to which of these two types of local control is chosen will affect the final determination of the number of new community colleges which will need to be created.

Finding an answer to the number of new community colleges which must be established in the next ten years, if the educational needs of American youth are to be served adequately, is admittedly a most difficult undertaking. At best, only a rough estimate can be produced. This is all that can be claimed for the effort made here.

The computation is based on the assumption that by 1974, 70 per cent of the age group eighteen and nineteen years will be enrolled in college, by far most of them in community colleges. One source reports that approximately 42 per cent of the high school graduates entered college in 1960. The U.S. Census Bureau estimates that the total population in this age group in 1974 will number about 8,000,000 (7,932,000). A 28 per cent increase in college enrollments of eighteen- and nineteen-year-olds (from 42 per cent to 70 per cent), results in a figure of 2,240,000. If community college enrollments are estimated at from 1,000 to 1,500 students, there will be a need for approximately 1,500 to 2,000 new community colleges, or between thirty and forty institutions in each of the fifty states.

Moreover, if a ratio of 20 students to 1 instructor is maintained, there will be a need for 112,000 teachers. On the basis of at least four top-echelon administrators per community college, the need in this category will be for anywhere from 6,000 to 8,000 persons.

If it may be assumed that an average operating cost of $800 per student will prevail, the annual bill for operating these community colleges will be approximately $1.8 billion. Capital outlay for building the physical plants will run from $4.5 to $6 billion.

These estimates provide a summary of the implications of universal higher education for community colleges in regard to the need for new institutions, size of staff, and approximate cost. It should be kept in mind that the estimates are rough approximations.

As the focal point in this analysis is moved from organizational factors to the elements of purpose currently proclaimed by community colleges, two conditions become apparent immediately. It will be observed, in the first place, that while the institutional purposes proclaimed by the community college in its catalog may coincide satisfactorily with the definition stated in this paper, in only a relatively small number of instances does the developed educational program reflect a full realization of what these stated purposes imply. The second condition which may be observed is the infrequency of the reassessment of the validity of the existing statements of purpose of the community college in the light of rapidly changing socioeconomic factors.

To assert that statements of purposes appearing in community college catalogs represent window dressing only, and were never intended to be taken seriously, would be to take a position which is completely indefensible. These statements usually result from serious efforts expended by faculty committees which had a sincere desire to capture the value-system underlying the community college, and to translate it into a list of institutional purposes.

This effort, moreover, receives impetus from regional accrediting organizations. Purposes hold a place of importance with these agencies, and the trend toward an ever-increasing number of community colleges which have become members of such associations attests to the necessary consideration by these colleges of the importance of purposes.

Despite these two circumstances, however, a substantial number of community colleges, probably a comfortable majority, have not given sufficient attention to what is implied in the way of a program by the stated purposes. An example of this criticized inactivity may be seen in the results of the publication of Burton Clark's *The Open Door College*.

This book popularized the term "open-door policy" in junior college circles, and while it probably found its way into few if any catalog statements, it was frequently discussed in considerations of community colleges. For a time it became almost a fetish in the apparent adoration accorded it.

Most of the discussions of the open-door policy coming within the purview of this writer's knowledge, however, were decidedly of the exhortatory type. Community colleges, as a matter of institutional pride, were urged to open wide their doors to all who sought admission. Very little time was devoted to an examination of the implications surrounding the adoption of such a policy. Very little consideration was given to the substantial broadening of existing community college educational programs if satisfactory educational services were to be provided for all who would be admitted by an open-door policy. The relationship between the implications of stated purposes for the educational program and the program itself is not always consistent.

The community college, if it is to achieve the criteria described above, must have an open-door policy. Of equal importance, it must accept an obligation to provide satisfactory educational services for the wide range of educational needs and the varying levels of student ability and motivation represented by all the students admitted. This, it must be acknowledged, is no small order.

The adoption of this policy and this obligation must be made in an educational environment in which two significant trends are in operation. The first comprises the greater persistence of students through high schools, their subsequent entry into college, and the consequent increase of college enrollments. As a matter of fact, increased college enrollments, from the time of the falling off of college entrance demands by veterans of World War II to the advent of the so-called war babies, can be attributed materially to this phenomenon.

In the absence of concrete evidence, it cannot be claimed that an inordinate number of those students who are responsible for this increase is made up of individuals who might at one time have been regarded as poor academic risks in colleges. It is highly probable, however, that the incidence of this category, those who are not good academic risks in the traditional sense, has increased substantially.

At the same time this trend is in operation, a second may be observed: the increasing disposition of four-year colleges, in and out of university organizations, to raise their admission standards. The implication is obvious. As the demand for college entrance increases, as this increased demand includes many students classifiable as poor academic risks, and as the admissions standards of four-year colleges are raised, those who cannot meet these standards will enter community colleges in increasing numbers.

A large number of students who may be described as good academic risks have always attended community colleges. Furthermore, there is no evidence whatever to indicate that this situation will change. The effects of the two trends mentioned, in so far as community colleges are concerned, will probably be observed in a substantial increase in enrollments with a concurrently increasing range of student ability measured by academic standards, or by any other set of standards.

Thus the policy (open-door) and the obligation (to provide educational services to all students admitted) advocated above will operate on community college campuses which will have increasing numbers and increasing diversity of students. To the extent that community colleges accept this policy and obligation as their basic purpose, it will become mandatory to examine program development in detail in the light of this purpose.

It was pointed out earlier that a second condition observable in any consideration of the stated purposes of community colleges is the apparent infrequency of reassessment of these purposes in the light of social changes which are normal in a dynamic society. One of the best evidences of the accuracy of this criticism is the lack of change in the catalog statement of purposes over a succession of several years of catalogs.

Obviously, any statement of institutional purposes for a collegiate organization will be broader in its nature—less detailed—than the statement of purpose for an academic or technical department, or for an individual course. Breadth of statement, however, can become so great as to make the statement meaningless, and as the author of the statements undertakes to avoid this status, he is forced to employ some degree of detail—of specificity—of conciseness in that which he writes. It is this very quality of specificity necessary for meaningful statements of purpose which ties them to the major aspects of the social environment at the time the statement is written. Moreover, as major changes occur in the social environment, an inescapable obligation arises to reassess the validity of the statements at frequent intervals, and to make changes in the statements as the reassessment reveals a need. This obligation devolves particularly on the community college whose program must include the provincialism of serving educational needs which are peculiar to the community in which the college is located.

This analysis thus far has undertaken to describe the nature of the community college and what must be done in regard to it if the implications made by the title of this paper are to be faced. In brief, the following has been suggested. From 1,500 to 2,000 new community colleges with an adequate complement of staff and finances must be added to the small number already existing. These must be located in such a manner as to be near the high schools from which their enrollees will come.

These community college students will continue to increase in numbers and a substantial number of them will be classifiable as poor academic risks, in the strictest interpretation of this term.

The purposes of these institutions will have to be determined in the light of the educational needs of all the students admitted. This action will have to be taken within the framework of an open-door policy, and with the acceptance of an obligation to provide appropriate educational services to all who are admitted.

The educational program developed will need to be kept consistent with these purposes, and the validity of the purposes will need to be reassessed periodically to assure its consistency with social change.

At this point in the analysis, one important consideration should be recalled. An open-door policy—completely open for all high school graduates—will result in the admission of a substantial number of students who have been classified as poor academic risks. If the community college accepts in full an obligation to provide an educational program appropriate to the needs and abilities of such students, it will be denied the "deck-clearing" device of removing at the end of the first term or semester all those who do not fit a restricted academic mold.

At the same time, most community colleges have for the sake of institutional respectability placed a heavy reliance on preparing students who can transfer successfully to four-year colleges. The juxtaposition of these two factors creates a real dilemma for an institution whose resources are limited. Service to the poor academic risks may cut down on the resources for transfer students, thereby jeopardizing respectability. Adequate service to transfer students may cut down on resources for the poor academic risks, thereby running the danger of violating the obligation to serve them educationally.

As one examines the nature of this dilemma, the parallel between it and that facing the American high schools in the early years of this century is striking.

The history of the emancipation of high schools in this country from the overriding domination of colleges is too familiar to require repeating here. It is an unfinished history with some major advances, and some equally major setbacks. It is a struggle in which the high schools operated consistently on the principle that every boy and girl who completed an elementary school education could profit individually from a high school education. This principle was applied individually, and also it was applied socially: Society in general would profit from its operation.

The campaign for emancipation was fought against both external and internal opposition. When gains were achieved, most often the advance came in the face of determined opposition from colleges acting individually or through regional accrediting agencies. Internally, the check on progress very frequently came from members of the instructional staff who viewed the high school's role solely in terms of serving those who had the ability and the motivation to go on to college.

While, as was pointed out above, the campaign is far from completed, one salient feature has been achieved which augurs well for the future. The atmosphere surrounding the campaign is characterized by a greater degree of tolerance from the external opposition. Leaders in secondary schools who want to find solutions to their problems experimentally have a great deal more freedom to conduct their investigations. The comprehensive high school stands as an example of one of the successes of their efforts.

One final factor of significance in the high school precedent needs to be noted. The campaign for emancipation from college domination was not really begun until a sharp change occurred in the frame of reference within which high school leaders operated. The frame was changed from looking inward at the success of high schools in serving all the pupils who were enrolled. So long as college demands concerned only those pupils who were college bound, leaders in high schools found an increasingly larger number of their enrollees unserved. The determination to serve these students as well as those who were college bound resulted in the initiation of the campaign for emancipation.

The implication of this consideration for leaders of community colleges is inescapable. Basic to any hope for success in reducing the magnitude of the problems previously defined is the necessity for far-reaching programs of experimentation. This experimentation cannot be expected to produce any substantial progress toward problem solving if it is constantly subject to the restrictive influence of satisfying the demands of four-year colleges governing transfer students. Success in experimental efforts requires freedom, and in this instance, freedom can come only through a sharp change in the point of view regarding the position of the community college in the educational hierarchy. We must cease to regard it as the first or bottom two years of the four-year undergraduate college, and view it instead as the top or culminating two years of a fourteen-year program comprising the elementary and secondary schools. In no other way can the leaders who are charged with curriculum development in community colleges attain the necessary freedom for contriving experimental programs to satisfy the needs of a large percentage of American youth.

The little melodrama created in the paragraphs dealing with the high school may be observed to be replete with the traditional cast of characters. First, there is the beautiful but put-upon maiden—the noncollege-bound pupil—who is portrayed as facing eviction from her new-found home—the high schools—due to the evil machinations of the slinking, mustachioed villain—the colleges—who is bent on foreclosing the mortgage found in the form of a program made up exclusively of college entrance courses. At the proper moment, the dashing hero—leaders of secondary education—appears on the scene, and at the great risk of professional, if not bodily, harm, throws out the interloper. It makes good melodrama, perhaps, and there may have been a time in the first decades of this century when there was a modicum of truth in the situation described. That period, however, is disappearing, and the villain, in many instances, has laid aside his cloak and dagger, and has moved over to the side of the hero. Possibly his action is but another illustration of the old maxim, "If you can't lick 'em, join 'em." And perhaps this is what is happening to the community colleges.

The freedom of the leadership of community colleges for contriving experimental programs to satisfy the needs of a large percentage of American youth advocated earlier already exists in part. Evidence of this may be observed in three educational developments currently taking place.

The first of these developments may be seen in the marked similarity of the first two years of the undergraduate program to the last two years of the high school. In some respects, this similarity is greater than that which exists between the first two and the last two years of the undergraduate program.

Specialization, *per se,* in many academic and professional disciplines is postponed to the third college year. The trend in respect to this phenomenon is in the direction of an increase in the instances in which this is the case. This trend leaves the first two years of college increasingly freer to provide a general education base with a few basic courses, usually non-specialized, which provide a stem for subsequent specialization. This condition increases the freedom of the community college leadership to carry on experimentation.

This trend also leaves the first two so-called collegiate years freer to develop elective courses and curriculums for community college students. The elective curriculums may well embody the vocational areas which must become an integral part of many more community colleges than is currently the case. The elective courses may well serve those students who will terminate their formal schooling with the community college, but who do not desire to take vocational courses.

The second development comprises frequent examples of junior college–four-year college cooperation in their attack on educational problems. Examples of this may be observed in such illustrations as the pact involving these two types of educational institutions in Florida in regard to general education programs. Junior colleges have been assured that if general education programs are developed, they will be accepted by four-year colleges and universities as a substitute for the senior institutions' requirements even though the two may not coincide. The acceptance by some universities of credits earned in junior colleges on the basis of advanced standing examinations is another example. Still another example may be seen in an application of the equivalency principle by senior institutions in lieu of identical prerequisite courses.

The third development is seen in the more appropriate standards imposed by accrediting agencies for junior colleges. Appropriateness, in this context, has to do with the broader educational programs which junior colleges provide for both transfer and terminal students.

Moreover, while what is about to be said is pure conjecture, it is nevertheless highly probable that junior college leaders could attain even greater freedom if they would but ask for it. Obviously, the granting of greater freedom on request would have to be accompanied by assurance to the four-year colleges that the bases for the individual requests were soundly conceived, and would not jeopardize the principles by which the four-year college operates.

It would be sheer ignorance, however, to assume that the only reason complete freedom has not been attained is because of the timidity of junior college leaders. There is a preponderance of evidence to justify the caution that community college leaders must exercise in many fields of the curriculum to avoid endangering the transfer credits of those students who do transfer.

The freedom for community college leaders considered here, however, involves more than relief from the fear of what might happen to transfer students in four-year colleges. It is rather the freedom emanating from a positive source: from finding the solution to educational problems within the framework of the community college itself, unfettered by the restrictive forces attached to the stereotype called higher education. In another sense, it is, rather, the freedom coming from constituting the culminating years of a fourteen-year program instead of the lowest years of a collegiate program.

It may be argued that paying no attention to the demands of higher education will inevitably result in the demise of community colleges. While investigation failed to discover any similar statements made about high schools in an earlier time, this writer is fairly certain that such warning must have been issued many times.

What the critic forgets in such a prediction is that the administrative and instructional staff of the community colleges are as concerned with providing high-quality education as are their counterparts in the four-year colleges. He forgets that the community college meets only one of its responsibilities when it serves as a feeder to four-year colleges. He forgets that community colleges have reached adult status, institutionally speaking, and their leaders may be depended on to judge alternative solutions to problems in an adult manner.

Much has been written on this point of "freedom to contrive appropriate programs," and "subservience to four-year colleges." As used, the terms have not been defined. It is thought that a definition of the latter term will define, by implication, the former.

In the first place, subservience has existed as the result of only a minority of community college students—the so-called transfer students —those who will continue their work in a four-year college. Studies show that they comprise no more than one-third of all the students enrolled in community colleges.

For this group, the community college curriculum must duplicate faithfully the first two years of the four-year college to which these students will transfer. That this responsibility has been discharged successfully will be attested by the numerous studies of the success of community college transfers in four-year colleges. Almost universally, these studies reveal that such transfer students do succeed in four-year colleges. Exceptions to this most often pertain to a very small number of individual community colleges, and not to community colleges in general.

The problem for the curriculum developer in community colleges, however, comes from the dissimilarity among four-year colleges in the organization of their curriculums for the first two years. It is probable that every community college administrator has wished many times that one of two things would happen: either the four-year college leaders would develop identical curriculums for the first two years, or that all junior college transfer students would attend the same four-year college.

Many, probably most, of the dissimilarities in the curriculums of the first two years of four-year colleges are of no great significance, yet in each instance, the unique aspects of separate curriculums result from a particular philosophy of curriculum organization held by the individual college.

There is no disposition to urge that four-year colleges lay aside the unique aspects of their separate curriculums, or lay aside the particular philosophy which produced the dissimilarities that exist. Certainly, one of the strengths of higher education in the United States is found in this very phenomenon of diversity, and no good end would be served by a move toward complete uniformity.

On the other hand, the extent to which differences are not really significant to a critical degree is the extent to which the principle of equivalency may be employed. One illustration of this has already been cited: the cooperative agreement in the state of Florida regarding general education programs. With a modicum of reasonableness on both sides—a quality which has been demonstrated to exist widely—so-called subservience of community colleges to four-year colleges, as it has been defined, may be reduced materially.

Not only do we have a precedent in the realm of higher education for this achievement, but it has long existed in the realm of secondary education. Secondary schools, like colleges, hold their own individual philosophies of curriculum organization. The net result is the existence of dissimilarities at this level. Moreover, the well-recognized factor of population mobility results in thousands of cases of high school pupils moving from school to school each year. Minor inconveniences occur, to be sure, but only exceptionally does a serious problem arise.

Thus, the freedom alluded to—the freedom from subservience to four-year colleges—may be seen to be not nearly so impossible of achievement as at first appeared. Given initiative by leaders of community colleges, and an attitude of reasonableness on both sides, much more along this line can be accomplished.

Mere freedom, however, with no consideration of the institutional framework within which this freedom is used, is far from comprising the whole story. Attention should be turned to the consideration of the desirable institutional framework of the community college. Since the restrictions on the length of this discussion prevent a detailed consideration of the topic, a brief summary of the most important aspects must suffice.

In the first place, curriculum planning should be conducted for an educational institution which constitutes the culminating two years of a fourteen-year educational span rather than the first two years of the four-year collegiate program. This approach logically suggests much greater cooperation with the curriculum of the high schools from which the community college students come than with the four-year colleges to which some of them will transfer.

One obvious objection to such a procedure is that the curriculum of the community college will consist of two additional years of high school courses rather than genuine college-level courses. The assumption made is that college-level courses are completely unlike high school–level courses; that the entering college student undergoes a far-reaching metamorphosis between June and September which makes an educational diet which had been digestible, completely indigestible.

The student who enters college in early fall is the same pupil who was graduated from high school in late spring. If the critical factor he encounters in the fall is a challenge to work up to his fullest capacity in a program which relies on his exercise of a certain amount of self-direction, it differs not one bit from what he encountered in good high schools, in good junior high schools, and even in good elementary schools.

The cooperation between curriculum developers in the community college and the high school should be directed toward reducing the gap between the twelfth and thirteenth years. It should be directed toward stress on the continuity of learning rather than on the separation of the two levels. It should be directed toward the elimination of needless duplication of curriculum elements, the presence of which has long been recognized.

The cooperation may well, in deference to the proximity factor, take the form of an organization in which an individual community college serves graduates from designated high schools, just as individual high schools serve those who complete designated junior high schools. This phenomenon can be created either with the community college as a part of a local school system, or as a separate district type.

It is possible that to encourage persistence of students through the thirteenth and fourteenth years, emphasis on high school graduation be reduced, but by no means, eliminated. On the other hand, the curriculum of the high school will be so ordered that those completing the twelfth grade may transfer directly to a four-year college.

The point has already been made that the wide range of student ability, interest, and motivation, which characterizes the community college student body currently, may be made even wider as a result of circumstances presently observable. In such a situation, the admissions policy of the community college, if it is to be governed by the recommended open-door principle, must be based on the assumption that every individual who has been graduated from high school can benefit from a community college education.

This principle means mandatorily that there can be no first- and second-class citizens in the community college. Each student admitted must be regarded as capable of success in some facet of the community college curriculum even though it may subsequently be proved that he was not. No artificial barriers to respectability may be permitted to exist.

The students in community colleges must be given the full benefit of a well-developed and comprehensive guidance and counseling program, a service which currently exists in all too few of the community colleges. With the wider range of student abilities, interests, and motivations, such a service is an absolute essential.

Teacher preparation programs for community college teachers should be based on a master's degree with a year or more of work beyond this point. This positive recommendation is based on the fact that over the years, this quantitative measure of preparation has been standard for about three-fourths of the faculty members in junior colleges. The remaining one-fourth have either an earned doctorate (about 10 per cent), no degree, or a baccalaureate degree. The latter categories include many members of the vocational education faculty for whom successful occupational experience is equated with academic degrees.

The community college faculty member will be almost exclusively a teacher. From the time of the earliest definitive treatments of junior colleges in the second decade of the current century, instruction has been cited as the major function of junior colleges. Very little research emanates from the faculty of these educational institutions.

Instruction, as the term is used, does not refer to the tasks undertaken in colleges with a highly select, highly motivated, highly academically oriented student body. As the term is used in the context of the community college, it refers to the procedure by which students, from the most capable to the least capable, are motivated to work up to their innate capacities. In involves working with diverse groups in classes in which equally diverse student orientations exist.

Teaching, in this situation, must also include specialists in diagnosing student learning difficulties. It seeks to help students to overcome these difficulties rather than to plan around them.

In all this emphasis on instructional skill, the teacher must be thoroughly proficient in his academic or technical field. The instructor need not be a research scholar in his field, but he must know his field well, including the results of the research done by others.

To all this array of competencies, two more need be included in the program of preparing community college teachers. These teachers must have a genuine desire constantly to improve instruction, and they must develop a keen sensitivity to discovering and satisfying educational needs of the community.

One of the critical factors in the institutional framework of community colleges is the position of director of curriculum, or dean of instruction, or whatever title this office may carry. This official's full-time job includes the selection and recommendation to the president of new faculty members. It includes assisting in the orientation of new faculty members. It includes evaluating the effectiveness of the instructional staff. It includes providing leadership to faculty members in the constant effort to improve the curriculum and instructional programs. It calls for a person of the very highest professional competence. Currently, such people are in critically short supply.

Much has been said about the nature of programs for the preparation of teachers for community colleges. It follows that programs for the preparation of administrators are of equal importance.

This need has received attention from the Kellogg Foundation in its subsidies for the Junior College Leadership Program. Centers have been established in ten universities, and have consisted of doctoral programs with exclusive emphasis on preparing junior college administrators for their work. In the main, however, the administrative position contemplated is that of president. These programs provide little or no preparation for the type of position considered in the preceding paragraph, the dean of instruction.

Another deficiency apparent in these programs is the lack of emphasis on developing abilities to analyze current practice and on developing a strong bent toward experimentalism in the operation of community colleges. Without these qualities, leadership in community colleges will not be likely to find answers to the legion of questions existing.

On the basis of the preceding considerations of the type of teachers and administrators needed, it may be protested that what is described is in no sense universal higher education, but in reality, the extension of secondary education for two years. There is no disposition to argue with this charge since it is exactly what is advocated. It is, however, a secondary education defined by three criteria, one of which is constant for all students; the second and third are optional for as many of the students as wish to make a choice.

The criterion which is constant for all students is the rounding out of a general education begun formally in the first grade. Of what shall it consist? There is no answer to this question. Probably it will vary among various groups of students. One thing is likely, however. If the answer to this question is dealt with experimentally in community colleges, the chances of finding it satisfactorily will be materially improved.

The criteria which are optional to students who desire to make a choice are (1) preparation for entrance full-time into the labor force, or (2) preparation for advanced work in academic or professional fields. Again, the answer to the numerous questions about the nature of these programs will constitute one of the major responsibilities for experimentation in community colleges.

What, then, are the implications of universal higher education for community colleges—universal higher education through the fourteenth year? The first implication is that the heaviest responsibility for finding solutions to the legion of problems entailing major revisions of the curriculum and instructional programs will come to rest directly on the professional staffs of the community colleges. The net effect of progressively rising admissions standards in four-year colleges and universities, of the adoption by community colleges of an open-door policy and an obligation to provide appropriate educational services for all students admitted, and the increase both quantitatively and qualitatively of students seeking admission to college assures that this heavy responsibility will fall on the community colleges.

Solutions to the problems which community colleges must solve are not available. The surest source from which these solutions can be determined is a carefully conceived and comprehensive program of experimentation. A further requisite for success in finding the best solutions to the problems is freedom for conducting experimentation.

The community colleges in which this experimental activity is conducted should be characterized by the following elements: (1) operation with a completely opened door to all high school graduates; (2) freedom from stereotypes of higher education through regarding the community colleges as the culminating two years of a fourteen-year program; (3) the freedom exercised through an institutional framework of the type described; and (4) the freedom used to find satisfactory answers to the legion of questions implied by the topic under discussion through a program of experimentation.

What happens to the other forms of higher education while community colleges seek experimentally for solutions to the problems described? Who can say? The topic assigned was that of community colleges, and all the efforts included in this discussion were confined to the assigned topic. There is a distinct possibility, however, that some of the solutions found might prove beneficial to other types of institutions of higher education.

How Will More Schooling Affect The High Schools?

HAROLD HOWE II, *Executive Director,*
Learning Institute of North Carolina and Adjunct
Professor of Education, Duke University

HISTORICAL PERSPECTIVES ON CHANGE IN SECONDARY EDUCATION

It is a heartening development in American education to be considering the problems we confront while there is still time to do something about them. Typically, we have worked the other way. Two excursions into the history of secondary education will serve to document this viewpoint.

The American high school, during the latter part of the nineteenth century and the early years of the twentieth, was a school for middle- and upper-class children, a small percentage of their age group. Its program was essentially academic, and those who controlled it operated on the assumption that students whose minds and interests did not fit its procrustean standards should not go to high school, let alone on into higher education. Although these rigid assumptions were attacked in the early years of the progressive movement and although some schoolmen saw the disparity between the education provided in the high school and the needs of millions of Americans, there was a strong tendency for the high school as an institution to keep its earlier shape.

By the 1930s the practices and theories of those responsible for second-ary education in the United States had reached the point where they ought to have been in 1912. Educators were emphasizing education for life, the needs of all the students, and diversified programs to fit the interests and abilities of adolescents with a variety of cultural back-grounds and an even greater variety of aptitudes. Even though some of the programs designed to provide high school education for all weren't very good, more boys and girls stayed in schools in the 1930s because there was, literally, nothing else to do.

While this movement to make secondary education serve everyone has never been completely successful, and probably never will be, it has come a long, long way. It has been accompanied by a steady growth in the percentages of an age group entering high school and finishing high school. But these adjustments in American secondary schools, which now make them more serviceable than they once were to a very high propor-tion of the teenage generation, came about long after both the needs of young people and the requirements of society demanded the kind of high school which had evolved in the United States by the middle of the twentieth century.

The same argument can be made with a second and more modern starting point. By the middle of the twentieth century it was perfectly clear that much of the curriculum of American high schools was obsolete. Eighteenth-century mathematics and nineteenth-century science charac-terized high school instruction, while the frontiers of these disciplines in the graduate schools had moved considerably forward. Teaching and learning in English language and literature, as well as in foreign lan-guages, were based on archaic methods and archaic assumptions, and whatever was going on under the banner of social studies was so far removed from the true disciplines of history and the social sciences that only the most optimistic friends of the schools could find the connection. More people were in school, but the levels of learning and the nature of learning, as well as the methods of teaching, were inappropriate for the time. Vocational high schools were running vast numbers of students through courses in agriculture as the farm population continued to de-cline. Those training for other vocations increasingly found the specific skills they mastered in school no longer useful in industry, which had changed its techniques radically during World War II and was looking by the 1950s to the brave new world of automation.

In this atmosphere, the high schools in the early and mid-fifties continued to emphasize better service to a larger proportion of young people, for which they had been battling during the twenties and thirties. School leaders failed to recognize that the need for change had shifted because of the demands of a society and a system of higher education that again made secondary education obsolete. What was really called for was a major curricular reform in secondary education, a reform which would bring the content of education up to date and which would in the process make use of the most modern methods of teaching and learning.

Here again we have an example of what might be called the momentum of educators in the *status quo*. Having dreamed up a new image, secondary school people tended to stick with it at a time when everything around them was demanding revised approaches to what is taught and learned and the ways to teach it and learn it. The invention of the transistor and the refinement in design of electronic circuitry were grasped and used by industry long before education made a real commitment to the possibilities inherent in these discoveries. When changes in method and changes in curriculum did come in the post–World War II era, again they came without the beforehand planning of school leaders.

The imaginative bribery of the Ford Foundation and of other groups interested in change, using points of leverage in the secondary schools, brought some new thinking into the methods of teaching and learning. As far as the curriculum goes, the instances are rare in which secondary school people took a leading role in the processes of change. What happened in the curricular arena was that secondary school leaders were frightened into acquiescence to change by the backlash from *Sputnik*. This created an atmosphere which allowed people like Professor Begle of Yale (since of Stanford) and Professor Zacharias of MIT to get a toehold in the schools. It is a toehold they have succeeded in expanding into a launching pad for major curricular reform; but the reform itself has come from scientists, mathematicians, linguists, and humanists working near the frontiers of knowledge in universities.

A happy exception to these gloomy generalizations was the development of the Advanced Placement Program, which had its beginning as a significant curricular reform in secondary education well before *Sputnik*. To this movement, the secondary schools made a major contribution; but in fairness it must be said that the schools first involved were a very small and specialized group of private and public institutions.

One way of summarizing this past history is to say that changes in curriculum, organization, and philosophy in American secondary education did not come about in the first half of our century through careful advance planning for future needs by educators. Instead, we school-masters grudgingly gave way, slowly altered our practices, and demon-strated that change in our schools is not much different from change in any other social institution. There is a time lag between demand and supply. The shifting requirements of society constantly make the schools obsolete, and the schools are constantly holding to so much of what they were that they can never be what they should. This is not a record to be proud of. It has confronted thousands of youngsters with inappropriate education, with endless frustrations, and with an unnecessary lack of success in school. But one should not be too harsh. For improvements and change in American schools, while not being what they might, have probably been more rapid and more flexible than in any other nation of the world, with the possible exception of the U.S.S.R.

This brief and oversimplified glimpse of past history argues that up to this time educators in the schools have provided followership rather than leadership in adjusting their institutions to the major needs of society and to the needs of the individual who must find his being within it. It is for this reason that I find it heartening that a group of educators in 1964 considered how their institutions should react to the fact that a larger and larger proportion of Americans are continuing with some form of educa-tion beyond the high school years.

Although this fact has been evident for some time, a large proportion of its demonstration has been in California, which is, after all, on the other side of both the Hudson and the Mississippi Rivers. Educational viewpoints from these regions are fortunately penetrating the frontiers of Eastern complacency a bit more rapidly than the West was settled. Clearly, the expansion of colleges and universities, the growth of commu-nity colleges, the development of various educational endeavors sponsored by industry, the rapid expansion of informal and unstructured education through TV, the multiplication of evening study programs, and similar developments have awakened us all. Something is going on. More people are getting more education, and here we are discussing what to do about it after it has begun to happen, as has been our wont. Yet in spite of this seeming repetition of the educators' proclivity for ex post facto adjust-ment, I am optimistic.

My optimism is based on the belief that it is not too late to bring about institutional change of a planned variety with a view to influencing the future. The movement toward education through the fourteenth grade or its equivalent by a very large proportion of people in the United States is just at its beginning. Both the numbers of people who will be involved and the kinds of activity they will undertake are in a flexible state. We are able to plan rationally for the revolution which is upon us rather than having to react in make-do fashion and as best we can.

THE DIVERSITY OF HIGH SCHOOLS
COMPLICATES THE PROBLEM

When Dr. Conant prepared his remarkably useful little volume on the American high school, he made one error. He should have added an *s* to the word *School* in his title. This discussion must start with the assumption that American high schools represent a variety of types of institutions. Depending on the pupils and parents of the communities they serve, depending on the states in which they exist, depending on local and regional traditions, and depending on the pressures from varying types of higher education, our secondary schools are found in many patterns. There is no such thing as *the* American high school.

This diversity of American high schools makes all simple generalizations about the institution suspect. When anyone says that the high school should do thus and so, it is a good bet that there is some high school doing it. Sometimes those of us who must write or speak about this illusive institution are tempted to advocate a national ministry of education which would impose a structure and a curriculum throughout the land. Such a system would certainly make a discussion like this one simpler; but diversity there is and diversity there will be. Therefore, in all that follows, I am talking about the broad middle range of schools in the American secondary school spectrum. These schools are publicly supported. They send 25 per cent or more of their graduates on to some form of higher education at the present time. They enroll 200 or more students, roughly in grades seven through twelve (I will not quibble about exact grade definition; my point is that I wish to include the junior high school in this discussion and not limit it to the three- or four-year high school.) They offer several programs or tracks adjusted to the interests or abilities or both of students with different talents and different objectives. They have been influenced in varying degrees by the post-*Sputnik* curricular excitements. But they still reflect a strong carryover of the commitment to "life adjustment" education typical of the three decades before *Sputnik*.

Schools of this type are providing a relatively high proportion of those youngsters now moving on to advanced education, and they will provide in the years ahead the major share of students who constitute the mass we expect to see continuing with education through age nineteen or twenty. It may be manageable to discuss high schools thus defined with some generalizations in a short paper. If we were to throw in the independent schools, the parochial schools, the specialized high schools, the slum schools with their special problems, the rural schools enrolling 200 or less students, and the schools of upper-class suburbia sending 95 per cent of graduates on to college, we would make the picture so complex that any generalization might not be particularly useful.

From this point forward, I would like to speculate under a number of headings about what can and should happen in American secondary schools as a result of rapid growth in the proportion of their students who will finish the high school, enter some form of advanced education, and complete as much as two years of that. This will be a statement which explores changes in school organization, curriculum, staffing, and student attitudes in the light of the assumption that for a majority of its pupils the high school will no longer offer a terminal education but will be followed by about two years in which education, rather than work, will be the main focus. In conducting this exploration I have found a distinct problem in trying to relate cause and effect. The question that has constantly arisen is: "Is this change one which will come about or should come about because more and more students will partake of more formal education; or is this a change which has its basis in the current shortcomings of the American secondary schools and is therefore related only tangentially or not at all to the emerging patterns of higher education?" While the discussion which follows attempts to disregard the latter category, it does not do so completely. The reason for this is that in a broad sense the major change we are discussing here shakes the whole web of education. And while we are shaking it we have the chance to set it right.

ORGANIZATION

It is probably natural for someone who has been a school administrator for the past twelve or fifteen years to start with what may well be the least important aspect for comment. After all, organization is a means rather than an end. And the professors of educational administration notwithstanding, I am inclined to think that it is an art rather than a science. But perhaps one or two ideas should be considered under this heading.

Two more years of schooling for most people should make possible at least one less year of schooling from kindergarten through grade 12. In spite of the arguments concerning the need for time to mature, about the

growing complexity of the world, about the amount there is to learn as
compared with a generation ago, and about the need for less pressure on
individuals in the schools, we have to admit that our schools waste time.
If, in A.D. 2000, we still have nine grades (K–8), four years of high
school, and four years of college, it will probably be more because it takes
four years to develop a good football team in high schools and colleges
than because there is any educational reason for such an arrangement.
Some of our stronger universities, Yale and Cornell for example, have
recently announced programs which allow able students to complete work
for the master's degree in four college years. The kind of thinking they
have done needs general application throughout education.

If society is to pick up the cost of an additional two years of education,
society has the right to ask that the education which exists, along with the
additions to be placed on top of it, be conducted with reasonable efficiency. Although there has been much talk about this matter, there has
been little action. A favorite topic of discussion is more efficient use of
our educational plant; another is abandonment of a school calendar based
on the needs of an agricultural society. Both these notions require more
energetic follow-up. Another hope for efficiency on the horizon, if not
actually at our front doors, consists of ways by which people can learn
more things with greater ease and in shorter periods of time. Intelligent
application of new approaches to learning and to the calendar should
promote efficiency in education and save at least one year in thirteen
(K–12) for most pupils.

Students now typically leave formal education with graduation from
high school at the age of eighteen. The two-year extension we are considering suggests making that age twenty. I suggest making it nineteen,
allowing one year to be cut out while two years are added. If I could
frame this discussion completely to suit my own prejudices, I would take
the year which is saved and add it before kindergarten, bringing youngsters into formal education at about age four and recognizing in the
schools such pressures in our society as the requirements of the working
mother and the need to overcome cultural handicaps by early schooling
for a significant number of Americans. In many American schools there
is no kindergarten, and this will have to be added as well. The romantic
notion that there is some special magic in having four-year-olds oppress
their mothers twenty-four hours a day needs a second look. There is some
reason to believe that the quality rather than the length of exposure to
mother is the determinant of a healthy childhood. In addition, we should
be less parochial about the fact that an early start in school has worked to
great advantage in some other countries.

The ideal pattern of schooling would start with an initial exposure to school at age four in a two-year nursery-kindergarten program. Next would follow a nongraded primary school which for some youngsters would require three years, for most four, and for some five (the large percentage of children would progress through this institution in four years). The third step would be another four-year school embracing approximately what is now accomplished in grades five through nine, but established on the assumption that some youngsters might progress through it in three years and some in five. Capping off the structure would be a three-year high school with sufficient diversity of program to allow for the very wide development of interests and abilities which prior schooling develops among adolescents. Some might spend four years in the high school.

In such a system, a large proportion of young people would start nursery school at age four and finish high school by age seventeen. Some, for reasons of different abilities, different personal problems, different rates of maturation, or different starting points in family environment, might spend one or two years more or less getting to this point. Built into the system would be a considerable effort to avoid having finishing times which are off the norm assume status implications. It is paradoxical to me that a society which is rapidly developing a profound respect for the individual and his rights, regardless of his abilities, his contribution, or his background, still operates an educational system so stratified in its organization that a large proportion of individuals lose status and lose interest because of unnecessary rigidities in the system. The result is that they lose their rights to an education. The flexibility I am advocating in organization is only one aspect of an effort to resolve this paradox. The addition of two years after high school can be the catalyst which promotes these changes in organization throughout the lower schools. The two additional years will take off the pressure; they will rid us of the irrational respect we accord a high school diploma; their emergence calls into question the patterns of education which precede and follow.

Let us assume, then, that the traditional years of schooling through what we now call grade 12 will require one year less for a large number of young people, and two years less for the better students. The resources which will be saved can help to pay for a much-needed earlier start for many if not all youngsters. Most students would be ready for post–high school opportunities at age seventeen. All sorts of arguments will be made against such changes. I have already mentioned the objections which will come from the athletic lobby. Chemistry teachers will assert that fifteen-year-olds just cannot study chemistry because they are not mature enough. The answer, of course, is that a great many can and some cannot, and some can do it at age thirteen or fourteen with great profit.

CURRICULUM

One of the interesting aspects of curricular change observable in American high schools since World War II has been the upward and downward flow of various topics of study as well as the introduction at various levels of new topics. Much attention has been called to the downward flow and not as much to the upward. We all know that sixth, seventh, or eighth graders are doing what we have for years called ninth-grade algebra, and that a good many twelfth graders are now doing mathematics which some years ago was typical of the freshman or sophomore year in college. We are also aware of the hop-skip-and-jump type of movement which brings into the high school years, or earlier, topics normally considered only in graduate school. This has been particularly typical of the sciences and mathematics, but evidences of it can also be found in the humanities.

Looking at the less familiar reverse process, we find eleventh graders successfully taking a normal eighth- or ninth-grade course in algebraic concepts and receiving therewith the tools to move forward into a deeper understanding of certain aspects of science. The upward movement of curricular topics in the school is based on the assumption that different rates of learning allow these youngsters, for whom mastery is difficult, successfully to attack studies normally not included in their education by giving them more time to understand the concepts involved. The downward movement recognizes the ability of many youngsters to grasp certain concepts and to use them at an earlier age.

This discussion is by way of introduction to the idea that two years of education beyond the high school offer a broader spectrum in which both the upward and downward flow can operate and, therefore, a greater opportunity for education to develop the varying potentials of the individuals it serves. The additional years beyond the high school should be thought of not just in terms of time to learn something salable on the job market, but as time available to the individual to plan for maximum development of his own powers of self-education. In addition, the two years beyond high school open a door to a much debated and much abused but still important concept of general education with two objectives: the enrichment of a person's own life and the development of a person who can and will enrich his society. As I think about additional time in formal education for most people, these are the concepts which seem significant. Perhaps they can be made more explicit by a few further observations which can then be examined for their effects on the secondary schools.

The personal experiences young people go through while they are eighteen and nineteen make them more receptive than they are earlier in their lives to certain fields of study. Psychology and sociology are good examples. Probably the same thing can be said about their potential interest in novels, in drama, in poetry, in music, and in art. More education for more people when they are more mature may help us to lead a larger proportion of our population to the kinds of interests which represent a really constructive use of our growing allocation of leisure time, currently regarded by many of us as a problem rather than a blessing. I am arguing, therefore, that for the purpose of arming more of our youngsters with learnings which have value, these years offer a very special opportunity. I am thinking also about the contribution which education can make to maturity and about the learning which may help youngsters to take a more responsible view of themselves, their society, and their personal obligations to each. We have tried without much success to provide all this in high school.

One of the distortions of the "life adjustment" movement with its overemphasis on utilitarianism has been its denial to a fairly high proportion of high school youth of many of the significant elements in their cultural heritage. It has been assumed that only those who are of "college caliber" can reach the levels of vocabulary and of capacity to handle abstractions which will allow them to partake of some of the most rewarding learnings in the school curriculum. Just as some youngsters must wait until the eleventh or twelfth grade to master algebra, so I think there are those who, if allowed extended time and different rates of expectation about their learning, may have experiences in the realms of both the humanities and the sciences completely untypical of what has been possible in the schools up to now.

This idea of a different pacing of education, when combined with the willingness to offer the same studies at several levels, brings an exciting new flexibility to serving the variety of pupils we know exists in the school population. It may be unrealistic to suppose that everyone can read T. S. Eliot and master PSSC Physics. But it is quite practical to assume that a very much larger number than now do so can draw meaning from these studies, the two-year extension of education offers us an opportunity to try.

What this line of argument means within the context of the existing secondary school is clearly a willingness to take things more slowly for some, to avoid getting excited about the fact that some people who are seventeen are working with ideas previously mastered by others at the age of thirteen. It connotes, also, for the secondary school rather extensive efforts to individualize learning whether these efforts be through novel teaching methods, through numerous curricular tracks in each subject field, or through a renewed emphasis on diversity of enterprise by individual students within the classroom of any one teacher. Each of these avenues will be pursued by those schools which are really successful in reaching objectives outlined here.

Still another possibility which the continuation of schooling will bring to the curriculum of the high school is a major shift in what goes on in the name of vocational education. If the personal needs and desires of young people are to be considered by educators, then the years added after high school will include for many the opportunity to earn some money while being educated. This possibility can be realized if patterns of cooperation between business and education are energetically explored. The result might be a kind of schooling in the post–high school years which uses a portion of a person's time for the general education I have been discussing, another portion for learnings directly related to employability, and still another portion for work on the job under supervision and with some pay. For people in skilled trades, for technicians in a variety of categories, and for office workers who will increasingly need training in the operation of complex data-processing systems, such a pattern makes a great deal of sense. The effect of its emergence will be to require of the junior high and high school considerably more emphasis on basic learnings in mathematics and science as well as in communication skills, and considerably less emphasis on working with actual techniques used on the job. A person will not have to be fitted for employment by the time he finishes high school, but instead will have the opportunity to use his introduction to actual work as a laboratory to fit himself in the two years after high school.

Students of eighteen and nineteen who are spending part of their time in offices or industries will be more acceptable to those organizations because of their greater maturity. They will flow successfully into full-time jobs after their school experience, and they will be benefited personally by the opportunity for some compensation while learning. Developments of this kind are, of course, already present in the eleventh and twelfth grades, but they contend with the immaturity of sixteen- or seventeen-year-olds on the job. They are present also in the best community colleges. They need to be expanded.

This reasoning would tend to make the high school years more academic in nature than they are now, and there is a real danger in any such development. For if the new emphasis up to age seventeen becomes a return to the rigid concept of college preparation for the few accompanied by rejection of a large percentage of aspirants, the results will be tragic. What is needed instead are variously paced curricula in mathematics, in the sciences, and in other areas, using materials which confront the individual with the opportunity for success as well as with some motivation to continue. Students with a secondary school background of experiences like these will tend to go on with education as well as fit better into the changing patterns of American life.

STAFFING

One of the most interesting contrasts in American education today is found in the requirements to be a teacher in grade twelve and the requirements to teach in grade thirteen. Typically a twelfth-grade teacher is certified by the state after taking a variety of prescribed courses and engaging in a certain amount of practice teaching to develop his skills. A teacher in grade thirteen receives little attention from the state and is, by and large, a person whom the institution in which he works chooses to appoint, whether or not he knows the subject, knows how to teach, or has any specific pattern of training. Usually, but not always, he has a degree of some sort from a college or university.

The existence of this illogical contrast will be more directly forced on the consciousness of professional educators and laymen as a larger and larger group of students continues beyond the high school to receive the attention of teachers who have had no training in how to teach after being ministered unto in high school by teachers who may have had too much of it. I would suspect that the growing awareness of this contrast might do something to break the rigidity of certification requirements now existing for grades twelve and below. It might also result in more recognition than now exists that something constructive can be done to help college teachers to be better teachers. It was refreshing to see that Harvard University recognized this fact several years ago and started a training program for its new instructors. Colleges of all kinds, vocational institutes run by industry, and all other after–high school educational arrangements may come to the realization that the amateur teaching performances they inflict on their students can be improved.

But in the high school itself what is needed is a chance to provide more flexibility of staffing than current patterns allow. A certified teacher is not needed for a great many functions performed by teachers, and there are categories of persons who can do excellent work for the schools if the schools could be allowed to have them. Pharmacists make good laboratory teachers. TV repairmen have much to contribute in an electronics shop. Native language speakers without methods courses and without a knowledge of the history of American education but with some practice teaching experience fare very well in the secondary school classroom. Perhaps the proximity of the two years after high school to the high school years will lead us to ask why these people can work in the colleges and not in the high schools. Asking this question with enough insistence can lead to new patterns of flexibility in the certification of secondary school teachers and thus to better teaching and learning in the schools. Let us hope it does not lead to the imposition of present secondary school certification rigidities on those who will teach in the post–high school years.

Special staffing for guidance purposes in the secondary school will assume additional importance as more students finish high school and go on to further education. There will be requirements for more counselors and a need for the retraining of the existing counseling staffs. Additional counselors will be required because of the added complexities within the high school growing from the flexibility of organization and curriculum already outlined in this statement. Young people who face a greater variety of choices will require help to decide on their personal objectives and the programs to meet them. Counselors now in the schools must be made aware that there will be new problems of articulation between the high school and the years of education which follow. In saying this I am assuming that the present confusing array of opportunities in the United States for education beyond the high school will be multiplied in the years ahead. This idea of a more advanced formal education for a very high proportion of our population makes sense only if the offering for eighteen-year-olds consists of a broad spectrum of institutional settings, learning programs, and work-study arrangements.

ATTITUDES AND VALUES

As we think of adding more time to the education of most people, we must ask ourselves whether the values which will be expressed in the additional years are those which look backward toward adolescence or forward toward maturity and responsible citizenship. Our high schools have become institutions for the perpetuation of adolescence. They treat their students in about the same way in the senior year that they do in the freshman year. Lip service to the idea of student self-government and to other responsible uses of freedom in many high schools makes the principal feel better when he is talking to other principals at conventions. But as far as having any meaning for the youngsters goes, too much of what happens in the name of responsibility for students consists of shuffling minutiae rather than a real opportunity for the demonstration of a developing maturity. The American high school is a high-security institution. It is about the only place outside of prison where the inmates are counted six or seven times a day to see if they are all there. Its long arm reaches out to return the sinner who has absented himself from the school's oppressive routines. It has helped to create the concept of education as an obligation or burden instead of an opportunity.

Somehow our high schools need to be jarred loose from the routines and practices which perpetuate the lack of maturity of fourteen- and fifteen-year-olds. But this won't happen if the years of education after high school fail to look toward adulthood and to assume more clearly than the high school now does that the individual student has and can take major responsibility for his own education. One of the tasks of an educational institution is to give people a chance to make mistakes rather than to hedge them about with so many rules and guardians that there is no opportunity to do so. A by-product of a freer atmosphere can be the feeling on the part of teachers and students that they are engaged in the same endeavor rather than being contestants. If these can become the ground rules of the years beyond high school, they can influence directly and immediately what goes on within the high school itself. In a high school with more freedom for its students, there is a fighting chance for them to demonstrate more maturity at an earlier age.

One way to help high school-age boys and girls to become more adult is to have them more with adults. On the face of it, this observation may seem almost self-evident, but adults and teenagers today live in separate compartments. Whenever they get together, there is a status relationship which destroys the value of the association. They need to do things together on a basis of equal status and mutual respect. A wide arena for possibilities of this kind can be found in the extracurricular activities program of the high school.

The high schools would provide better education and both younger and older generations would benefit, if community-centered activities mixing adults and teenagers were to take over orchestras, choruses, dramatics, some publications, radio clubs, and the like. Even some sports such as golf, tennis, rifle shooting, badminton, and skiing could mix the generations. There is plenty of room for discussion groups which cut across ages, and there are some surprisingly successful examples of such groups. The only necessary ingredient is the clear respect of the older person for the ideas of the younger and vice versa. Although it may be heresy to say so, one wonders whether volunteer adults with training might not be able to teach young people to drive cars, thus eliminating from the school's responsibility one of the most expensive and more questionable tasks taken from the family by education. Efforts like these could have a considerable effect in leading young people to maturity through association with it. They would, of course, disturb a good many sacred cows in the present system of extracurricular activity. I submit that this present system has become as rigid, stereotyped, and stratified as the rest of the high school, and that all concerned will benefit from a shake-up.

In this context, it is pertinent to ask whether some of the efforts for education beyond the high school should not take place as a normal development within the high school itself. The presence of older students engaged in more advanced programs and their association with young people of normal high school age in the same educational institution will frighten some parents and educators. They will fear that students in their "middle teens" will emulate their older associates in unconstructive ways. This is a fear with its counterpart in six-year junior-senior high schools, where the mothers are concerned lest seventh graders learn from sophomores the habit of using lipstick. But the mothers don't seem to think about the constructive models in the same way that they emphasize the destructive ones. My own experience is that a school containing youngsters from twelve to eighteen years of age calls forth more positive emulation than negative among its younger members, and I would guess the same thing would be true in a school mixing students of high school and junior college age. Certainly some experimental institutions with this characteristic should be tried, even though experience with this type of organization has not always been successful in the past. Those who think that the social interests of the more mature students will contaminate the high school group don't know their teenagers. After all, 20 per cent of all seventeen-year-olds are married today. Within a school with a spread from age fourteen through nineteen or twenty, there will be new opportunities to find the right educational prescription for those students whom the three- or four-year high school is hard put to serve. The one real danger in such a system is that the older students will be captured by the immaturities of the younger ones.

A possibility now selected by a very small minority of high school students should become more manageable and more important as the years of formal education for the large proportion of young people are increased. This is the opportunity to interrupt formal schooling in the American high school or college with some experience which brings a wider exposure to the world. Ten years from now every place in the world will be within less than a day's convenient travel from any place in the United States. The major cultural centers of Europe and South America will be reached between meals, and people who want to see an entire movie on the way to London will have to board the plane half an hour early. Right now the accessibility of an experience in another culture is so convenient that we are negligent in allowing so few young people to have the opportunity.

Living and learning abroad in association with one's peers from another national tradition is an experience which can help to make our young Americans better citizens of their own country and better citizens of the world. In addition it can give them new horizons and new motivation for continuing education. All sorts of evidence supports this latter point. The growing number of able students who leave our colleges in mid-course because of vague feelings of dissatisfaction and lack of fulfillment seem to find a new purpose in learning when they return after diverse activities at home and abroad. The veterans who came to formal higher education late and with more maturity demonstrated surprising capacity for academic success. These lessons about student attitudes would seem to require educational leaders to build into the American system of schooling wider opportunities than now exist for more young persons to include in their education the exposure to other lands and people which has come to only a few fortunate upper-class youngsters and to the recipients of limited private support for such experiences. To accomplish this end we shall have to be less rigid than we are about credit counting and other academic arithmetic which interferes with education. In addition, we must be willing to accept the idea that public funds can be used quite legitimately for this purpose. Our congressmen find it necessary to spend considerable time on trips abroad at public expense. They might be more statesmanlike legislators if they had been there while still in their formative years at age seventeen or eighteen.

Another possibility to be kept in mind by those planning the emerging educational patterns of the United States is that of volunteer public service during the period when a boy or girl is finishing high school and starting on some form of higher education. School programs which allow a young person a year's service in VISTA (Volunteers in Service to America) or in some venture with similar purposes may provide more

real education than does the typical senior year of high school or first
year of college. Particularly for able students who can complete their
academic requirements more rapidly than others, such an experience
could seem to be both worthwhile and practical. There is something tragic
about the blinders our very able young minds can so easily find perma-
nently attached to their thinking. They become so guided and prodded
down the road to academic success and professionalism that they lose the
chance to include in their education what the eighteenth-century charter
of a great private secondary school, Phillips Academy at Andover, calls
"the great end and real business of living."

CONCLUDING OBSERVATIONS

The facts we confront say to us that modern society needs and will use
an ever greater proportion of persons with more education and find little
use for persons without it. The young people who will constitute the
better-educated adults of the latter years of this century are now in our
schools, and we are attempting to face the problem of changing the
schools to serve them better while the schools are in active operation. This
is a very different problem from that of a motor company which can shut
down its production line while it retools for a new model. We must retool
and reorganize while operating, something no automobile magnate in his
right mind would attempt. What is more, we must accomplish this miracle
in an enterprise which has no central planning body with authority to
enforce its decisions. Our points of leverage for change are limited, and
we need to take full advantage of them. In oversimplified form they are
three in number: (1) the development of a rationale for change;
(2) the provision of funds from private and public sources to encourage
implementation of the new rationale; and (3) the building of models
through the use of the funds to spread by example but on a voluntary
basis the practices which stem from the rationale. I take it that this
conference is concerned with developing the rationale. If it takes the first
steps in that direction it will be useful.

As a final word I must observe that a major issue in American education receives very little emphasis in the foregoing pages. It is the special
concern the schools must continue to have with that segment of the
population with whom they are unsuccessful. Too often we have said that
the students have failed rather than the schools. Whereas some of the
suggestions made here for flexibility of organization, for varied pacing of
curricular offerings, and for changes in methods of teaching and learning

have implications for this issue, those implications are not developed in depth. As we think about the larger number of students who will take advanced education, we must keep in mind the large remaining group for whom even high school education fails to take. Only if the members of this second group can become members of the first will American schools really accomplish their mission.

Admission to College

RICHARD PEARSON, President,
College Entrance Examination Board

It approaches the commonplace, then, to observe that the factor of relative abundance is, by general consent, a basic condition of American life. As to the fact itself, we have demonstrated it in a thousand measurements of our own plenty. But it may be that we have emphasized this too much as an economic fact and not enough as a social one—that we have not sufficiently considered the pervasive influence of abundance upon many aspects of our lives which have no obvious relation to the standard of living. For certainly it is an influence that impinges upon all American social conditions and contributes in the most fundamental way to the shaping of the American culture and the American character.[1]

One manifestation of abundance in American society is the trend that is moving us from an era of scarcity to one of broad opportunity for formal education beyond the secondary school. This trend is discernible from national statistics of college enrollments and from a perusal of the growing variety of programs and facilities at the educational level we have known as "college." It is also discernible from developments in a number of states, notably California, where fourteen years of full-time education are now available to the great majority of the population. Barring nuclear or economic catastrophe, it seems inevitable that this trend will continue

[1] David M. Potter, *People of Plenty: Economic Abundance and the American Character* (Chicago: The University of Chicago Press, 1954), p. 84.

nationally to the point that half or more of the country's youth will continue their education through at least two years beyond the high school.

It is my purpose to explore the implications of this trend for college admission: to consider whether present practice is sufficiently relevant and comprehensive to provide the means by which the generality of American young people can move through elementary and secondary school and, then, into an appropriate college or university program.

We shall approach the subject in two stages. First, we shall consider the characteristics of the present college-going population, with an emphasis on changes in the makeup of this group that have occurred in the last ten to fifteen years. Second, we shall consider the process by which students move from school to college. In this instance we shall seek to identify the major barriers that may impede an open, continuous, and rational movement of young people into various elements of the higher educational system.

THE DIRECTION OF CHANGE IN THE COMPOSITION OF THE COLLEGE-GOING POPULATION

Two factors dominated the college admission scene during the past ten to twelve years. In the first place, the number of students entering college each year increased steadily, both in absolute and in relative terms. Second, we have been engaged in a series of innovations in education and in admission practices: curricular changes in the secondary schools, increased emphasis on educational guidance, expanded programs of financial assistance for college students, and a considerable diversification of facilities for postsecondary education. The effect of these developments was to change significantly the characteristics of the college-going population, compared with those of the early 1950s.

The basic figures on the number of students attending college are presented in Table 1, where it can be seen that the number of first-time college entrants increased from 381,000 in 1939 and 517,000 in 1950, to 1,038,000 in 1962. In 1939 the number of first-time college entrants amounted to 16 per cent of the age group and 31 per cent of high school graduates. By 1950 these proportions had increased to 25 per cent and 43 per cent, respectively. By 1962 these proportions reached 37 per cent and 54 per cent, respectively.

A prominent change in the characteristics of the college-going population relates to the number of very able students who are now entering

TABLE 1.   Number of First-time College Entrants, 1939 to 1962

	1939	1950	1955	1960	1962
Number of young people 17 years of age (in thousands) [1]	2,403	2,034	2,270	2,862	2,762 *
Number of high school graduates (in thousands) [1]	1,221	1,200	1,415	1,864	1,930 *
Number of first-time college entrants (in thousands) [2]	381	517	675	930	1,038 †
Proportion of 17-year-olds who are college entrants	16%	25%	30%	33%	37%
Proportion of high school graduates who are college entrants	31%	43%	48%	50%	54%

* Estimated.
† U.S. Office of Education, *Opening Fall Enrollment* (Institutional), 1962.
SOURCES: 1. U.S. Office of Education. *Digest of Educational Statistics,* 1963 (figure for high school graduates in 1955 is actually 1956).
2. U.S. Office of Education, *Opening Fall Enrollment In Higher Education, 1960* (1939 includes students in continental United States).

college. Byron Hollinshead, writing in 1952, estimated that high-ability students graduating from high school were about as likely to go directly into employment as they were to enter college; that is, a ratio of about 1 to 1.[2] John C. Flanagan's work with Project Talent, conducted among high school graduates in 1960, suggests a sharp change in this ratio. Table 2 presents the results of his comparison for the Project Talent students. There it can be seen that 23 per cent of the college-going group scored in the top tenth of the aptitude distribution, whereas only 3 per cent of the noncollege-going group scored at this level. If we extend the definition of "high ability" to include students scoring in the top fifth of the aptitude distribution, then 42 per cent of the college-going group scored at this level, whereas only 9 per cent of the noncollege group did so. Thus the tendency of high-ability students to attend college now ranges from a ratio of 4 to 1 to one as high as 7 to 1.

It seems likely that this change in the characteristics of the college-going population is at least partly the result of efforts made to increase financial aid funds for prospective college students. The Project Talent survey goes on to report that "at the highest aptitude levels, only a very

[2] Byron S. Hollinshead, *Who Should Go to College?* (New York: Columbia University Press, 1952), pp. 38–39.

small percentage of boys and a small percentage of girls do *not* enter college, regardless of income level." [3]

The various educational innovations of the 1950s assured that this increased movement of high ability students into college was accompanied by a substantial improvement in the level of their academic preparation. An indication of this trend is given by the rapid growth of the Advanced Placement Program. In 1955, 925 students from thirty-eight secondary schools took college-level courses in school and then took Advanced Placement Examinations. In 1963, almost 29,000 students from over 2,000 secondary schools participated in this program.[4] The statistics for the Advanced Placement Program undoubtedly understate the results of curricular change in the secondary school to strengthen the academic

TABLE 2. Comparison of 1960 Aptitude Distributions for High School Graduates Who Entered and Did Not Enter College*

Aptitude percentile rank	Percentage of high school graduates	
	Who entered college	Who did not enter college
90.0–99.9	23	3
80.0–89.9	19	6
70.0–79.9	16	8
60.0–69.9	12	11
50.0–59.9	9	12
40.0–49.9	7	12
30.0–39.9	5	13
20.0–29.9	4	12
10.0–19.9	3	12
0.0– 9.9	2	11

* The percentages are based on 4,162 high school graduates who entered college in 1960–61 and 4,060 students who graduated from high school in 1960 but did not enter college in 1960–61. The group entering college is probably a representative sample of all high school graduates entering college that year. The group that did not enter college is probably representative only of high school graduates who did not go on to college. It excludes all students who dropped out of school before high school graduation.

SOURCE: John C. Flanagan et al., *Project Talent: The American High School Student* (Pittsburgh, Pa.: The University of Pittsburgh Press, 1964). Derived from Table 11–5.

[3] John C. Flanagan et al., *Project Talent: The American High School Student* (Pittsburgh, Pa.: The University of Pittsburgh Press, 1964), pp. 11–19.
[4] *55th Report of the Director, 1956,* and *Annual Report of the College Board, 1963–64,* College Entrance Examination Board.

program for students of above average ability. Beyond this national program, there are a variety of honors courses and local efforts that have
resulted in stronger preparation. This trend has been accelerated in the
recent past because of the cumulative effect of improved instruction in
many elementary and junior high schools, particularly in foreign languages, mathematics, and science.

As a consequence of all these factors, we would estimate that between
100,000 and 150,000 of the 1 million students entering college in 1962
are both very able and well prepared to undertake college-level work. One
of the negative aspects of this development is that these students are
coming from a proportionately small number of the country's secondary
schools—probably no more than 5,000 of the country's 25,000 or so
schools. Indeed, there is reason to believe that the differences between the
strongest and the weakest of the secondary schools have grown greater
during this era of curricular change. The proportion of able, well-
prepared students may rise from 10 to 15 per cent up to 20 per cent or
more, but it will require successful effort to reduce this difference.

A second significant change in the characteristics of the college-going
population has occurred at the lower end of the ability range. Referring to
the aptitude distributions from the Project Talent survey which appear in
Table 2, it can be seen that the full range of student ability among high
school graduates is now represented in the college-going group. As many
as 5 per cent of the students who entered college scored in the bottom one-
fifth of the aptitude distribution, and as many as 21 per cent scored in the
bottom half. The Project Talent evidence makes clear that these students
of modest ability were not admitted to college only to fail in their academic work. The college dropout rates in the college-going sample ranged
from 4 per cent for students in the top tenth of the aptitude distribution to
28 per cent among students in the bottom quarter. In other words, 72 per
cent of the students with modest ability were performing satisfactorily at
the end of one year of college work.[5]

It should be emphasized that these students of modest ability all succeeded in graduating from high school. The Project Talent sample does
not include students who dropped out of school before graduation. Allowing for this qualification, however, it seems apparent that the expansion of
facilities for higher education during the past ten to twelve years has
proceeded in such a way that the full range of ability among the high
school graduating class is paralleled by a full range of instructional offerings given at the postsecondary level. To a large extent, the public com-

[5] Flanagan et al., *op. cit.,* Table 11–2, p. 11–5.

munity colleges have succeeded in working effectively with these students.[6]

An increased mobility constitutes a third significant change in the characteristics of the college-going population, a mobility that is part of, though distinct from, general migration trends within the country. The high-ability students with strong preparation now range over the country in their transition from school to college. Some of this mobility is occasioned by an imbalance between facilities and enrollment demands among the several regions of the country. For example, students from New England and the Middle Atlantic states are, to an increasing extent, attending college in the South, the Middle West, and the Far West. Another aspect of the mobility among these students is the competition among colleges and universities for them, wherever they may live.

Geographic mobility is accompanied by temporal mobility when we consider the students who alternate study and employment. The Project Talent survey reports "studies made by the National Science Foundation indicate that about 25 per cent of boys and 6 per cent of girls who do not enter college immediately after high school graduation do so later on." [7] In California, where opportunities for higher education are broad, there are indications that alternating study and employment continues for some students over a period of years following high school graduation. In this state, where an unusually high proportion of high school graduates matriculates at college, some students intentionally take anywhere from three to five years to complete a two-year community college program and others from five to ten years to complete a four-year undergraduate program.[8]

The mobility of the college-going population, both geographical and temporal, is inadequately charted by available statistics. Nonetheless, the writer would advance an hypothesis drawn from general observation: that the college-going population is increasingly mobile with respect to geographic movement and increasingly likely to alternate full-time study, part-time study, and employment in varying proportions.

A fourth change in the characteristics of the college-going population has both positive and negative aspects. On the one hand, there are indications that low-income families are increasingly able to send their children to college. On the other hand, there is ample evidence to suggest that the

[6] See, for example, Morris Meister, Abraham Tauber, and Sidney Silverman, "Operation Second Chance," *Junior College Journal,* October, 1962.

[7] Flanagan et al., *op. cit.,* p. 11–1.

[8] Based on a conversation with Dean Edward J. Sanders, of Pomona College, who is studying this question in connection with a survey for the California State Scholarship Commission.

very low income groups, particularly from culturally deprived backgrounds, are not now sending children to college in numbers that approximate their proportions in the general population.

Table 3 presents a comparison of the 1960 income distributions for
families from a general sample and for families with college-going students. This table clearly shows that college-going is still highly related to
level of income. Only 2 per cent of families with college students had
1960 incomes of less than $2,000, whereas the proportion among families
in the general population with incomes at this level was 6 per cent. At the
other end of this scale, 41 per cent of families with college students had
1960 incomes of more than $10,000, whereas the corresponding propor-
tion in the general population was only 22 per cent. Students attending
college today are drawn from families with middle or high income to an
extent that is disproportionate to the distribution of income in the general
population.

The striking thing about the comparison in Table 3, however, is that
the differences between the two groups are not sharper. Children from low-
income families are now represented in the college-going group to a

TABLE 3. Comparison of 1960 Income Distributions for Families in a General
Sample* and for Families of College-going Students†

Family income	Percentage of families	
	In a general sample	Of college-going students
Over $10,000	22.1	41.1
$8,000–$9,999	17.5	17.7
$6,000–$7,999	19.0	19.1
$4,000–$5,999	21.8	14.1
$2,000–$3,999	13.2	6.0
Below $2,000	6.4	2.0

* Families in the general sample are urban residents between forty-five
and fifty-four years of age and are quoted by Moon from Herman Miller,
*Trends in the Income of Families and Persons in the United States, 1947 to
1960*, U.S. Bureau of the Census, technical paper no. 8, 1963.

† Families of college-going students are estimates derived by Moon for
2,527,000 full-time undergraduate students enrolled in 1960. Estimates are
based on a questionnaire study among twenty-three colleges and universities
conducted by the Educational Testing Service in 1963.

SOURCE: Rexford G. Moon, Jr., *A Model for Determining Future Student
Aid Needs in the United States for the Support of Full Time Undergraduate
Education* (New York: College Entrance Examination Board, 1964),
(Mimeographed.)

considerable degree. This table also shows that 8 per cent of students enrolled in college in 1960 came from families with incomes of less than $4,000, and 22 per cent from families with incomes of less than $6,000. Comparable figures from earlier years are not available, but it seemed likely that these represent a recent trend. Low-income families could not send their children to college in even these numbers without the availability of low-cost education or widespread financial aid. These two elements have been generally present on the educational scene only since the early 1950s.

We have noted earlier that students with very high ability, but with low incomes, are now attending college in impressive proportions. Thus the financial barrier to college attendance bears most heavily on high school graduates of average or below average ability. As we have seen, there are now college programs that can be taken successfully by a great majority of these students.

The foregoing figures on family incomes are encouraging because they represent considerable progress since the early 1950s in removing financial barriers to college attendance. On the negative side, however, it is apparent that large numbers of low-income students are dropping out of high school before graduation either because of poor educational programs, poor motivation, or severe financial burdens, or a combination. As is well known, this problem is most prevalent in urban areas and rural sections and is highly related to the status of minority groups and the problem of cultural deprivation. Negroes, Puerto Ricans, Appalachian whites, Spanish Americans, and American Indians are undoubtedly underrepresented in the present college-going population. We have been unable to find reliable national statistics on the extent to which such students are now attending college. An indication of the disparity, however, is given in the report of Harlem Youth Opportunities Unlimited, an analysis of the Negro community in New York City.[9]

There is an additional characteristic of the present college-going population that does not represent a marked change, but which is relevant to our inquiry. This is that students of average ability are now about as likely to go directly into employment from high school as they are to attend college. This tendency can be seen in Table 2, which gives the aptitude distributions from Project Talent for 1960 high school graduates who entered and who did not enter college. Looking at the middle aptitude ranges in this table, it can be seen that the proportions are roughly

[9] *Youth in the Ghetto: A Study of the Consequences of Powerlessness,* Harlem Youth Opportunities Unlimited, Inc., New York, 1964.

the same for students entering college and students going directly into employment—if anything, the comparison favors the latter group.

Any explanation of this characteristic is undoubtedly complex. The one thing these students have in common is that they probably can complete college-level work successfully if they can enter the right program. Otherwise the differences among them are many and varied. Some have undoubtedly gotten into nonacademic programs in high school and will move into jobs of a clerical or technical nature; if postsecondary education is looked on by these students as a gateway to better vocational opportunities, they will undoubtedly consider college attendance. In other cases, there may have been motivation for college, but inadequate facilities available nearby. Expansion of facilities for higher education has proceeded unevenly across the United States, and the student with particular interests faces different opportunities, depending on where he lives.

In considering the composition of the present college-going population, we have identified five characteristics of this group. (1) Most high-ability students are now going to college and most of these students are better prepared academically than their counterparts ten to fifteen years ago. (2) Students of modest ability are now entering college in impressive numbers and are performing successfully through the first year. (3) There are signs of a growing mobility in the college-going group; this mobility has both geographic and temporal implications. (4) There is evidence that financial barriers to college attendance are being breached, particularly in the case of high-ability students. On the other hand, there are large numbers of students from minority groups, with culturally deprived backgrounds, who do not stay in school long enough to become part of the college-going group. And (5), we have seen that students of average ability are now about as likely to go directly into employment from high school as they are to attend college. To a considerable degree, future enrollment increases will come from this group of average-ability students.

We believe that the foregoing discussion suggests the conclusion that the present college-going population already possesses many of the characteristics that would obtain if the generality of high school graduates were to attend college. The differences are differences of degree rather than kind, and most of the future increases in college enrollment will be made up of students very much like those who are now attending college. The important exception to this generalization is the group not now reaching the point of high school graduation: principally members of several low-income, minority groups.

THE IMPLICATIONS OF CHANGE FOR THE COLLEGE ADMISSION PROCESS

The movement of young people from schools into colleges and universities in the United States is not a single step that is taken between the end of high school and the beginning of college. Rather, it is a long-term, intricate, and loosely organized movement, characterized principally by a variety of individual decisions made by young people and their parents, by schools, and, eventually, by higher institutions. Further, there are great regional and local differences in the way this process operates across the country. Frank Bowles has proposed a descriptive model of the operation of this process that is an oversimplification but which is useful in gaining a broad perspective and in considering the stress and strain that underlie much of this process.[10]

This model considers that the college admission process is divided into two stages: an antecedent stage that ranges from the early elementary school years to the middle secondary school years, and a formal admission stage that ranges from the middle secondary school years to the middle years of a four-year undergraduate program. The *formation* of the college-going population occurs chiefly during the antecedent stage; this is the period when college potential is recognized and when students take academic work which places them in one or another of several college-going streams. The formal admission stage, though not unconcerned with the identification of college potential, is principally concerned with the *distribution* of students among the various higher institutions. The operations in the formal stage are divided between the secondary schools and the colleges. For their part, the schools are concerned principally with college guidance, which seeks to relate an individual student's interests and abilities to the requirements of particular colleges. The colleges, acting through their admission offices, undertake recruiting, selection, placement, and the administration of financial aid programs. The operations of both schools and colleges in the formal admission stage are supported by a number of external agencies and programs, such as the College Entrance Examination Board, the National Merit Scholarship Corporation, the American College Testing Program, the Advanced

[10] Frank H. Bowles, *Admission to College, A Perspective for the 1960's,* and Frank H. Bowles and Richard Pearson, *Admission to College, A Program for the 1960's,* biennial reports of the College Entrance Examination Board for 1957–1959 and 1959–1961.

Placement Program, the College Scholarship Service, among others. Rapid growth in the number, variety, and activity of these groups was a feature of the educational innovations of the 1950s.

With respect to the formal admission or distributive stage, Mr. Bowles's model identifies three distinct levels of college admission operation: advanced, standard, and postsecondary. In his words:

> The advanced level of college admission may also be described as the competitive level. It is a level at which candidates for admission have covered half or more of the work of the freshman year as offered in most colleges. This is already an operating level with respect to a number of colleges which between them admit approximately 100,000 students each year. By 1970 it may be expected that the standards of these institutions will have risen still further and that their admissions will be at an academic level equivalent to the present requirement for admission to their sophomore class.
>
> The standard level of admissions is the present normal level of preparation of the average high school graduate who followed a college preparatory program in high school. It may be expected to continue with about the same qualitative and quantitative requirements over the next decade, pressure for change having been removed by recognition of the advanced level for superior students, and the now emergent post-secondary or continuation level for students who are now marginal and sub-marginal with respect to college entrance. About 500,000 students are now admitted at this level each year.
>
> The post-secondary or continuation level of admissions can be equated with the standards of the so-called general course of the secondary schools, now admitting about 250,000 students each year. A considerable number of the candidates for admission, who will be added to college-going rosters during the 1960's will of necessity enter at this level of preparation.[11]

Using this formulation, we shall now examine the implications for the college admissions process of future changes in the size and composition of the college-going group.

Formation of the College-going Group

To an increasing degree, the various decisions affecting college going are being made at earlier and earlier ages. We have become aware that children from culturally deprived backgrounds enter the primary grades with handicaps in reading ability that become greater as they progress through the elementary school. Many of these children are effectively selected out of the college-going group before they are twelve years of age. This is an extreme example of the fact that, early in the game, a great many social, economic, cultural, and educational factors influence the size and composition of the group that later will attend college.

[11] Bowles and Pearson, *ibid.*, p. 8.

Of the actions that might be taken to support the idea of universal higher education, those that would strengthen the elementary school experience for large numbers of our children in our cities and rural areas are likely to be the most effective. The period between ages five and twelve is the time when the formal educational system has the opportunity to develop the abilities, knowledge, interests, and attitudes that will lead most young people into continued education. It is probable that, for the majority of young people who do not now attend college, an improved elementary school experience would have been a determining factor. Detailed exploration of the changes that might be made at this level are both beyond the scope of this paper and the competency of the author. We can only assume that such efforts will be made and will be successful.

The period between ages twelve and eighteen, the junior and senior high school years, is the time when the college-going group begins to take form and when three levels of future college admission can first be seen. The curricular innovations of the 1950s have reached deeply into this period, and advanced classes, particularly in mathematics, science, and foreign languages, are not uncommon. At the other extreme, we are beginning to recognize that the opportunities for remedial work to overcome reading and other deficiencies are greatest during the early part of this period; they become sharply and progressively less during later years.

This is also a period when important decisions affecting future educational opportunities are made. All too often students are directed to secondary school programs which restrict or preclude certain educational choices beyond the high school; for example, the student of average ability who elects a general course in high school may find he will not later qualify for many college programs. These circumstances are often the result of poor information, low motivation for further schooling, or even an inadequate awareness that important decisions are being made. The situation is aggravated by tendencies in large school systems to classify students in mass terms, with the result that rigid grouping restricts future movement and choice.

Educational and vocational guidance are widely used at higher levels of education, where they are found useful in dealing with problems of student choice and decision. There is need for a substantial adaptation of guidance during the junior high school years. We stress the word "adaptation" because this is not a simple problem of transferring techniques that have worked well at higher levels. An effective adaptation of guidance at this level will require making it an organic part of the school program in grades seven, eight, and nine, and, at the same time, an integrated part of the decision-making process that runs through an individual's educational experience and into his career planning. Such an adaptation will be no mean accomplishment, particularly if we are to keep important decisions in the hands of individuals.

Stated in general terms, the need in guidance during this period is for broad descriptions of student interests and capabilities, which can be related to the broad spectrum of educational opportunities which lie in the secondary schools and beyond. The schools need to understand the varied educational opportunities and how they relate to various vocational choices. They need to communicate what they learn to the student and his family in terms they can understand. The student and his family, in turn, need to relate the student's interests and capabilities to choices that will be realistic for him. This is both a massive and a delicate task: massive because of its scope, and delicate because we must not force unnecessarily restrictive choices on young people at this age.

It should be emphasized that such an approach could not rely exclusively on the development of new and better tests, although these may well be needed. It will also have to rely on such other techniques as self-descriptions, informational publications, and films. Further, the testing cannot be limited to the assessment of skills and achievements normally associated with academic progress, although these would obviously have to be included. The effectiveness of such a guidance system may well rest more on our small but growing understanding of student interest and motivation than on our traditional concern with performance in conventional school courses. Special attention in this effort should be directed to the problems of minority groups and children with culturally deprived backgrounds. Better techniques for the identification of latent abilities among these children are needed and probably can be obtained through extended research and development work.

The Distribution of Students at the Advanced Level

The appearance of a substantial number of able students with advanced academic preparation for college is one of the most important outcomes of the various educational innovations of the 1950s. Many of these young people have made distinguished records in college and have moved on in gratifying proportions to graduate and professional schools. They thus represent a continuing source of high-level talent, one that should be nurtured and expanded if at all possible.

These students are admitted to college today under highly competitive conditions. They are sought after by many first-rank institutions, both public and private. There is considerable tension and uncertainty, both on college campuses and among these students and their families, before the formal admission offers are tendered and accepted. On the other hand, these students now do have a wide choice among possible colleges and, when they need financial assistance, this is usually forthcoming. The formal admission procedure for these able, well-prepared students is crude, individualistic, and breeds considerable anxiety but it does work after a fashion.

The formal admission procedure for these able students would be improved if better information were made available to them about the colleges they are considering. This is a mature group of young people and they are capable of making sound decisions about choice of college, if they can act on adequate information. What they now receive is often fragmentary, exaggerated, and erroneous, and this despite great improvement in school guidance programs. The work of Robert Pace and others in measuring the characteristics of college environments promises to provide a scientific basis for better information about colleges that can be related to student interests and capabilities. The "fit" between the able student and his college will, at best, be a precarious business. The colleges could do worse than entrust accurate information about themselves to the able student while he is still in school. There, with the aid of professional counseling, he should be able to make reasonable choices.

From the point of view of the colleges admitting these students, there is also need for broader information about the students themselves. The admissions officers are using informal and highly subjective means of reducing their reliance on conventional tests and school grades. We have probably adopted an unduly restricted image of the potentially creative student that may just be a horrible reflection of the image *he* has of his formal educational experience.

Like many basic admission problems, this one has some of its roots in matters academic. A major difficulty in the admission of these students to college today lies in the area of articulating the academic programs of schools and colleges. The faculties at colleges and universities have been slow to respond to the significant changes that have already occurred in the curriculum of many secondary schools, changes that are now making their way into some junior high schools and, in the case of foreign languages, science, and mathematics, into some elementary schools. In at least some cases, the work during the eleventh and twelfth grades is superior to many first-year offerings on college and university campuses. The actions recently taken at Yale and at Cornell to accelerate the completion of graduate studies for able students are exceptions. Far more common is faculty resistance to changes in the undergraduate program which would build upon the improvements already made in the secondary schools.

In two contrasting papers, Clark Kerr and William C. DeVane touch on this problem.[12] President Kerr, writing about the "multiversity," identifies undergraduate instruction as a university function which is not now thriving under the pressures of size, research, and public service. Dean DeVane, who worries about preserving the liberal arts tradition, sees this tradition threatened by the pressure of early specialization from the graduate schools, on the one hand, and the existence of advanced courses in secondary schools, on the other. The fact is that we have moved to a position where the liberal studies, or general education, are now in the joint custody of the strong secondary schools and the undergraduate colleges. For the able student, the last two years of secondary school and the first two years of an undergraduate program will soon constitute what we have thought of as a traditional undergraduate program.

The conservatism of college faculties under these circumstances is reflected in the reluctance of the secondary schools to broaden their definition of what constitutes an able student and to experiment with *further* curricular changes that would seek to define a broad liberal education in terms appropriate to the secondary school. As a result, much of the momentum that was gained during the 1950s, indeed much of the excitement that then surrounded work with these students, may be lost. We may be moving into a thoroughly conventional and inflexible means of dealing with these students academically during this four-year period, one that stresses early specialization.

The underlying problem, of course, is the legal demarcation which separates the secondary school from the undergraduate college. We face the problem of designing a curriculum that would be a coherent experience for the student, when that curriculum is the joint responsibility of two distinctly different levels of education. Granted that this curriculum is, ultimately, the responsibility of teachers, there would seem to be reason to look to external means of compensating for the legal demarcation between the two levels.

The immediate need is for a comprehensive, authoritative review of the course offerings during the last two years of secondary schools and the first year or two of college. This review should be followed by a series of recommendations aimed at formulating a program of general education for the able student during this period, one that would provide a continu-

[12] Clark Kerr, "The Frantic Race to Remain Contemporary," and William C. DeVane, "The College of Liberal Arts," *Daedalus,* Fall, 1964.

ous, progressive movement for him, and one that would draw on the resources and the opportunities available at both strong colleges and strong secondary schools. Finally, there should be several continuing external arrangements (of which the Advanced Placement Program is presently the only example) that would provide articulation between school and college, in behalf of the individual student.

The Distribution of Students at the Standard Level

Students entering college at the standard level account for somewhat more than half of the college-going population. As we have seen earlier, this group has not grown as rapidly as the admission groups at the advanced and postsecondary levels. The Project Talent evidence suggests that only about half of the high school graduates of average ability are entering college today: the other half are proceeding directly into employment. If substantial increases are to occur in the size of this group, it seems evident that these will have to be preceded by continued expansion of the varied facilities for postsecondary education, and, further, that these opportunities will have to be related by the students to various career choices. It seems quite likely that both of these outcomes will occur.

If this is the case, we can then question whether the means by which these students are distributed among the various colleges and universities will prove to be adequate under substantially larger numbers than exist today. The present admission procedures applying to this group are very much decentralized and quite inefficient. Despite major gains in college guidance at the secondary schools, it remains true that college choice for students in the standard group is a risky business and multiple applications for admission are the rule, not the exception. Despite efforts on college campuses to mechanize admission procedures, it remains true that there is a considerable duplication of clerical effort among the colleges as the result of multiple applications. And, despite the continued expansion of facilities for higher education, it remains true that there is a real likelihood of regional and local imbalance between available facilities and student demand for those facilities. The latter problem is becoming particularly acute in the heavily populated Northeastern section of the country, where numbers of applicants and numbers of available places on college and university campuses are now out of balance.

It seems evident that serious study and consideration should be given to a central clearinghouse for admission applications at the standard level, one that would relate the student's choices among particular colleges to a college's choices among particular students. Such a possibility has been considered in the past and rejected because of undue restriction on the freedom of action of both students and colleges. That objection remains valid, yet is softened by the prospect that expansion of facilities for higher education may lag behind enrollment pressures from high school graduates of average ability.

The Distribution of Students at the Postsecondary Level

Many of these students are now entering college in their own communities as the result of the rapid expansion of the public community colleges. There is every indication that this movement will continue as additional states and local communities act to make junior college education available to their residents.

The community college does not face an admission problem of the traditional sort. Typically, these institutions will admit all students of age eighteen or older and sometimes regardless of the fact of high school graduation. As has been frequently observed, the junior college itself performs an admission function for the four-year institutions by distinguishing between students who pursue a so-called terminal-technical program and those students who undertake a transfer program leading ultimately to an undergraduate degree.

Because of its emphasis on guidance and identification of student potential, and also because of the clientele which it serves, the junior college contributes to the formation of what we have earlier termed the migratory student population. Many postsecondary students, studying at junior colleges, are part-time students who will take longer than the customary two years to complete their junior college work. Some are adults, studying in evening programs. Still others are transfer students, who will enter the admission process at the upper division level, i.e., the last two undergraduate years. The migratory college population, however, is not confined to those students who undertake junior college programs. Rather, it extends to include the substantial number of students who transfer among the four-year colleges and universities and, beyond these, to include the individuals who undertake college-level work through university extension programs, adult education programs, educational television courses, and independent study. Recent studies have shown that the number of adults, both young and old, taking college courses on a part-time basis or by studying independently, has increased substantially in recent years and probably has reached a figure five times as large as full-time enrollments.

The traditional four-year undergraduate experience on the campus of a single college or university is true now for only a minority of the individuals who make up the college-going population.

It seems likely that the mobility of the college population can only increase during the years ahead. Under these circumstances, the traditional procedures for the award of college credit and the transmission of this information among higher institutions through official transcripts of record may be placed under great stress, so that decisions affecting the admission, placement, and degree status of migratory students will be adversely affected.

As an initial step in coming to grips with this problem, the College Entrance Examination Board has acted to form a Council on College-level Examinations for a three-year period of study and experimentation. The Council represents the interests of individual colleges and universities, both two-year and four-year, in the academic and psychometric standards of examinations to be commended to the country's higher institutions for use with migratory students. Working with a small professional staff, the Council will undertake surveys to determine the need for examinations in particular areas, including the need for a broad-based aptitude test. It will also study alternative ways for administration of the tests and for their utilization in college and university decisions. The eventual objective is a depository of college-level tests and examinations which could be drawn upon, as needed, for use with migratory students.[13]

Such a depository of examinations could become the core of an admission and placement system at the college level. The tests will need to be supplemented by additional activities. There should, for example, be provision for a central transcript service for the cumulative reporting of scores made by a given individual over a period of years. Such a transcript might well become a valuable supplement to the official transcript issued by a college or university. There is great need for better educational counseling for individuals in the migratory population, and steps should be taken to extend the counseling services now available to resident students to members of the migratory group. The already existing arrangements affecting transfer students, particularly between two-year and four-year colleges, will have to be taken into account, so that the new effort will be constructive, rather than disruptive. It will be a matter of one or two years before the full scope of this new activity will be known.

[13] Jack N. Arbolino, *A Report to the Trustees of the College Board: The Council on College-level Examinations,* November, 1964. (Mimeographed.)

Toward a Strategy for Future College Admission

We have observed that the college admission process should be strengthened in several important respects if the movement of students from elementary and secondary schools into some form of higher education is to be a universal movement. First, there should be an extensive adaptation of guidance and testing at the junior high school level in order that children not be selected out of the college-going stream at this level. Second, there is need for improved academic articulation between school and college, if able students are to receive an integrated program of general education during the last two years of secondary school and the first year or two of college. Third, we should be prepared to deal with great pressures of numbers at the standard level of college admission by developing plans for centralized clearinghouse operations that can quickly be put into effect if the situation deteriorates. And fourth, we have identified the need for the extension of formal admission operations to include a large, amorphous, migratory element in the college-going population, an element that may seek to enter at any point in the undergraduate program.

These suggestions, in sum, represent a considerable augmentation of existing admission practices. It is difficult to evaluate them, however, without relating them to a broad, long-term strategy for college admission in the United States. The same difficulty arises in evaluating many present practices which have not been referred to in the present paper. Ideally, such a strategy should encompass a number of elements: the young people themselves and our aspirations for them; the adult world they will enter and its requirements; the effectiveness and relevance of formal education prior to the college years; and the resources at the level of higher education that we are willing and able to put at their disposal. Such a strategy is clearly out of reach. We should be able, however, to work toward the definition of such a strategy (or perhaps a series of alternates) at a more practical level as a means of assuring that admission to college is open, rational, and fully effective. The definition of a strategy for college admission would be a useful outcome of the present conference.

Selective Higher Education
for Diverse Students

C. ROBERT PACE, *Professor of Higher Education,*
University of California at Los Angeles

Since the advent of mass testing some fifty years ago, millions of individuals have been measured along hundreds of dimensions. Most commonly in schools and colleges we have measured individual differences in general intelligence, scholastic aptitude, school achievement in many different subjects, a variety of special aptitudes and talents, vocational and other interests, various attitudes and values, and assorted characteristics of personality. From this long experience we know that college students differ greatly from one another, that in scholastic aptitude, for example, they range from rather modest talent to the highest levels of potential genius. We know, further, that within the student bodies of some colleges nearly the full range of this talent can be found, whereas in other colleges the range of talent is much narrower.

It stretches our credulity too far to suppose that any college student, from the brightest to the dullest, can find equal stimulation, reward, and personal enrichment at any institution of higher education. Institutions differ from one another just as individuals do, although we have not yet developed a comparable body of knowledge about the nature and dimensions of these institutional differences. Usually we have just classified institutions—as universities, colleges, junior colleges, teachers colleges, technical schools, or public versus private, or coeducational or not, or denominational versus nonsectarian, or residential versus commuter campuses. But these are structural or categorical differences. It is as if, in describing individuals, we merely classified them as men or women, adolescent or adult, fat or thin, rich or poor. Yet we know that there remains a great diversity within these categories—that not all women are alike, nor are all universities alike, that not all fat people are alike, nor are all denominational schools alike.

That there is some kind of selective distribution between students and colleges, however, is a fact. There are selective students as well as selective institutions, and the number of both has increased in the recent past. For the present, selective distribution is better described as a phenomenon than a system, a loosely individualistic and informal process than a national program, a competition among possible choices than a matching of particular students to particular colleges. As more students have sought admission to college there have been more opportunities to influence who goes where. How we should respond to these opportunities—whether with enthusiasm or caution or rejection—needs to be discussed now. The facts of diversity and the phenomenon of selectivity form a curious dilemma. In some ways it can be argued that both are desirable but incompatible, and that each has liabilities as well as benefits.

In exploring this dilemma of diversity and selectivity we need first to remind ourselves about who is going to college today, who went yesterday, and who is likely to go tomorrow. Briefly, about a generation ago 60 per cent of the young people graduated from high school and about a third of the high school graduates went on to college. Today, about 70 per cent of the young people are graduating from high school and about half of the high school graduates are going to college. A generation from now we expect that 80 per cent of the young people will graduate from high school and that about two-thirds of these high school graduates will go to college.

Paradoxical as it may appear, many of these increases over the past generation in the number and proportion of high school graduates who entered college were accompanied by increases in quality as well. The reasons are quite simple. A generation ago only half of the brightest high school graduates (those who would rank in the top 15 per cent of the general population in measured intelligence) went to college. Today, more than two-thirds of those students are going to college. In another generation we can be confident that almost all of those in this top segment of intellectual talent will go to college. The same rise in quality can be seen in relation to high school achievement. Not long ago only half of the students from the upper half of their high school graduating class (measured by their high school grades) went to college. Today about 70 per cent of these students are going to college. And tomorrow it is likely that 90 per cent or more of this upper group will go on to college. In the expansion that has occurred so far there has been lots of room at the top, but we have rapidly been filling it.

Because this has been the recent pattern of expansion many institutions have become more selective and also more homogeneous in the level and range of scholastic aptitude in their entering classes. On the College Board's Scholastic Aptitude Test, scores can range from 200 to 800, a spread of 600 points. If we eliminate a few scattered extremes, we can say that the range within which 95 per cent of the scores would fall is 500 points. Looking at the freshmen test scores at fifty-three colleges and universities reported for 1961, I found that in half of these schools the range (95 per cent) of scores of admitted freshmen that year was 350 points or more. At these same fifty-three schools in 1964, however, only one-third had a range of 350 points or more in the scores of their entering freshmen.

More specifically: seventeen schools had lopped off the bottom 50 points in their range; nine schools had increased the top 50 points in their range; twelve had lopped off the bottom 50 points *and* also increased the top 50 points, and fifteen schools had no change in the range of scores. In brief, thirty-eight of the fifty-three schools had become more selective and seventeen of the fifty-three schools had become more homogeneous. The upward trend in selectivity has been happening at large universities as well as at liberal arts colleges. Of fourteen universities, in this group of fifty-three institutions, twelve went up and none went down; of the thirty-nine colleges, twenty-six went up and none went down. In the range of scores of entering freshmen, five of the fourteen universities were more homogeneous; and twelve of the thirty-nine colleges were more homogeneous. The consequence of this trend is that the importance of college choice has increased but the range of college choice for some students has decreased.

While the competition for top talent has become tougher, we know that the major increases in enrollments from now on must inevitably come from the broad middle segment of high school graduates. In a sense, we have been living in a fool's paradise where numbers and quality have both increased. This does not mean that existing institutions must become less selective. The vast population growth assures an even larger supply of all kinds of students, including the very brightest; and it is quite probable that many new and highly selective institutions will be needed. It does mean, however, that institutions which serve a broader segment of youth will be in even greater demand.

Although colleges of all kinds may increase in number and in the size of their enrollments, most forecasts agree in believing that the bulk of new enrollments will be absorbed by the public junior colleges and public universities. Private colleges can increase their enrollments about as much as they want; but for many of them their policies and their financial resources will lead them to expand more slowly than the public institutions.

Granted these probabilities about the distribution of students among various types of institutions, we can turn next to a closer look at the institutions themselves. Earlier we noted that the common way of describing institutions was to group them in broad categories—such as junior colleges, liberal arts colleges, and universities—but that these groupings probably contained a great deal of diversity and overlap within and between them on more fundamental characteristics, fundamental in the sense of having greater relevance to the educational impact of the institutions.

In the past, accounts of what life was really like on the college campus were found mainly in novels, short stories, and memoirs. More recently, sociologists, psychologists, journalists, and others have attempted to characterize the atmosphere of different colleges and universities. David Boroff, for example, has visited various campuses, talked with assorted students and staff, and written journalistic impressions from his observations. David Riesman, from his observations, has written character vignettes of several colleges. Howard Becker has analyzed the student culture of a medical school by observing students from day to day and identifying characteristic ways in which they responded to the demands made upon them. Burton Clark and Martin Trow have classified student groups into four types according to their major value orientations which they describe as vocational, collegiate, academic, and nonconformist; and studies made by the Educational Testing Service have shown that colleges differ markedly from one another in the proportion of their students expressing preferences among these value orientations. Many of these character sketches are not easily reproducible for they depend on the particular style and perspective of a single observer. The descriptions are often fascinating to read, but they may or may not be as perceptive as a good novel. By and large, also, the methods have been too elaborate for use on a large scale and so have given us knowledge about only a few places.

Over the past several years I have been experimenting with a somewhat different way of characterizing college environments. It is similar to a public opinion poll in that students act as reporters about what they believe to be characteristic of their college. Typically, the students are upperclassmen who presumably know what the environment is like because they have lived in it for several years. The poll, or test, consists of a list of statements about college life; and the students indicate whether each of these statements is generally true or false with reference to their college. What the students are aware of, and agree with some unanimity of report to be generally true, defines the prevailing campus atmosphere.

The concept in back of this approach is that the college environment can be thought of as a stimulus. It is a complex stimulus consisting of professors, books, laboratories, social and public events, student organizations and extracurricular programs, housing and feeding, counseling, curricula, examinations, lectures, discussions, interpersonal relationships, and many other conditions which impinge in varying degrees upon the lives of students. Cumulatively these conditions—rules and regulations, policies and practices, features and facilities, activities and interests—tend to encourage and reward some kinds of behavior more than others, and in this sense they define what may be called the effective environment of the college, effective because students are aware of it and have to cope with it.

After several hundred statements had been tried out in many colleges it was possible to select a cross section of institutions which was reasonably representative of the variety of environments students live in—public and private, large and small, and geographically distributed in appropriate ways. By studying how these environments differed and noting only those statements which most clearly reflected these differences, we arrived at five factors or dimensions which seemed to be most relevant. Each of these dimensions is defined by thirty statements. The score for any institution is the number of statements reported to be characteristic of the school, with "characteristic" defined as a consensus among the reporters of 2 to 1 or greater. The instrument is called CUES, which stands for College and University Environment Scales, and it is distributed by the Educational Testing Service.

The dimensions, or scales, are these: Practicality, Community, Awareness, Propriety, and Scholarship.

The *Practicality* dimension suggests an instrumental emphasis in the college environment in which procedures, personal status, and practical benefits are important. Apple-polishing, having assigned seats in class, being in the right club, having special privileges, offering many practical courses—these are illustrative features in this type of environment.

The *Community* dimension describes a friendly, cohesive, group-oriented campus. The environment is supportive and sympathetic, with feelings of group welfare and loyalty about the college. History and traditions of the college, group spirit, borrowing and sharing, helping others—these are illustrative characteristics.

The *Awareness* dimension suggests an emphasis on the expansion and enrichment of personality, of societal horizons, and of expressiveness and sensitivity. Many opportunities for creative and appreciative relationships to paintings, music, drama, poetry, sculpture, and so on are provided. Much concern about events around the world and about the present and future condition of man is evident.

The *Propriety* dimension suggests an environment that is polite and considerate. Group standards of decorum are important. Caution and thoughtfulness are evident. There is a minimum of rebellious, risk-taking, or convention-flouting behavior.

The *Scholarship* dimension suggests an emphasis on competitively high academic achievement, intellectual discipline, and the rigorous pursuit of knowledge and theories for their own sake. Professors really push the students' capacities to the limit. There is a lot of studying over the week ends. Class discussions are typically vigorous and intense.

Since there are thirty statements in each scale, the scores for an institution can range from zero to thirty. Surely there is a great difference between the atmosphere of a school in which none of the statements in the scholarship scale, for example, is identified as characteristic and a school in which all thirty of these same statements are identified as characteristic. At least we can say that the environment in which learning and development occurs would be strikingly different in the two cases. We have actually found differences this great, or almost this great, on all the dimensions in the test.

Looking at the scores obtained from ninety-nine institutions we can see how much diversity there really is among schools of presumably the same type. The ninety-nine schools include thirty-two junior colleges, forty liberal arts colleges or others offering work no higher than a master's or first professional degree, and twenty-seven universities offering advanced professional degrees and the Ph.D. The extent of their diversity is shown in Figure 1. The dotted line on this chart is drawn at the approximate average score of fifty institutions that were selected to comprise a representative cross section of four-year colleges and universities. Junior colleges, for example, spread over only half of the possible range. On three of the scales their scores cover the middle segment of the distribution—from moderately low to moderately high. On the other two scales, Aware-

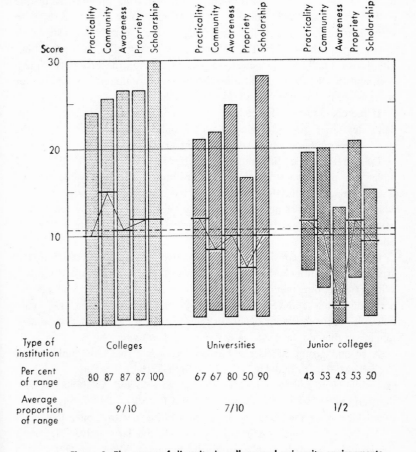

Figure 1. The range of diversity in college and university environments

ness and Scholarship, their scores fall almost entirely within the lower half of the possible range. Universities spread over seven-tenths of the possible range. On four of the scales their scores range from zero or close to zero to quite high. On the Propriety scale their scores range from close to zero to just beyond the middle of the possible range. The colleges are the most diverse set of institutions, spreading over nine-tenths of the possible range, and going on every scale from zero or close to zero up to very high scores. We can also note from Figure 1 certain ways in which the average profiles differ. The colleges are typically high on the Community dimension. The universities are typically low on the Propriety dimension, and to a lesser extent also on the Community dimension. The junior colleges are typically low on the Awareness dimension.

If the character of the college environment has any influence on students' learning, then it obviously could make quite a difference to the student depending on which college or university he attended.

Despite the wide differences in environments which are still found under the usual ways of classifying institutions, it is possible to find several classes of schools each of which has a roughly similar profile, and which are much more homogeneous on at least some of the five characteristics. Figure 2 shows the range of scores for several groups of institutions.

One such group consists of highly selective, private nonsectarian liberal arts colleges. Antioch, Swarthmore, Vassar, and Oberlin are examples. Without exception they stand very high on the Scholarship and Awareness dimensions and very low on the Practicality dimension. The main differences between them occur on the Community and Propriety scales, ranging as they do on these scales from very low to very high.

A second group consists of academically selective large universities. Cornell, Michigan, and UCLA are examples. These institutions, without exception, stand relatively high on the Scholarship and Awareness dimensions and quite low on the Community and Propriety dimensions. On the Practicality scale their scores range from quite low to moderately high.

A third group consists of relatively less selective large universities, both public and private. Examples would be Syracuse, Miami of Ohio, Ohio State, Southern Methodist, and Kentucky. Typically, institutions in this group obtain their highest scores on the Practicality dimension and their lowest scores on Propriety and Scholarship. On the Community and Awareness scales they range from relatively low to well above average.

A fourth group is a somewhat more heterogeneous one, consisting mainly of liberal arts colleges which have some loose denominational connection, and of teachers colleges. DePauw, Denison, and Ball State

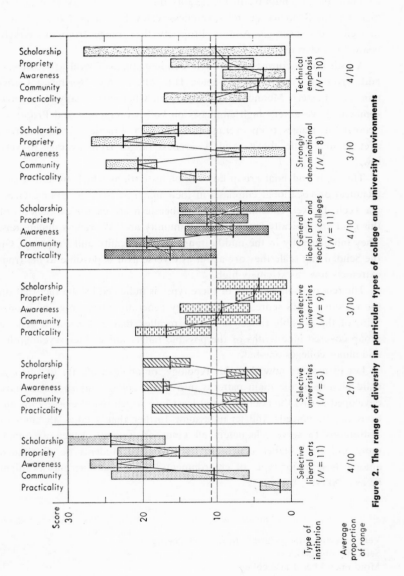

Figure 2. The range of diversity in particular types of college and university environments

Teachers College are examples. These schools typically have a strong emphasis on Community. In Practicality they range from average to very high. On the Scholarship and Awareness scales they range from very low to well above average. And in Propriety they range from moderately below to moderately above the average.

A fifth group consists of strongly denominational liberal arts colleges, both Protestant and Catholic. Seton Hill, Mt. Mercy, Northwest Christian, and Eastern Mennonite are examples. Characteristically their environments have a very high emphasis on both Community and Propriety. Scholarship ranges from average to quite high. Practicality ranges from average to a little above. And Awareness ranges from average to very low.

The sixth and final group consists of institutions which have a strong technical or vocational emphasis in their undergraduate programs. Georgia Tech, Drexel, Cincinnati, and Northeastern are examples. Schools of this kind are typically low on the Community and Awareness dimensions. They fall generally in the middle range on Practicality and Propriety. On the Scholarship scale they are about as diverse as it is possible to be, from extremely low to extremely high.

The relative homogeneity of these types is indicated by the fact that on the various CUES scores combined they generally cover only about one-third of the possible range. It will be recalled that colleges as a general group covered nine-tenths of the possible range, universities seven-tenths, and junior colleges one-half.

Let us assume now that this typology, or one reasonably like it, is a valid picture of the main patterns into which college environments have developed across the country, or at least into which many existing institutions can be placed. And let us assume further that it takes all kinds of institutions to serve adequately all kinds of students. When we attain more universal higher education how will the students be distributed among these major types of environments? Some plausible guesses might be as follows:

Type of institution	Per cent of students
Very selective nonsectarian liberal arts colleges	5
Selective universities	15
More open liberal arts colleges	10
More open universities	35
Strongly denominational colleges	5
Schools with major technical emphasis	5
Junior colleges	25
Total	100

In every segment except the very selective liberal arts colleges and universities, we would also estimate that there will be a fairly wide range of student talent, and that in all types of institutions there will be some students from the very top level of academic ability. Between the various segments of higher education there will also be considerable student mobility, except perhaps at the very selective liberal arts colleges and private universities. About one-third of those who graduate from junior colleges will move on to four-year institutions. And about one-fifth or more of those who begin at one four-year institution will transfer to another at some time.

The opportunity for students to choose where they will go depends on several conditions: on what is available near at hand, on knowledge of what is available elsewhere, and on the students' talents and financial resources. The combined possession of high academic talents, money, and scholarships will enable some students to make national choices among the best public and private institutions. At this level of national choice the public institutions are about as exclusive as the private ones, for they have all erected tariff barriers against interstate commerce in talent in the form of substantially higher tuitions for out-of-state students, and in some cases quotas on the number they will admit. One useful form of Federal aid to higher education might be the payment of these excess out-of-state tuitions so as to counteract the present restraint-of-trade policies.

Opportunities for choice are important because the character of the college environment has an influence on the course of students' learning and development. Many years ago in a study of students in forty-three Pennsylvania colleges it was shown that students did better in good company. Students who went to colleges where the average ability of the student body was high performed significantly better on comprehensive tests of achievement than did students of the same initial ability who went to colleges where the average ability was low. In Minnesota's General College, where pressures on students to be interested in current affairs came from many aspects of the total program, students' scores on a current affairs test were close to the 70th percentile of national sophomore norms despite the fact that the average General College student came from the lower half of his high school graduating class. In a recent study of my own involving nine different colleges it was quite clear that students at colleges which had the strongest and most pervasive environmental emphasis in, for example, a humanistic-aesthetic direction were precisely the ones who felt they had made the most progress toward the attainment of goals relevant to that emphasis. The same was true for other environmental emphases in relation to other relevant attainments.

Certainly at the extremes it is also clear that the goodness of fit between the student and the college has a bearing on the student's success and retention. In places that have had the most opportunity to be selective and the most experience in choosing appropriate students—medical schools, for example, or Harvard College—it is common to find that 90 per cent or more of those who are admitted eventually graduate. It is in the more heterogeneous institutions, where the goodness of fit cannot possible be as sharp, that we find the largest numbers of students who transfer elsewhere, drop out, or otherwise fail to complete the program.

Although selective distribution has merit, it can only be promoted by policies which enlarge the range of individual choice. Any national effort toward selective assignment, which told people where to go and what was good for them, would be contrary to our deepest traditions of freedom and morality. Distinctive institutions and distinctive individuals will just have to find one another, as they often do now; and they will be more likely to do so as information about each becomes more available to both, and as the resources which permit mobility are increased.

For most students going to college, however, the choices open to them will be more limited—based mainly, as they are now, on the circumstances that the place is near and the price is right. And most people continuing beyond high school will be enrolled in relatively open and accessible state universities, junior colleges, or other generally large, complex, and comprehensive institutions. Large public institutions will become larger, but the demand for higher education will also spur the construction of new institutions so that the opportunity for local choices both city wide and state wide will be greater than it is now.

Just as there is diversity across the national scene, so also is there diversity within single institutions between one part and another and between students within different parts of the institution, especially in the large institutions where most students are and will continue to be. And we find here the same kind of relationships and problems we have just described. Within a single complex institution the progress of students toward various objectives is in part dependent on the degree to which major parts of the environment are mutually supportive in their emphasis, and on the compatibility between the student and the particular subculture within the environment in which he finds himself.

By major parts of the environment we mean three things: first, an administrative environment which consists of policies and procedures, rules and regulations, and overall features and facilities; second, an academic environment which consists of that part of the institution in which the student is doing his major study, such as engineering, business, nursing, science departments, humanities, social sciences, and so on; and third, a student environment which consists of one's major circle of friends and student activities. When these three parts of the environment are mutually supportive, students' attainments are consistent with their combined direction of influence to a greater extent than with any one part alone.

By subcultures we mean the different academic fields and the different circles of friends and activities. In the nine colleges and universities we studied in this particular research, we found that the academic subcultures most often deviant from the college as a whole were the various vocational groups and the sciences. The humanistic and social science groups were not so often deviant from the college as a whole.

When we looked at the personality characteristics of students in five of the colleges we also found internal differences, and again mainly in certain vocational groups and in the sciences.

When we looked at the attainment of various objectives we found that differences in attainment were most frequently in relation to (1) understanding science and technology, (2) vocational preparation, and (3) developing an enjoyment and appreciation of art, music, and literature.

Within complex institutions, then, whether we considered the major subgroups, or the students in them, or the attainment of various goals, we typically found three cultures—vocational, scientific, and humanistic.

Now when we examined the environmental characteristics of different subcultures and the personality characteristics of students in them in relation to the attainment of goals judged to be relevant to those characteristics, we found an interesting and significant set of associations.

1. Environment and attainment scores were consistent (both above the college average or both below the college average) as opposed to inconsistent in a ratio of 2⅓ to 1.

2. Between personality and attainment scores the ratio was 1⅔ to 1.

3. When both the environmental emphasis of a subgroup and the attainment of objectives relevant to that emphasis were really deviant from the college average (significantly different in the statistician's terms), the ratio of consistent to inconsistent relationships was 6½ to 1.

4. When both the personality characteristics of a subgroup and the attainment of objectives relevant to those characteristics were significantly different from the college average, the ratio was 2½ to 1.

5. The personality and environmental characteristics were more likely to be congruent than incongruent: 60 per cent to 40 per cent. When they were congruent, attainment was consistent with their combined influence in a ratio of 3½ to 1. When they were not congruent, attainment was consistent with the environmental emphasis in a ratio of 1⅓ to 1. The

difference between these last two ratios suggests the increase in relevant attainment that might result from a more appropriate distribution of students among the various subcultures of the university. And this in turn suggests the importance of opportunity for lateral movement across various parts of complex institutions. The pattern and direction of a student's attainment within a diverse environment seems to depend a little more on where he is than on who he is.

At the beginning of this essay we said that the facts of diversity and the phenomenon of selectivity comprised a curious dilemma, that, in a sense, both were desirable but incompatible, and that each had liabilities as well as benefits. The development of new colleges and the enlargement of existing ones, particularly in the metropolitan centers, will increase the options for many students. As we more nearly approach universal higher education, we must also provide a wider range of opportunities for many different kinds of people. We cannot limit our programs and our rewards to academic book-learning. In Nevitt Sanford's words, "We shall provide further education for youth not because they are bright but because they are our children."

The freedom we have had in recent years to stress academic selectivity has been a mixed blessing. One serious liability in the concentration of academic talent has been uncovered in a nationwide survey of college graduates conducted by the National Opinion Research Center. One aspect of the survey dealt with influences on students' choice of science as a career, or more specifically, the decision to continue the study of science in graduate school. The most startling discovery was that the high-prestige intellectually elite colleges were serious underproducers of future scientists in relation to their talent supply and the initial interests of their students. The most influential factor on the student's choice was encouragement from a faculty member. The faculty members rarely gave such encouragement to any but their A students. And, of course, faculty members tended to distribute their grades along a more or less normal curve. Even though all the students might be in the top 10 per cent or so on any national scale of scientific aptitude and achievement, many of them got B's, C's, and even worse. This produced a lowering of the students' self-esteem, and a lowering of their career aspirations. The same phenomenon did not occur at the more heterogeneous state universities because most students there who would fall in the same top 10 per cent of talent and achievement were quite likely to get A's, and thus be encouraged by a faculty member to go on to graduate school. One counterforce to this unhappy condition might be to give students a national grade as well as a local grade, so that even if they were C at Swarthmore they would at least know (and so would their professors) that they were A nationally; and such knowledge might influence the professors' judgment as well as lift the students' self-esteem.

On this same line of revising our standards of judgment, we might suggest that the College Board's Scholastic Aptitude Test be interpreted along a more universal scale. Many students, parents, and counselors seem to think that a score of 500 is "average." Actually, a student who scores 500 ranks just inside the top 15 per cent of American youth; and "average" in this larger perspective is really about 325.

There is one last bit of information from our own research which may be especially pertinent. When we examined the characteristics of college environments in relation to students' satisfaction with college life, rather than in relation to students' achievement of certain objectives, we found that satisfaction was most clearly related to a friendly, congenial atmosphere, to a sense of community within the college campus. Satisfaction was also related to whatever the opposite might be of a scientistic, independent, competitively aggressive atmosphere. In view of the increasing urbanization of higher education, paralleling the larger society in its concentration of people in bigger and often more impersonal groupings, we may well pause briefly to reflect on this small bit of research data: The extent to which students like and feel satisfaction with their college experience seems to depend primarily on their finding in the college environment conditions which reward their own needs for friendship and communal experience. Yet it seems to be precisely this human need that is in danger of being unfulfilled by metropolitan concentrations, whether civic or collegiate. Impersonality, privacy more than community, things more than lives—such emphases are often found in the large institutions of modern society, but they do not generate satisfaction with or in the institution. In the academic setting it is usually the science subcultures which have these emphases; and students in these subcultures are usually least satisfied with their college life.

No doubt science needs humanizing, as some philosophers have said since the beginning of science, and urban complexes made more fit for the human spirit; but neither the subject matter of science nor the size of the institutions are necessarily the main contributors to students' dissatisfaction. What is really needed, we believe, throughout the college and university environment, is a greater acceptance of multiple responsibilities—for personal and social development as well as for the mastery of things and theories, for human rewards as well as academic rewards. Not until we accept these multiple responsibilities will we be ready for universal higher education.

Significance for High School and College Teacher Preparation

WILLIAM J. HAGGERTY, *President,*
State University College, New Paltz, New York

A discussion of how many teachers will be needed, how they can be recruited and retained in the teaching profession, and how they should be prepared for teaching in a system involving expanding secondary and postsecondary enrollments must follow the prior consideration of just how many youth are anticipated at various educational levels, what their academic and vocational interests and capacities are, and what kind of educational programs are to be expanded or constructed for them. The present patterns of preparing teachers for existing schools and colleges are being challenged today by Dr. Conant and others, and such challenges are stimulating examination and evaluation of these existing patterns. If much larger numbers of teachers will need to be provided, and if the educational institutions they will man will be more varied, and if the youth they will teach will have greater ranges of abilities, interests, and motivations —all of which seem likely—then a serious attempt to evaluate our present teacher preparation programs and the proposals for improvement that have been made is even more pertinent and timely.

THE SIZE OF THE PROBLEM

When one speaks of universal higher education it is universality in terms of school attendance rather than singleness of educational purpose or uniformity of curriculum or method that is involved. Indeed, as larger proportions of school- and college-age children and youth attend school and college, the more varied must the educational programs become.

Universality in school attendance appears to be both a tradition and a goal in United States society. The time has long passed since anyone seriously discussed whether all the children in this country did or should continue in school through at least the first eight grades. State compulsory education laws have merely confirmed the universality of elementary education and have suggested, where the school-leaving age is seventeen or eighteen, the desirability of universal education for the secondary level. In fact, regardless of compulsory schooling laws, universal secondary education for all is becoming almost a reality. Figure 1 gives a general picture of how high school and college enrollments have gradually increased in actual numbers and in percentages of their respective age groups since 1900.

More than 95 per cent of high school–age youth are expected to be in attendance by 1970. This percentage was less than 50 in 1930, and less than 10 in 1900. At the college level the goal of universal attendance appears to be almost the same as that for elementary and high school education but percentage of attendance figures for college-age youth are about thirty to forty years behind those for secondary school–age youth. For example, the proportion of college-age youth in college in 1950 (27 per cent) was approximately the same as the proportion of high school–age youth in high school in 1920 (28 per cent); the estimated proportion of college-age youth expected to be in college in 1970 (49 per cent) is about the same as the proportion of high school–age youth in high school in 1930 (47 per cent). While the gap between the number of youth of high school age and the number in high school is almost closed, the gap at the college level is not. Although about half of the college-age youth in 1970 are expected to be in college as far as the nation as a whole is concerned, this represents very rapid growth in recent decades. In 1960 about one-third of college-age youth were in college; in 1950 about one-fourth were in college; and in 1940 less than 15 per cent were in college.

The goal of universality of opportunity for college education has recently been restated by two major political leaders. Speaking at the Amer-

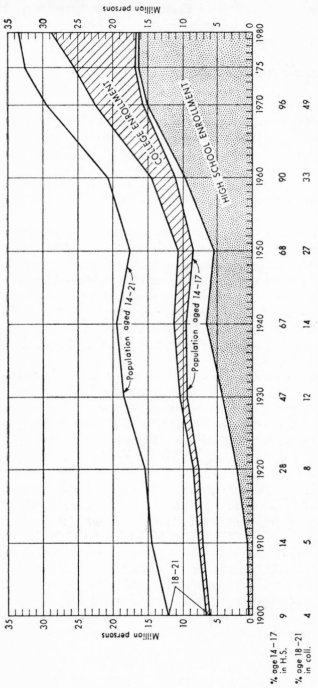

Figure 1. Population and enrollment data for high school and college-age levels for the United States for the period 1900–1960 and estimates for 1970–1980 (Data from U.S. Office of Education)

	1900	1910	1920	1930	1940	1950	1960	1970	1980
% age 14–17 in H.S.	9	14	28	47	67	68	90	96	49
% age 18–21 in coll.	4	5	8	12	14	27	33	49	

ican Council on Education meeting in San Francisco in October, 1964, Governor Edmund G. Brown of California said,

> The fact is that over the years California has developed a unique system of tuition-free education for all who can make the grade from kindergarten through graduate school. That system was not developed overnight nor was it the invention of any one governor or state administration. It results from the determination of the people of California to make a massive investment in education which cuts down the ancient barriers of social standing, race, or personal income. Long ago we rejected the idea that only a select few shall go to the universities, or that you dilute the quality of education when you offer it to every qualified student.

Also in October, President Lyndon Johnson, speaking at the dedication of the new Florida Atlantic University at Boca Raton, Florida, said that, "advanced education is no longer a luxury to be enjoyed by the children of fortunate families." He said it had become a "necessity" and was "the right of every American boy and girl." Referring to the GI Bill of Rights, he pointed out that the country was challenged to develop a "program of loans and scholarships enabling every young man and woman, who has the ability, to move beyond the high school level."

It should be noted that in both these statements the reference was not to the need for providing higher education for every youth of college age but, as the Governor said, "to every *qualified* student" or, as the President indicated, to "every young man or woman *who has the ability.*" The definition of *ability* or *qualifications* is left undetermined in this context. In terms of goals the United States tradition has, in some state universities, and in a rapidly increasing number of community and junior colleges, made the high school diploma the primary index of ability or qualifications to continue into higher education. State and national surveys have recommended that educational opportunities of some kind should be available to all high school graduates for at least two years of postsecondary education. The elimination of social and financial barriers to higher education, which is being achieved at varying rates of speed throughout the country, is gradually removing former obstacles to universal higher education. The steady trend to automation and the increasing technicality associated with almost all forms of employment are removing many job opportunities that required little education and which, therefore, constituted alternatives to continuing in school and college for many youth.

For well over half a century the educational gap represented by those young persons aged fourteen to seventeen not in school, and the gap represented by those aged eighteen to twenty-one not in college have been closing. The barriers have been and are being eliminated and the traditional social commitment to universal educational opportunity is being reaffirmed and extended. It is, I think, unlikely that any restrictive educational philosophy as to who should be educated or any particular set of economic conditions will halt or reverse the long trend toward universal opportunity for higher education. The actual numbers or percentages of youth who will be in attendance at postsecondary institutions by 1980, or 1990, or 2000, will be affected by many factors, including particularly the employment situation throughout the nation and the availability of sufficient numbers and varieties of educational programs in terms of the number of young men and women graduating from high school and the variety of their educational needs. Providing the appropriate kinds of educational opportunities for the total range of aptitudes, abilities, and interests of the youth involved will constitute a crucial challenge to the members of the educational profession and others involved in educational planning.

As larger percentages of youth attend school and college the actual number of persons in each age group has also increased throughout most of the decades of this century. The combined population of both high school and college-age groups has increased from 12 million in 1900 to 20.7 million in 1960, and is expected to rise to 33.5 million in 1980.

Where these statistics are translated into the need for preparing teachers for high school and college youth it is possible to ascertain some idea of the magnitude of the task as far as numbers go. It is estimated that during the five-year period from 1965 to 1970 about 100,000 new high school teachers and approximately 125,000 new college teachers will be needed on the basis of increased enrollments in high school and college alone. For the whole decade, 1965 to 1975, the corresponding figures would be more than 165,000 new high school teachers and about 235,000 new college teachers. In addition to these estimated numbers of new teachers needed to provide for increased enrollments, much larger numbers of new teachers will be needed to replace members of the profession who die or retire, or who leave the profession for other reasons. The fact that more new college teachers than new high school teachers will be needed in the years immediately ahead reflects a new condition in United States education—the large size of the gap at the college level compared to the relatively small size of the gap at the high school level between the actual and potential numbers of young persons enrolled—and creates certain implications for the total problem of preparing teachers for universal education at the upper levels. The basic conclusion here is that the number of high school teachers needed will continue to increase because the number of students will increase for at least another decade, and that this will be accompanied by a very rapid and comparatively large increase in the number of college teachers needed—the result of the increasing enrollments during the next decade and beyond as the long-term trend toward the goal of universal higher education continues.

THE CHARACTER OF THE STUDENT BODY

With everybody's children in school through high school, which, it appears, will be almost the case in the next few years, the schools will have the problem of providing educational programs suitable to the interests and abilities of the entire population, excluding a few who may be judged incapable of profiting from organized schooling. The elementary schools of the country have been facing this problem of the universality of education at the earlier years for a long time and have learned some of the ways to deal with situations involving almost the total range of individual human differences. The high schools are enrolling, or will soon enroll, practically all youth of high school age with all their problems of adolescence and their greater range of individual differences, and are seeking appropriate educational answers to the problems with which they are confronted. Universality of education at this stage means, among other things, that the young people who are destined to become mechanics, filling-station attendants, architects, professors, lawyers, doctors, taxi-drivers, bookkeepers, industrial leaders, bankers, hairdressers, waitresses, homemakers, and just plain socialites, as well as those later to be elected as mayors, councilmen, senators, governors, and even presidents, are together in the same high schools. Those of meager and great ability, of weak and strong motivation, of timid and aggressive personalities, of robust health and vigor, as well as those who are physically weak, are also in the same high schools. Indeed, all these varied people have been in school together for almost twelve years by the time they finish high school, and the varieties of their individual differences have determined to a great extent the characteristics of the groups they compose, be it a ninth-grade history class, a senior class about to graduate, an athletic team, a French club, or an entire student body. It appears from the evidence at hand that in the future most (more than half by the early 1970s) of those completing high school will go on together to the colleges and universities of the country and create in those institutions another cross section of the nation's citizens.

With universal education at the high school level and an approach to universal education at college level, the former concept of higher education institutions catering to a selected few of common background is no longer useful. Those responsible for both the high schools and the colleges must develop educational programs which take account of the wide variations in interests, abilities, intended vocations and professions, and personality traits that characterize our total population. This is not an easy task. Goals such as preparation for responsible citizenship may be the same for every student in school or college. But if the acquisition of intelligent habits of thinking is a part of that goal for all, certainly the means for achieving it will be different with young people of different degrees of intelligence and different cultural backgrounds. There are probably few educational goals, if any, whose most effective achievements can be accomplished in the same way for all students. Even the content of the curriculum, as well as methods of teaching and learning, may be different for different students, even for the same goal.

For a long time psychologists and educational psychologists have been pointing out and describing the individual differences that characterize the members of our human race. This has been done in detail and has been verified by successive generations of testers, experimenters, and evaluators. Furthermore, the implication of such individual differences for educational method and procedure and content has been pointed out to everyone in the educational profession. It is frequently difficult, however, to find that recognition and awareness of the individual differences of the students have resulted in sufficient adaptation of program and method to provide the equal educational opportunity generally aspired to. With all the youth of the country in school the teachers at the high school level, as well as those at other levels, will be confronted with large majorities of young persons whose characteristics fall within a middle range and who pursue their studies, their vocations, and their lives with equanimity. At the same time they will also have responsibility for some who might be classed as delinquents, as late-bloomers, or as delayed adolescents, or who are characterized as inner-directed, precocious, mentally retarded, emotionally deprived, unmotivated, overly aggressive, or just plain disorganized.

All the variety of personalities, abilities, interests, motivations, and ambitions that human beings possess are coming to be reflected in the student bodies of the nation's high schools and colleges. This creates a new and expanding challenge to teachers—a challenge for which they must be prepared by the program of preparation they follow in anticipation of entering the teaching profession.

THE CHARACTER OF CURRENT HIGH SCHOOL
AND COLLEGE PROGRAMS

Since the turn of the century the traditional academy, high school, and college have undergone continuing changes, expansions, and proliferations, many of these having been caused by the broadening segment of the total population in attendance. Many new subjects have been included in the curriculum; knowledge and the content of courses have expanded by large ratios; departments and fields have been divided and subdivided; and new goals, many of them vocational or occupational, have been accepted. At both high school and college levels new types of institutions have been established. The multipurpose high school with its separate "tracks," the vocational schools of many types, and other specialized schools have been developed in answer to the variety of the needs and interests of the expanding school population. The two-year college appeared early in this century and expanded rapidly in numbers, in enrollments, and in variety of programs offered. Enrollments increased in these institutions from 8,000 in 1920 to more than 400,000 in 1960, and are projected to climb to more than 1 million by 1970 and 1.5 million by 1975. The testing and evaluation movement was developed and expanded and has had a profound influence on the organization as well as the methods of education. More recently there has been greater attention given to new approaches to teaching and learning and evaluation through programming, learning machines, educational television, proficiency examinations, advanced placement, independent study, and other arrangements and methods that provide for greater recognition of the individual differences among students. There is a growing notion that students should be given freedom for more individual initiative in learning on their own and at their own pace, and that the educational system should provide the opportunity for this to take place.

When a large expansion in postsecondary enrollments is contemplated several questions which have relevance to the preparation of teachers arise: How many of these new college-level students will enter existing institutions and follow existing college-level programs, whether in two-year or four-year institutions? If large numbers enter existing institutions will this cause a lowering of the expectation of what college students should achieve? Or will existing institutions, as they expand, create new and different programs, as the comprehensive high schools have done, for students with abilities and aptitudes quite different from those of existing students? Or will new types of postsecondary institutions be developed which will be designed particularly for students whose ability and aptitude levels are below those of present student bodies? If the last alternative is followed will this create new social distinctions, based on intellectual levels, which are inconsistent with traditional notions of equality of opportunity? In terms of the democratic ideal there are certainly some values to be achieved in having all types of college students on the same campus, even though they may be pursuing quite different programs.

As these changes in educational institutions take place the functions the teacher is called on to perform expand and the amount of knowledge the teacher is expected to master and understand increases. This, in turn, will call for extensions of and changes in the programs of preparation for teaching. It is against this changing picture of the student bodies of high schools and colleges and the character of those institutions, then, that the preparation of high school and college teachers must be discussed.

RECRUITMENT FOR AND RETENTION IN THE TEACHING PROFESSION

Providing teachers for a system of universal education at the high school and college levels involves: (1) locating and recruiting adequate numbers of persons who have the basic personalities needed for successful teaching; (2) seeing that they are admitted to programs of teacher preparation without social, racial, and economic barriers; (3) locating them in the profession on completion of their preparation; and (4) providing the conditions that will make it possible for them to achieve satisfactory lives and to desire to remain in the profession.

It is difficult to estimate with any degree of certainty, at least in detail, what "adequate numbers" will turn out to be. Based on estimates of the United States Office of Education of projected high school and college enrollments for the next decade—and using the assumptions that one teacher is needed for every twenty-five high school students and every fifteen college students and that approximately 15 per cent of the high school and college teachers will leave the profession each year—the estimated number of new high school and college teachers that will be needed per year during the next two five-year periods is shown in the table on page 183.

Considering that in recent years some teachers have been employed,

New teachers needed	High school	College	Total
1965–1970			
Per year for replacements	82,500	60,000	142,500
Per year for increased enrollments	20,000	25,000	45,000
Total per year	102,500	85,000	187,500
Total for period, 1965–1970	512,500	425,000	937,500
1970–1975			
Per year for replacements	95,250	78,000	173,250
Per year for increased enrollments	13,000	22,000	35,000
Total per year	108,250	100,000	208,250
Total for period, 1970–1975	542,250	500,000	1,042,250
Total for period, 1965–1975	1,054,750	925,000	1,979,750

sometimes temporarily, at both high school and college levels, who were not fully qualified according to desired standards, and that the replacement of those teachers would add to the total number of new teachers needed, the task of recruiting persons for the teaching profession at high school and college levels has become a formidable one.

Teachers for high schools have traditionally been recruited from among young persons about the time they were finishing their high school education and preparing to enter college. In general it has been assumed that decisions to prepare for and enter the teaching profession could be made intelligently at about the time of high school graduation. Obviously this may be done wisely in some cases. For many individuals in today's complex society, however, ultimate decisions concerning professional careers may be postponed until the time of college graduation or beyond.

Two types of programs designed to make it possible for college graduates to enroll in programs of preparation for the teaching profession have been developed in recent years. The first, constituting an answer to the extreme teacher shortage following World War II, was inaugurated in several states as an emergency measure. College graduates who had not prepared for teaching were given an opportunity to attend a summer session during which they would pursue professional courses and work with children's groups and, if successful, receive a temporary license allowing them to teach for a year. Work during subsequent summers and in extension courses made it possible for these new teachers to become fully certified. Through these emergency programs substantial numbers of persons, who ordinarily could or would not have become teachers, joined the profession. The few studies that were published concerning these emergency programs indicated that, after a year or two of teaching experience, there was very little difference in teaching competence between those teachers who had entered teacher education programs at the time of graduation from high school and those who first studied to be teachers after college graduation.

The second type of teacher education program designed for college graduates was the Master of Arts in Teaching (M.A.T.) program which was carried on with foundation help by certain universities which accepted college graduates for a year's work of courses, study, and contact with teachers and children in the classrooms of local school systems. As in the other programs described, these programs also produced some good teachers who would have been lost to the profession if they could not have followed a choice which was made only after completion of their undergraduate education.

Some very able persons, married women in some cases, decide to prepare for teaching after they have reached maturity and even after they have raised families. Others, who have followed a profession other than teaching, are sometimes attracted to teaching as a second career and, because of their useful experience in some cases as well as their general abilities, become good candidates for the profession. As the general citizenry lives longer and in better health the possibility of recruiting teachers from older than high school and college-age groups grows. It is important that the opportunity to become teachers is not denied these late recruits. Returned Peace Corps volunteers may also provide many good recruits for the teaching profession. Since larger percentages of youth are completing high school and college, the increase that creates the need for more teachers also provides a larger educated group from which to secure teachers. As groups who have been denied education because of racial, social, or financial barriers take advantage of new opportunities they will also provide a share of the new teachers that are needed to man the nation's schools and colleges. For some types of teaching positions, particularly for foreign language teaching positions and for courses dealing with other regions of the world, persons recently arrived in this country may have excellent qualifications, providing they can meet licensing or certification requirements. It has been suggested that if educational institutions could have enough flexibility in their programs, they might use some very capable people who would be available on a part-time basis only. This would probably be more easily arranged in colleges than in high schools.

The problem of recruiting for the teaching profession is not really whether there are enough persons who might be available. The real problem is the competition between teaching and other professions and occupations. If the teaching profession is to get its needed share of persons for high school and undergraduate classrooms alone, it will need to recruit a substantial proportion of all students graduating from college each year. The need for guidance workers, administrators, and other professional academic personnel is in addition to the numbers of teachers estimated above, and shortages of qualified persons for those positions constitutes a problem by itself. The numbers needed for elementary classrooms constitutes still another addition to the needs of the teaching profession. If schools and colleges should adopt any one of the varieties of year-round operation that are currently being experimented with across the nation, this in itself would make it necessary to increase the estimates of future teachers needed by an additional 25 or 30 per cent. The total needs of the profession for new and adequately prepared people each year is equal to a very large share of all the young persons in the nation entering on their working careers.

It is important to know what factors are primarily responsible for influencing young people to choose the teaching profession for themselves; what factors discourage people from entering the profession; and which ones play the greatest role in determining whether a successful teacher remains in the profession or leaves for what are, or appear to be, superior working conditions in another profession.

Since children and youth sit before teachers in classrooms for thousands of hours—almost a thousand hours a year for twelve or more years—they undoubtedly evaluate, consciously or unconsciously, a good many members of the teaching profession, both as persons and as teachers. Undoubtedly this long-term evaluation in depth is a strong factor in some cases in a decision to become a teacher or a decision not to. Some teachers, by example, create a desire on the part of students to emulate them. Other teachers provide guidance to some of their students to consider the teaching profession as a satisfying career. On the other hand, unfortunately, some teachers, by example or otherwise, create a distaste for teaching and teachers and prematurely influence young people not to consider teaching as a goal for themselves. Very likely the total influence of teachers on the decisions of their students to enter or not to enter the teaching profession is not known or understood by many teachers. Potentially it would seem that here is an undeveloped opportunity to recruit the best potential teachers possible if present members of the profession would go about it in a systematic way.

Apart from the example and conscious influence of members of the teaching profession themselves, salary is agreed by most persons who have studied the problem to be the most influential factor in attracting young people to teaching. Beginning salaries in teaching, in most states, compare favorably with the beginning salaries in other professions. For the able and diligent person who has spent five or more years after high school preparing for the profession, however, the possibilities for salary advancement in teaching are not as attractive as in several competing occupations. For the year 1962–1963 there were sixteen states where the average annual salary of full-time elementary and secondary school teachers was less than $5,000. In four states the average salary was less than $4,000. And these average salary figures were based on salaries paid teachers who had been teaching for many years as well as those paid new teachers. Salary, then, may be considered to some extent a positive factor in recruiting for the teaching profession, but it is certainly an unfavorable factor when it comes to retaining some of the most able persons for a lifetime in the teaching profession, as compared with the financial emoluments of other professions.

We all know that conditions for advancement in the teaching profession are different for teachers in the high schools from conditions for faculty members at the college level. In the public schools the normal plan of advancement is within fairly fixed limits or schedules, usually related to exact amounts of preparation and experience, with the usual procedure being for the teacher to start at the bottom of an appropriate schedule and proceed automatically by regular increments to the maximum of the schedule. Although some school systems have attempted to add optional increments at the top of their salary schedules and have experimented with so-called "merit increases," no real degree of flexibility has been developed whereby exceptional ability, industry, or inventiveness can be rewarded. The teachers themselves, as represented through their organized professional associations, have resisted any attempts to develop such flexibility.

At the college level, on the other hand, the system itself usually has a built-in plan of flexibility in starting salaries and in rate of salary advancement, and a system of academic ranks that satisfies some and frustrates others for whom status or prestige is an important value.

The question of work load is a perennial one. It is not so much a factor in the competitive position of the teaching profession vis-à-vis other professions. It is more of a factor between different types of institutions and between different positions within the teaching profession. For any given situation, however, it may be a very important factor in retention.

These factors which create the image of the profession for both those in the profession as well as those outside, and which determine the rewards and satisfactions accruing to the successful teacher, are extremely important for recruitment and retention in the profession. To a large degree they determine the quality of teaching our youth will have. First they help to determine who becomes a teacher and whether he stays in teaching, and then they help to determine whether the teacher is sufficiently free of personal problems and frustrations to make the best contribution he is capable of to his students. It cannot be overemphasized in our highly competitive society that if teaching as a profession is to attract sufficient numbers of able and dedicated persons to meet the needs of our youth in school and college, the competitive factors of salary, status and prestige, and opportunity for advancement will have to be enhanced.

PREPARING TEACHERS FOR UNIVERSAL EDUCATION

Given the forecast of numbers of teachers needed at both high school and college levels, and with some notion of the problems of attracting adequate numbers and keeping them happily at work in the teaching profession, it is appropriate to turn to what is probably most controversial in the whole problem of relating the preparation of teachers to the concept of universal education at the high school and college levels, i.e., the programs, or curriculum, whereby people are prepared to become teachers.

Most of the current discussion and controversy over various aspects of teacher education programs relates to the preparation of teachers for the high schools rather than the colleges, although, with the very acute and growing shortage of college teachers, more thought is being given to the question of where future college teachers are coming from and how they should be prepared for their responsibilities.

It is generally agreed by many persons that there should be four essential elements in the preparation of the high school teacher: (1) a certain amount of general or liberal education that is essential to all educated persons (which teachers must be) and which is also a necessary possession of adults in a democratic society (which teachers are); (2) such mastery of subjects, ideas, and concepts which the prospective teacher will be called on to teach as will enable him to impart the knowledge and values of that subject in ways which will help his students gain an effective understanding of it; (3) knowledge and understanding of those aspects of the history and science of the field of education as will give him the resources and background to practice his profession; and (4) acquisition and mastery of the skills and arts of teaching through guided practice.

The first two elements just mentioned are least controversial although there are some differences in points of view as to how much general or liberal education is desirable or necessary and how much and how broad or narrow should be the requirement in the teaching subject. Within the faculties of teacher-preparing institutions, more specific discussions and arguments take place as to the details of requirements of general education, of majors and minors, and of all of the various aspects of curriculum patterns. But the controversies here are not of the same magnitude, nor do they become issues of great public concern, as are the questions of content in education and acquisition of the skills and arts of teaching. With respect to the last question the controversy is not whether the teacher should acquire the skills and arts of teaching; everyone is in favor of this. The basic argument is over where and when and under whose supervision these arts and skills should be acquired and practiced. Traditionally, practice teaching has been an integral part of an undergraduate teacher education program with the practice teaching being done in a laboratory school attached to the teacher-preparing institution or in the classrooms of nearby schools, and with the activity being supervised by a faculty member from the professional department of the institution. A cooperating teacher from the school where the practice teaching is taking place is usually associated with the supervision process. Recent suggestions regarding this aspect of teacher education propose that the supervision responsibility be transferred in larger measure to school systems which would "contract" with the teacher-preparing institution to handle the function of supervising practice teaching. A "clinical professor" from the college or university would supervise the activity, but it would be under the general direction of the cooperating teacher who would be given a higher salary and a reduced work load as compensation for directing the practice teaching program.

Other suggestions contemplate the postponing of practice teaching until the prospective teacher has completed his formal education, after which he would take a position in the school with less than full-time pay and perform his practice teaching in somewhat the same way that a prospective physician goes about his internship.

The greatest controversy currently being waged (see item 3, p. 187) is that over the question: "Is there a legitimate professional content or body of knowledge about education as a field of study and, if so, can that knowledge be taught, learned, and understood?" and the succeeding question, "Should the acquisition of that knowledge be an essential part of a teacher education program?" The answer to both questions has been a clear affirmative for more than a generation as far as those responsible for setting up teacher education programs are concerned. They would argue that the literature abounds with knowledge, recent and historical, concerning education and that it has long been included in professional courses for those preparing to teach. The subject matter of education is ordinarily subsumed in the following categories: (1) the history and philosophy of education (much of the material here enjoys full respectability when it is included in the courses of the departments of history and philosophy); (2) knowledge about human behavior—how children and youth learn and how the learning process can be influenced (most of this knowledge is deemed completely valid, educationally valuable, and proper for college courses when found in the offerings of psychology departments); (3) principles that are involved in carrying on the teaching process (even if teaching as a process is considered to be a skill and an art rather than a science, the possibility of analyzing, discussing, and attempting to evaluate the process—that is, the skills and the art—is as legitimate as analyzing and discussing the process of painting in a class in painting, or the principles involved in the art of writing in a creative writing class, or the skilled techniques involved in a course in surgery); and (4) knowledge about the way United States citizens and their various agencies have gone about organizing, administering, and financing the great enterprise of education in this country.

I would suggest that some of the criticism of education courses comes from people *in* the profession who do not really have, and perhaps don't even believe they have, a case against the "content" of education courses. Rather they would like to make a case against the attempt to investigate the educational process at all lest such investigation spread to all aspects of the process and at all levels. Some criticisms of the proliferation of education courses and of overlapping content between education courses is no doubt legitimate, but such criticism might be justly applied to the offerings of other departments and fields as well. What, one might ask, does this have to do with implications of universal education for the preparation of high school and college teachers? Only this—the historical squabble between the critics of education departments, education courses, and education as a legitimate field of study and teaching, and the objects of their criticism has not led to much of anything but the abolition of fraternal good will between college colleagues and a spate of published charges and defensive reactions that has confused the public, lowered the morale of teachers, and raised doubts in the minds of young persons contemplating entrance into the teaching profession. The job of preparing teachers is a staggering one in terms of numbers; it is crucial in terms of its effect on our youth. Many voices are being raised, including Dr. Conant's, concerning the ways in which teachers are being prepared in the

United States. What has largely been a concern regarding the preparation of elementary and secondary teachers now involves teachers for college students. It has been suggested that the task of preparing teachers involves many agencies—state legislatures, state departments of education, local school boards, departments of education and other pertinent departments in teacher-preparing institutions, and voluntary professional organizations —and that *each* of these agencies should examine its own role in the overall process of preparing teachers and that representatives of these agencies should sit down together in a multilateral effort to improve the process of teacher education throughout the country. It would be hoped that some consensus could be reached on the basic issues involved.

Most of what has just been said pertains to the preparation of high school teachers rather than college or community college teachers. The preparation of the former has been strictly regulated by the fifty state education departments in accordance with almost unchanging traditions as reflected in certification requirements which everyone must meet who hopes for a teaching career within the various states. The preparation of teachers for postsecondary levels, on the other hand, has never been organized as a truly professional program. The assumption that master's degrees and graduate majors and doctor's degrees constitute the necessary requirements for the profession of college teaching has been questioned from time to time but no alternative has become generally acceptable. No other major professional group in the country has been able to maintain its public support with as little in the way of organized professional preparation as the college teaching profession.

Some persons who have pointed out that there is a very abrupt change in the concepts regarding the preparation of teachers for grade twelve and below as compared with grade thirteen and above, have suggested that perhaps the former have been required to complete too many courses in professional education subjects and the latter too few.

With regard to teachers for the community college level there have been two approaches to the problem of teacher preparation. Where such institutions were extensions of the public school system the tendency has been to seek teachers with backgrounds similar to those of high school teachers; where the community college was established with sponsorship other than the local school board, the tendency has been to seek teachers with backgrounds similar to those of college teachers.

Probably neither of these alternatives is a good one at the present time. On the one hand the legitimate criticisms of the present programs for the preparation of secondary school teachers would apply with even greater force if these programs became the main source of securing community college teachers. On the other hand, the assumption that the Ph.D., or some point on the road to the Ph.D., is the best possible measure of a person's qualification to be a college teacher is also of doubtful value. It is probably not even a good measure of the qualifications of a person who teaches students in the upper levels of college and university. At any rate, the universities turning out Ph.D.'s cannot provide enough personnel to come anywhere near meeting the need for all the new college teachers that will be required. With neither of the presently existing alternatives adequate and with the very large numbers of teachers that will be needed, particularly at the level of the first two years of college, within the next decade and beyond, it would seem to be singularly appropriate and timely for those concerned with the problem to put forth a major effort to devise, as a matter of national policy, an appropriate new program for the professional preparation of community college teachers.

A well-thought-out plan to develop such a program might commend itself to some foundation interested in the improvement of education through improved programs for the preparation of teachers. If and when such programs could be developed for the preparation of teachers at the community college level they would no doubt have very salutary effects on the preparation of teachers for the secondary school and also for the senior college level.

In conclusion I would suggest that plans for developing new approaches and new programs for the preparation of community college teachers—which, with those teaching in the first two years of four-year colleges, is the level for which the great bulk of new teachers will be needed in the next fifteen years—should take into consideration the following:

1. Programs for teacher preparation should recognize that teaching is a profession, even at its higher levels, and should include an appropriate professional component.

2. Programs for preparing community college teachers should seek to turn out teachers who can be sufficiently flexible to deal with students having a broad range of abilities, interests, motivations, and backgrounds.

3. Teachers should be prepared to experiment with new educational ideas and methods and not to accept today's or yesterday's educational methodology as the final word. The relating of educational methods and procedures to optimum achievement on the part of students should be uppermost in the teacher's mind. This means, of course, that educational goals relating to student achievement must be very clearly defined.

4. It is important that all education in the United States today be carried on in a setting that reflects the growing international interdependence of the people of the world. This is perhaps more important in programs for

preparing teachers than for any other profession. It would be desirable, where possible, to include some kind of service or experience abroad as a part of the preparation of teachers.

5. In any major consideration of new programs for the preparation of teachers the practical possibilities of preparing persons at the level of technicians of various kinds and para-professionals associated with the teaching profession should be adequately examined. It is not possible, nor even desirable, that all school personnel who deal with children and youth have exactly the same skills and professional background. If this fact is recognized it should not be difficult to devise a variety of programs to prepare a variety of professional and subprofessional workers for the nation's schools and colleges.

It would seem possible that in trying to meet the urgent need for large numbers of well-prepared teachers for the next phase of universal higher education a major advance in teacher education will be achieved.

The Economic Aspects

ALGO D. HENDERSON, Director, Center for the
Study of Higher Education, University of Michigan

The prospect of having 6 to 10 million college and university students by 1980 confronts the nation with a large financial problem. It will not be easy to solve. But on the optimistic side, it can be noted that when the demand for something is pressing and when the total national income is large and growing, ways are found to solve the financial problem. The allocation of huge portions of our income for such things as national defense, the construction of highways, and the exploration of space are vivid examples.

This study will be concerned mainly with the potential sources of funds for the support of higher education. Consideration will also be given to the theory that the expenditures for higher education represent a social investment. Finally, some discussion will be given to the question: Can the nation afford the cost?

In my analysis, I am assuming some reasonable continuity in the rise of the gross national product, and in the disposition of the national income. A war, or a prolonged depression, would change the outlook. Even in war, however, the educational institutions are used heavily for training and for research; and in a depression it is in the national interest to solve some of the problems of unemployment, of morale, and of delinquency by encouraging attendance at school and at college.

REVIEW OF THE PAST AND ESTIMATES FOR THE FUTURE

A brief summary of the achievements of the past will help provide an orientation. A review of some estimates of costs for the future will give an impression of the magnitude of the task.

First, we should note the achievement in public secondary education. It was only ninety years ago (1874) that the Kalamazoo Case in Michigan decided that boards of education had authority to spend public funds in building and supporting public high schools. In the interval, a system of comprehensive public high schools, with complete geographical coverage, and free to the students, has been built in the United States. The total enrollment in 1962 included 92 per cent of youth of the age group.[1]

The same faith in education is now developing a system of public community junior colleges. In some states, these colleges are free to the students; in others, the charge is far below the cost to the community. In California, the Master Plan for Higher Education proposes that by 1975, 68.9 per cent of the total full-time, lower-division enrollment should be accommodated in junior colleges.

At the level of the senior colleges and universities, the institutions have been growing in number and in size as the need becomes apparent. Furthermore, the quality of the institutions appears to have been maintained, and they have improved their facilities, libraries, and faculties.

Although solutions to the financial problem have been found to date, we are confronted with serious questions about the future. These arise for various reasons. Charges to students have been increasing faster than other prices. Private philanthropy has been a significant source of income for plant, endowments, and operations, but governmental policies have reduced the ability of individuals of wealth to contribute to charity.

In a similar vein, the states and the local communities have been facing an increasingly difficult financial problem. The tax systems generally lack flexibility or impose regressive types of taxes; and much of the budgets of payments become fixed commitments, leaving inadequate margins of revenue with which to expand the appropriations for higher education.

In the past, the assistance to higher education from the Federal government has been meaningful, and such programs as those of the two Morrill Acts, 1862, and 1890, the Service-men's Readjustment Act of 1944, the

[1] 1962, ages fourteen to seventeen years. *Statistical Abstract of the United States,* 1963, p. 116.

National Defense Education Act of 1958, and the tremendous growth of federally sponsored research programs have given substantial aid and encouragement. The benefits to higher education have been not only financial. The Morrill Acts, for example, are an instance where the Federal government assumed the leadership in establishing a program in higher education that has had profound significance in developing the agriculture and industry of the nation and in extending educational opportunity. In the past, however, the policy of Federal assistance to higher education has been highly controversial. Such unresolved issues as those relating to the dangers of Federal control, to the separation of state and church, and to the segregation of the races have stymied more positive action. Not until the Eighty-eighth Congress has substantial progress been made in resolving these issues.

The financial contributions that have been made to higher education by various of the above sources, and the trends for a period of years, are shown in Table 1.

It is apparent that the institutions of higher education in the United States receive their income from many sources and that the burden does not fall heavily on any one. The increase in the Federal portion is due largely to the scholarship program and to payments for research.

The problem for the future is the amount of money that must be devoted to higher education. The President's Committee on Education Beyond the High School (1957) estimated that the total of annual operating cost for educational and general purposes would become $6.2 billion by 1970.[2] At the present rate of growth, this figure will have been reached several years before that date.

Seymour Harris made a calculation to show that the annual cost by 1969–1970 would be $9.8 billion, as contrasted with the total of the educational and general budget for 1957–1958 of $3.6 billion. He then added, "A more realistic estimate is a 20% inflation in ten years and hence a total operating educational and general budget of $11,760,000,000." [3]

Still another authoritative spokesman is Marion B. Folsom, former U.S. Secretary of Health, Education, and Welfare. He has stated, "Higher education teaching costs . . . of $7 to $9 billion are likely for 1970; by 1975 these costs may reach $8.5 to $12.5 billion, if we consider only the increase in enrollment and in costs per student necessary to gain and retain a more competitive salary level for those on faculty and other instruc-

[2] President's Committee on Education Beyond the High School, *Second Report of the President*, 1957, p. 85.
[3] Seymour E. Harris, *Higher Education: Resources and Finance* (New York: McGraw-Hill Book Company, 1962), p. 20.

TABLE 1. Current Income of Higher Education Institutions by Source and Per Cent Distributions

(In millions of dollars)

Year	Total current income	State and local	%	Federal	%	Student fees	%	Private gifts and endow-ments	%	Sales services, other	%	Auxiliary enterprises	%
1935–1936	598	141	24	43	7	158	26	97	16	52	9	106	18
1939–1940	715	176	25	39	5	201	28	112	16	44	6	144	20
1949–1950	2,390	562	24	527	22	396	17	215	9	147	6	543	23
1959–1960	5,813	1,541	27	1,041	18	1,162	20	590	10	379	7	1,100	19

SOURCE: *A Fact Book on Higher Education* (Washington: American Council on Education, December 1, 1962), p. 63.

tional staffs of colleges and universities." [4] None of the above estimates of operations included organized research and auxiliary activities.

The President's Committee also estimated the annual need for facilities to 1970 as $1.3 billion. A recent prediction by the U.S. Office of Education for the period 1965 to 1970 totals $11,862,284,000, or an average of $2.4 billion per year.[5]

In considering these estimates, it should be remembered that additional items will need to be provided. Student housing and food services will be essential for at least a portion of the students. These costs are usually paid by the students (including the amortization of loans with which the plant has been built). Research continues to expand at a rapid rate; organized research ordinarily is not undertaken until the funds have been committed by government, by industry, or otherwise. In addition, substantial programs for scholarships, fellowships, and loans to students may be advisable. The finances required for these programs could be quite large, as is shown by the generous provisions that have been made for them in New York State, by the GI Bill, and by the other fellowship programs of the Federal government.

It is the enormity of the prospective bill for higher education that causes many persons to question whether the previous sources of funds will suffice.

ECONOMIES IN THE PATTERN
AND OPERATION OF INSTITUTIONS

Before seeking funds elsewhere, it makes good sense for the institutions themselves to examine whether they could put into effect some economies that would reduce the total cost to the students and to the public. Such possible economies may be considered from two points of view: the overall organization of higher education and the possibility of effecting operating economies.

Let us first note a principle that should guide the organization of and interrelationships among institutions. This principle requires the decentralization of programs and facilities at the undergraduate and master's-degree

[4] Marion B. Folsom, "Who Should Pay for American Higher Education?" in Selma J. Mushkin (ed.), *Economics of Higher Education* (Washington: U.S. Department of Health, Education, and Welfare, 1962), p. 196.

[5] *A Fact Book on Higher Education* (Washington: American Council on Education, May 16, 1960), p. 152. This figure was compiled from data supplied by the colleges and universities.

levels, and the concentration of resources behind selected programs of advanced studies and organized research.

The reason why education should be decentralized at the post–high school level is twofold: a large portion of the students need to have the opportunity to attend college near their homes, and a better economy in the distribution of the costs for facilities is secured through having local and regional participation.

On the first point, it is clear that young people from higher socioeconomic families have had good opportunity to attend college. In a study in New York State the startling fact was revealed that a higher percentage of youth from the lower half of the high school, but where the family income was $9,000 or above, was attending college than was attending from the top quarter of the class when the family income was $5,000 or less.[6] Thus attendance is related to socioeconomic status. If most of the children from the high-income families are already attending college, the great bulk of the additional students will come from the lower socioeconomic families.

The relevance of this fact to the location of the institution is apparent. There is a tremendous saving to the student when he can commute to a college, and especially to one that is free of tuition. Table 2 shows the data from one study.

Students who remain in their home communities find it easier to get part-time and summer jobs. By living at home, and working part time, a student may pay his own way through a low-cost community college. This preserves a good American tradition.

TABLE 2.   Annual Expenses by Students at New York Colleges
(Typical budget 1950–1951)

| Expenses | All colleges | | University of City of New York |
	Resident	Commuting	
Tuition and fees	$ 630	$ 520	$ 10
Meals, or meals and room	700	140	200
Other expenses	480	590	480
Total	$1,810	$1,250	$690

SOURCE: P. A. Cowen and L. H. Conger, *New York Studies, 1950–51* (Albany: State University of New York). These data are not recent, but the cost differentials are accurately shown.

[6] Elbridge Sibley, "The Relation Between College Attendance and Economic Status," in *Matching Needs and Facilities in Higher Education* (New York State Legislative Document No. 31, 1948).

As for the cost of the plant, there is a tendency for senior institutions to use more expensive plant and equipment.[7] At the junior college level the courses of instruction require laboratories and libraries that are limited to the needs of the underclass student. Ordinarily, dormitories are unnecessary, and the food services may provide only for lunches and snacks. On the other hand, somewhat greater provision may have to be made for student union and study facilities.

There is a further relief in that the burden of financing can be well distributed among the students and the local and state governments. In some instances, local philanthropists and corporations have made substantial contributions.

The above argument applies specifically to the location of public community junior colleges, but it relates also to undergraduate institutions located in population centers, whether public or private, and to the public colleges and universities that are distributed regionally within the state.

The benefits arising from decentralization help account for the nationwide movement to transform the regionally placed teachers colleges into complex institutions.

Another factor of importance is the advantage to the nation in seeking talent among its young people wherever they may be located. Numerous studies have shown that where there is a college, whether public or private, that is within commuting distance of the homes of students, the rate of attendance from that community rises sharply, and often is double that of other communities.

Looking into the future, it seems probable that the increase in the number of low-cost institutions will be much greater than will be the increase in the number of high-cost institutions.

The other part of the principle stated above arises from the need to have the best possible quality of faculty, laboratory, library, and other facilities for the programs of advanced studies, and in the major professional schools such as medicine, engineering, law, and so forth. The same reasoning applies to the method of organizing for significant research.

At a more modest level of operation, many specialized programs need not be duplicated in large numbers of institutions. For example, in the study of rare languages, or for the training of optical technicians, it is

[7] In California, estimates of 1958 construction costs for educational plant were: for junior colleges (per 8,000-ADA), $2,500; for state colleges (10,000 campus, per full-time student), $4,050; and for University of California (10,000 campus, per full-time student), $7,100. (Report of the Technical Committee on Costs in Higher Education in California, 1960). (It is not implied that the differences in unit costs at the *underclass level* for the respective types of institutions would be as large as shown.)

more economical to serve the students at a central place where good programs are established than it would be to initiate numerous duplicating programs.

The conclusion is that there should be an identification of the roles of particular institutions or groups of institutions. An example is found in the state of California, where the legislature has differentiated the functions of the junior colleges, the state colleges, and the University of California.

A discussion of possible economies in the operation of institutions is more difficult. Generally speaking, the goals of the education of students and of research are intangible. Effectiveness in attaining the goals is of greater importance to society than is a high degree of efficiency in operation.

Nevertheless, the principles of scientific management have a degree of applicability in the administration of space and services. In this phase of administration, norms of costs can be established and used as measures of relative efficiency.

Some changes in modes of instruction, in the utilization of specialized services, and in the college calendar can result in economies. There is a detectable trend, for example, toward an increase in the student-faculty ratio. Whether this is good or bad is a disputed point, but in many institutions the admission of a larger student group results in a more nearly optimal ratio of students to faculty. Unfortunately, the results of research on the relation of class size to the learning of students are inconclusive.

Whether the use of teaching aids and of programmed instruction will reduce the total cost is uncertain, but a principal benefit might be that they can result in utilizing the more expensive faculty members more fully for the services for which they are professionally prepared.

Some studies of the utilization of plant have shown that classroom, laboratory, and recreation space tend to be unused for significant portions of the day, week, or year. This has led to a movement for calendar reform in as much as space can be used more fully and without any detriment to the educational program. It seems illogical to ask the public to pay for more space merely to duplicate space that is being wasted.

In an effort to utilize space more efficiently, therefore, a number of institutions have been converting to a year-round operation. Not enough is as yet known about the responses of students and faculty to this change to enable us to evaluate fully the increased enrollment that becomes possible, but the potential results are significant. A private college, for example, that has not had a summer session, through the introduction of one additional semester might conceivably increase its total student enrollment by approximately 50 per cent. Obviously, also, in an institution where tuition payments constitute a substantial portion of the income, the college can benefit materially from the increased tuition fees. A public university, likewise, can increase its enrollment considerably; but because tuitions are low or nonexistent, additional appropriations would be needed to supply the additional faculty and other operating costs. However, in both cases the plant would be utilized more fully. The year-round operations would also distribute the overhead costs among more students.

The institutions of higher education are examining these various possible economies. Undoubtedly, many efforts will be made to economize further in the internal operations. However, the savings thus effected can, at best, reduce by only a small portion the total money that will be needed to do the job in higher education during the foreseeable future.

TUITION AS A SOURCE OF INCOME

Private colleges and universities depend heavily on tuition payments by students to provide the necessary operating income. Public institutions depend far less on tuition, and, in some instances, only small fees are charged to the students.

In at least some states, the state university was originally conceived to be the capstone of a system of public education, all levels of which would be free to students. Some of these universities do not use the term "tuition" for this reason. They began with a nominal matriculation fee, but later inserted additional fees and these have been increased at intervals. Some of the state legislatures have made certain increases in appropriations contingent on a rise in fees. Thus public policy for free higher education appears to be changing.

The rise in tuition among the public institutions has been general, as has that at private colleges and universities. Table 3 provides more specific data.

The Office of Education reports that this trend is continuing. For example, the increase in tuition in private men's colleges during the five-year span ending in 1963–1964 was 25 per cent.

The relationship between the charge for studying at a private college and prices for consumer goods generally is shown by two studies. One involved twenty-four private liberal arts colleges where during the ten years ending in 1963 the average increase in tuition had been 124 per

TABLE 3.   Annual Tuition and Fees
(Averages)

Year	Large institutions		Smaller institutions	
	Public (res)	Private	Public	Private
1928	$ 77	$ 267	$ 86	$206
1940	106	332	129	302
1952	145	553	183	517
1960	248	1,008	247	935

SOURCE: Compiled from *A Fact Book on Higher Education* (Washington: American Council on Education, November 4, 1960), pp. 217–220.

cent, and the rise in the consumer price index had been 15 per cent. In another study made of the period 1940 to 1960, the average charge for tuition by ninety-nine selected private colleges had tripled, whereas consumer prices had risen 110 per cent.[8]

The costs to students of room and board have also increased very substantially. Formerly, college students could anticipate living in housing that was at least partially provided through public subsidization. Today, the policy of erecting dormitories with loan funds—usually from the Federal government—is so uniformly the practice that the cost of amortizing the loans becomes a heavy additional charge in the student's room rent. In some legislatures, the question has been raised as to whether classrooms and laboratories could not also be built with borrowed funds, the loans to be amortized through student charges over a period of years.

On the average, college students in the United States provide 20 per cent of the current income of the institutions. With respect to how much they *should* pay, there are two contrasting views: The first of these is that the students can and should pay for a larger share of the cost of their education. In some part, this is a matter of expediency based on the belief that other sources of income will not be sufficient. However, there are additional arguments. The average family personal income after taxes has risen from $2,320 in 1929, to $4,070 in 1950, to $6,400 in 1962.[9] The incomes are more evenly distributed among the population than was formerly the case. The families do seem able to buy television sets and automobiles.

More particularly from the viewpoint of the student, there is the argument that it pays him to get a college education, since this considerably enhances his earnings (see Table 4). Even two years of college, after

[8] *A Fact Book on Higher Education, op. cit.,* September 29, 1961, p. 263.
[9] *Survey of Current Business,* April 1963, p. 15.

TABLE 4.   Lifetime Incomes of Males as of 1956
(From age 25 to death)

Length of schooling	Percentiles		
	25th	Median	75th
High school, four years	$149,000	$199,000	$270,000
College, four years or more	195,000	291,000	417,000

SOURCE: Adapted from Seymour Harris, "Returns on Investment in Education," in *Economic Aspects of Higher Education* (Paris: Organization for Economic Cooperation and Development, 1964), p. 49.

training for technical and semiprofessional work, increase the probable initial earning rate from $300 to $425 per month.[10]

It is sometimes contended that students can well afford to borrow the money with which to pay the cost of their education, and that lending agencies could afford to schedule the repayments on the loans over a long period of years, coincident with the earning period of the individual. One plan that has been advanced is for the government to guarantee such loans in order to assure a low interest rate and the avoidance of risk on the part of the lending agency. Another is for the government to lend the money, and perhaps collect from the student annual sums that depend on the size of his earnings year by year.

The contrasting view is that society should pay for higher education, or at least the substantial share of it. The presence of high costs to students would tend to skew the enrollments in favor of the higher socioeconomic classes. In 1962, 20 per cent of the families in the United States, or 9.3 million of them, had incomes of less than $3,000 [11] and could hardly afford college tuitions. High charges—especially if coupled with hangover loans, something that Marion Folsom has called "indenturing of the student for life"—may have the effect of channeling students into occupations and professions that bring large economic rewards. The children of poor families would begin life after college heavily in debt, whereas the children of wealthy families would be free of it. The existence of unpaid loans might also handicap women in their plans to marry and raise families.

From the student's point of view, he already suffers a substantial cost in two forms: his outlay for clothing, travel, books, room, board, and usually some fees, and the income that he forgoes through unemployment.

[10] Norman C. Harris, *Technical Education in the Junior College* (Washington: The American Association of Junior Colleges, 1964), p. 28.
[11] *Economic Report of the President,* January, 1964, p. 59.

Other arguments, to be discussed more fully later, are that higher education is of substantial advantage to society because of the cultural, economic, and other benefits. Higher education produces human capital. It prepares staff for the professions. It gives the citizens substantial additional preparation with which to act wisely in voting and in civic affairs. It helps to assure continuing progress toward a higher stage of civilization in the world.

The arguments in favor of maintaining as low as possible a cost to the student are impressive. It would seem most unfortunate to abandon—or even injure—our great tradition of extending widespread, and equal, opportunity in higher education.

As the balance in enrollments between private and public institutions shifts more heavily toward the latter, it may be that the private colleges and universities will have to turn more and more to emphasizing distinctive purposes, exceptional quality, and experimentation. While doing a lesser share of the total job, they can nevertheless continue to be highly influential in the evolving pattern of higher education. They should be able and indeed may have to charge tuition on a scale that will alleviate the financial problem, and still serve the essential purposes just noted. Undoubtedly, substantial scholarship and loan programs will help solve the financial problem for a portion of the students.

Public institutions, on the other hand, should continue to operate at as low a cost to the student as possible. The trend toward placing more of the burden on the student should be stopped, if not reversed. The policy of Soviet Russia to provide free higher education follows good American tradition, although the Russian system of allocating graduates to jobs would not be acceptable to us. However, it would be unrealistic to assume that we shall ever go back to a completely free system.

THE ROLE OF PHILANTHROPY

The colleges and universities in the United States have been most fortunate in having had from the beginning substantial support from philanthropy. The founding of dozens of institutions was made possible by substantial gifts and bequests of funds. For these colleges and universities and a multitude of other institutions, buildings have been provided, endowments have been created, and operations have been supported by gifts and bequests.

While the above is characteristic of the private colleges and universities, there are many instances of gifts and bequests of significant size that have gone to public institutions. For example, more than half of the physical plant of the University of Michigan has been provided through private funds. Among the public community junior colleges in the state of Michigan, several—including Henry Ford, Flint, Alpena, Kellogg, and Lake community colleges—have recently received gifts and bequests that total in each case well in excess of $1 million.[12] In 1960–1961, the total of private contributions to forty-nine public, state-controlled institutions was $58,702,116.[13] While the large, private universities are receiving more and more of their income from governmental agencies, the public institutions are beginning to benefit somewhat more fully from private gifts.

In general, philanthropy has recently accounted for about 10 per cent of the annual total income received by the institutions of higher education. The annual gifts and bequests to selected colleges and universities during the twelve years from 1950 to 1962 have approximately trebled in amount.[14] However, income from this source as a percentage of the total income of institutions has decreased from 16 per cent before the war to the present 10 per cent.[15]

There is no reason to predict that the total amount received through gifts and bequests will diminish—indeed, the expectation is the contrary. This conclusion is based on several things. The total amount of disposable personal income continues to grow, having increased from $207.7 billion

---

[12] At Flint, the contributions for plant for the total community higher educational-cultural program have included the following:

Mott Memorial Building (University of Michigan)		$ 1,201,760
Other college plant (primarily for the Flint Community Junior College)		2,787,511
College and Cultural Center	$6,053,721	
Additional under construction (est.)	4,500,000	
		10,553,721
Expansion of the Art Center (under construction)		800,000
Total:		$15,342,992

If the gifts and bequests for endowment were added, the total amount would exceed $20 million.

[13] *Guide Lines to Voluntary Support of American Higher Education* (New York: Council for Financial Aid to Education, Inc., 1963), p. 38.

[14] *A Fact Book on Higher Education, op. cit.,* May 15, 1962, p. 64. (Quoting studies by John Price Jones Co., Inc.)

[15] *Ibid.,* December 1, 1962, p. 63.

in 1950 to $431.3 billion in 1964.[16] Through the New Jersey case, Smith versus Barlow, decided in 1953, the directors of corporations were given legal freedom to make contributions to colleges and universities, and they have responded in good measure. The tax laws continue to be so worded as to encourage the making of gifts to exempted, nonprofit institutions. There seems little danger that these conditions will be drastically changed. In the meantime, the United States continues to enjoy prosperity, and devices have been found by the Federal government to smooth the fluctuations in the business cycle.

The situation respecting philanthropy has, however, shifted rather considerably. Formerly, individual donors were able to provide large gifts to particular institutions, and foundations gave money that accounted for significant portions of the needs of individual institutions. Relatively, these grants of funds have diminished in coverage, and much of the total now is for experimental or special projects rather than for general support. In addition, the policies of the Federal government, beginning with the New Deal days, have been directed toward the wider distribution of income and toward the graduated income tax as the major source of revenue. A result has been that the institutions, individually or collectively, must organize and engage in "drives" for money. Large numbers of donors must be brought onto the list in order to yield the needed sums. This method of raising money is much more costly than the former.

It seems probable that the need for funds by the colleges and universities will grow at a more rapid pace than will the funds available through philanthropy. A substantial portion of this growth will occur in public community junior colleges and in other public colleges and universities. The proportion of the total income of higher education that comes from philanthropy probably will not increase, and may diminish.[17]

In spite of all the commendable things that can be said about philanthropy as a highly important support for higher education in the United States, we should not overlook the fact that to lean heavily on this source of funds is to make of education a charity. In our society, such a view is no longer tenable. The provision for higher education is becoming more and more a matter of public policy and a function of government.

[16] *Federal Reserve Bulletin,* August, 1964, p. 1079.

[17] The Council for Financial Aid to Education, Inc., takes a more optimistic view. Estimating the annual need by 1970 for educational and general expenses for plant and for additions to endowment to be $9 billion, the Council envisages that 22.4 per cent of this total might be expected from private gifts and grants. See *Guidelines to Voluntary Support for American Higher Education* (New York: The Council, 1963), p. 25.

THE RESPONSIBILITY OF STATE AND LOCAL GOVERNMENTS

The Northwest Ordinance is best known for its ringing words, "the means of education shall forever be encouraged." It was this ideology that caused the several states to establish state colleges and universities. In addition, there were the needs of providing teachers for the public schools and for research that would develop the natural resources of the region. A further stimulation was provided through the federally encouraged land-grant college and university system.

More recently, many of the states have begun to establish a system of public community junior colleges. Many of the state surveys proclaim that the system of public education should now be available to all youth for at least two years beyond graduation from the high school. The President's Commission on Higher Education (1947) agreed.

Another evidence of the public desire to encourage education lies in the exemption from taxes granted by the states to colleges and universities, whether public or private.

The principal support from local communities has been in behalf of public community junior colleges. Typically, the local community has initiated a college, and then sought state aid. In a few states, the first two years of college are uniformly financed by the state.

Because of the influences already described, the various states have been under strong pressure to increase the appropriations in behalf of the state colleges and universities. To a surprising degree, they have succeeded. Selma J. Mushkin states, "In current dollars, state and local funds going to colleges and universities in 1957–1958 were twenty times as high as they were in the early 1920s, and three times as high as they were after World War II. In the four years from 1953–1954 to 1957–1958, the increases in these expenditures averaged about 10% a year, and the increases in enrollment in public institutions averaged about 12% a year." [18]

M. M. Chambers has collated the appropriations of state funds for the operating expenses of higher education in the fifty states for each of several years. The total for the fifty states for the year 1962–1963 was $1,808,825,000, and the gain over two years was $375,499,000 or 24½ per cent. The above appropriations did not include the state aid to local junior colleges. These appropriations in twenty states showed a two-year gain in state aid of 41½ per cent.[19]

[18] Mushkin, *op. cit.*, p. 240.
[19] M. M. Chambers, "Progress in State Tax Support of Higher Education," *School and Society*, March 23, 1963.

Although this performance is a most impressive one, Dr. Chambers notes that the differences among the states varied from an increase of 75 per cent to a decrease of 1½ per cent. The high figure was for New York State, and the appropriation there included a large, new scholarship program in which private colleges and universities could participate, and where the intent seemed to be to provide a device by which the state indirectly could give assistance to the private institutions in a manner that would enable them to increase their tuitions. The latter action may be suggestive of a way to overcome the constitutional question of using state funds in behalf of private institutions.

As shown in Table 1, it has required this large increase in annual appropriations to keep the proportion of current income received from the states at a fairly constant level.

In spite of the increases in appropriations, the states have been lagging in their provision of plant, considering the impending increases in enrollment. Certain other problems should be noted, including (1) the efforts of certain states to erect barriers against out-of-state students for the purpose of avoiding the subsidization of students from other states; and (2) the pressure brought by the states on many institutions to operate at lower per-student costs. The latter influence may cause the institutions of superior quality or with the more advanced programs to offer a deterioration over a period of years. The reason for this is that a way to secure low unit costs is to emphasize underclass enrollments, employ inexpensive faculty, increase teaching loads, and minimize research.

It will be extremely difficult for the local communities and the states to raise the needed additional income through taxes. For one thing, there is a general tendency to oppose increases in taxes because the communities and the states are competitive for the location of industry. Second, some of the taxes, such as those on real estate, do not relate to the on-going production of wealth and hence do not keep pace with the needs; and the sales taxes are regressive and hence limited in application. Since each state and community has large commitments that are static and other pressures that are politically potent, the margin of income out of which the appropriations for higher education can come, is definitely limited.

Because of the disparity in provision among the states, the quality of the institutions varies. Because the population is mobile, the quality of education in one state is of concern to another state. The need is for Federal equalization. However, the states that protest the immigration of insufficiently educated persons are apt to be the same ones that resent having their income tax money go out of the state.

Undoubtedly, the local communities—and especially the states—will continue to provide a substantial portion of the income needed by the institutions of higher education. This portion has been about 27 per cent. There is general acceptance of the belief that the primary responsibility for higher education lies with the states. The states have demonstrated a surprising ability to respond to the needs. The institutions, however, are not satisfied with this performance. The state surveys have emphasized the need to find additional sources of income.

THE ROLE OF THE FEDERAL GOVERNMENT

The Federal government began to participate in the financing of education as early as 1787 when Congress granted lands for educational purposes in the territory of Ohio. It began in earnest to support higher education with the passage of the first Morrill Act in 1862.

Kenneth Little has identified five major types of Federal programs: (1) research, (2) education and training, (3) student financial aids, (4) loans and grants for facilities and equipment, and (5) international programs.[20] He points to two major patterns of relationships between the Federal government and institutions of higher education: Federal-state relationships, as, for example, in the land-grant college programs, and Federal-institutional relationships implemented through contracts and grants. His report further reveals a tremendous variety of types of programs that are supported in one way or another by the Federal government. These include specific institutions such as the military academies and Howard University; assistance programs related to national defense, such as ROTC training, and research on missiles; plus a variety of other things, including the partial subsidization of programs in the field of health, programs of fellowships for students, and loans for housing.

Congress has passed several bills in support of higher education in recent years. The National Defense Education Act of 1958 was a major breakthrough in Federal participation. Although limited to special areas such as science, foreign languages, and so forth, the NDEA provided the format for future Federal involvement. This takes the form of Federal support for programs where the Federal government has specific need of services or where the programs are distinctly in the national interest.

An even more significant development occurred in the Eighty-eighth Congress when four highly significant measures were passed: the Health

[20] J. Kenneth Little, *A Survey of Federal Programs in Higher Education,* Office of Education Publication, no. 50033 (Washington: U.S. Government Printing Office, 1963).

Professions Educational Assistance Act of 1963, the Higher Education Facilities Act, the Vocational Education Act, and the extension and enlargement of the National Defense Education Act. The Economic Opportunity Act of 1964 will prove to be of some significance to higher education since one of its aims is to provide education as one of the means of assisting persons to find employment.

The volume of Federal support for higher education for the year 1960 was $544,273,000.[21] This annual total will, of course, be considerably increased as a result of the new legislation just mentioned.

Indeed, the appropriations for the Office of Education for 1965 were $1.5 billion as compared with $692 million in 1964. Much of this large increase can be attributed to the new legislation favoring higher education.

Illustrative of the kind of growth in Federal interest that may take place in higher education is that which has been taking place in medical and health-related research. Here the annual Federal expenditures, portions of which have been channeled to universities, have increased from $22 million in 1947 to $1.13 billion in 1962.

Earlier, I described some of the reasons why there has been considerable reluctance on the part of colleges and universities to seek Federal aid. The reluctance was clearly evident in the reports of the Commissions on Financing Higher Education (1952) and in that of the President's Committee on Education Beyond the High School (1957). This sentiment, however, appears to have undergone pronounced change within the past five years, which may account for the favorable actions taken by the United States Congress during the past session. Thus the fear on the part of educators of Federal encroachment in the field of higher education appears to be diminishing. At the same time, colleges and universities are beginning to recognize that the Federal government must provide a considerably larger portion of the money required by higher education if the needs are to be met.

The several reasons why the Federal government should participate much more actively have already been given, or will be discussed while considering the concept of social investment. In one sense, there is the very practical reason that it is only the Federal government which has funds adequate for the purpose. Such funds might be made available in one or more ways—direct appropriations, matching aid, or money distributed to the states for the purpose. In this respect, aid to higher education is analogous to Federal aid for the development of transcontinental highways or to take care of problems of welfare and security. In another

[21] Mushkin, *op. cit.*, p. 206.

sense, it has become clear since World War II that the colleges and universities of the country are highly important agencies of national defense and national welfare. To the extent that higher education is a social investment, it raises persistently the question whether there should not be considerably increased Federal support.

I believe there would be national advantage in having a limited number of outstanding universities designated as Federal institutions and assured of genuinely substantial funds for advanced studies and research. These should consist of high-quality programs available to selected students from any state and from other countries. This plan would offset the pressures from the state to reduce the number of out-of-state students, and reduce unit costs to norms that would be common to all institutions within the state. For implementation, the plan would encounter a very difficult political problem.

In passing, it should be noted that the Federal government supports higher education in indirect ways. The most important of these is the provision for deductions by individuals and by corporations on the income tax returns for donations made to nonprofit tax-exempt institutions. A proposal to extend this kind of privilege would allow parents to take tax credits in relation to tuition charges paid. This plan would benefit private colleges because it would enable them to increase tuition. The opponents contend that the plan would benefit high-income families and increase the burden on low-income families.

To repeat what has been implied before, the Federal government would seem to be much the best potential source of the additional income that will be needed for the further development of higher education.

President David D. Henry, of the University of Illinois, has said:

> I shall assume that the case for increased and more orderly Federal involvement has been made, that the unprecedented anticipated enrollments—which must be accommodated if educational opportunity is not to be curtailed— require unprecedented assistance, that the demands for the specialized competence in research, consultation, and leadership must be met to gird the national interest in science, in the professions, and in many other areas of service, and that these goals, which are essentially national, cannot be reached by the institutions of higher education without increased Federal expenditure.[22]

In his message to Congress, January 29, 1963, recommending comprehensive legislation in support of education, President John F. Kennedy said:

[22] David D. Henry, "A Program of Action for Higher Education," in *Higher Education and the Federal Government, Programs and Problems* (Washington: American Council on Education, 1963), p. 99.

Fundamentally, education is and must always be a local responsibility, for it thrives best when nurtured at the grassroots of our democracy. But in our present era of economic expansion, population growth, and technological advance, State, local, and private efforts are insufficient. These efforts must be reinforced by national support, if American education is to yield the maximum of individual development and national well being.

HIGHER EDUCATION AS A SOCIAL INVESTMENT

Historically, higher education has been thought of primarily as an opportunity for the individual to prepare himself better for life and for an occupation or profession. During a century and more, the United States has experienced the full impact of the Industrial Revolution, and subsequent to World War II it has witnessed a tremendous technological advance. In the meantime, we have also been advancing in culture. These basic achievements in our society are bringing about a revision in attitude toward the essential mission of higher education. It can now be seen more clearly than in the past that colleges and universities are primary agencies for the on-going evolution of society. They are also an implementation of the concept of democracy in meeting the aspirations and needs of the people.

From the viewpoint of economics, higher education is a "social investment." This is because it makes contributions to the development of the economy and to technological advance. Education becomes embodied in the labor force. Higher education produces human capital. It increases the current input of human capital, and provides the nation with a store of human capital in support of the economy.

It is difficult to prove through precise data the economic value of higher education. An improvement in man's intellectual competence differs from an improvement made in a machine for two reasons: The man himself receives many benefits from the improvement, and, second, the intangible values—cultural and otherwise—cannot be separated from the economic ones. In analyzing the subject, we must, therefore, rely heavily on reasoning and on the opinions of authoritative persons.

Persons who argue against the hypothesis continue to subscribe to the view that the benefits to the individual are primary. They may contend that we are educating too many persons, especially at the college level, and that we cannot afford to do this. Inasmuch as the real cost of higher education lies in what is foregone by devoting the resources of the nation and the potential services of the students to higher education, it would seem that the opponents of this view favor utilizing the services of youth in activities that demand less intellectual competence and devoting the resources to other goods and services.

Shortly following the war, a number of writers were attracted to a theory advanced by Walter Kotschnig [23] that to educate more persons than were needed would lead to unemployment, feelings of frustration, and the danger that these persons would turn against society. As yet, these predictions have not come true. With the evolution of our technology and the continuing rise in our gross national product, the overall demand for educated personnel continues to exceed the supply. In many areas, there are decided shortages.

Indeed, it would seem to be distinctly in the social interest to promote higher education in a positive manner for several reasons: (1) to assure a continuing supply of educated personnel of all kinds; (2) to search for the best possible talent that exists, regardless of socioeconomic class, to assure that these youths have the opportunity to continue in education, and to encourage persons of the best quality to enter the several professions; (3) to educate for breadth of vision and versatility in application, thus assuring greater mobility and ability to adjust to new developments as the social needs change; (4) to provide institutions that will assist individuals on a part-time basis to acquire additional competencies, and displaced persons to secure fresh training that will fit them for reemployment; (5) to assist all individuals to reach their highest potential as human beings and as members of a democratic society; and (6) to foster growth of knowledge in all fields because of the contributions that fresh knowledge can make to the economy and to the health, welfare, and happiness of the people.

Recognizing that there are genuine benefits to individuals, the opinions of economists and of educators are nevertheless overwhelmingly in support of the concept that higher education is a social investment. I shall quote a few of these opinions.

Theodore W. Schultz said: "Investment in schooling is presently in the United States a major source of human capital." [24]

J. Philip Wernette pointed out that some nations with large natural resources but low achievement in education (Brazil, China) have an inadequate economy, whereas other countries with high provision for

[23] Walter Kotschnig, *Slaves Need No Leaders* (London: Oxford University Press, 1943), and Seymour Harris, *The Market for College Graduates* (Cambridge, Mass.: Harvard University Press, 1949).
[24] Theodore W. Schultz, *The Economic Value of Education* (New York: Columbia University Press, 1963), p. 46.

education but with low natural resources (Norway, Switzerland) have a high per capita income.[25]

Richard S. Eckaus supported this view:

> It may appear somewhat strained to treat educated labor, even in some limited aspects, as if it were a capital factor. From the viewpoint of the individual and of society as a whole, however, education is similar to the production of physical capital goods. Both require the use over a period of time of facilities. . . . Both necessitate the sacrifice of goods and services that might otherwise have been produced. . . . To gain an appreciation of the significance of education treated as a process of capital formation in humans, it is helpful to use an analogy with the natural resources of a nation—its farmland, mineral deposits, rivers, and so on. Virtually none of these, by themselves and unimproved, yield useful outputs. Yet after they are worked upon by men and equipment, they produce crops, ores, and power. After developmental work, natural resources become a kind of capital. . . . Over a period of time, education will improve the productivity of labor, and will result in services that could not otherwise be performed.[26]

Edward F. Denison attributed about 18 per cent (net) of the growth rate of the United States economy between 1929 and 1957 to advance in knowledge.[27]

John W. Kendrick found for the United States economy from 1889 to 1957 that the combined input index increased at an average rate of 1.9 per cent per annum, and the output index increased about 3.5 per cent per annum. The inputs consist of costs of labor and capital. The excess of 46 per cent may be attributable to education.[28]

Svennilson, Edding, and Elvin correlated GNP/capita and enrollment ratios for various countries, and found a positive relationship, although there is also considerable dispersion, particularly among the countries falling in the middle range.[29]

The Robbins Committee Report, in recommending a large further investment in higher education in England summarized as follows:

[25] J. Philip Wernette, *Growth and Prosperity Without Inflation* (New York: The Ronald Press Company, 1961), p. 27.

[26] Richard S. Eckaus, "Education and Economic Growth," in Mushkin, *op. cit.*, p. 103.

[27] Edward F. Denison, "Education, Economic Growth and Gaps in Information," *Journal of Political Economy* (supplement), LXX, October, 1962.

[28] John W. Kendrick, *Productivity Trends in the United States* (Princeton, N.J.: Princeton University Press, for the National Bureau of Economic Research, 1961), Table 6, p. 79.

[29] I. Svennilson, F. Edding, and H. L. Elvin, "Targets for Education in Europe in 1970," paper prepared for Washington Conference of the O.E.C.D., Fall, 1961, p. 75.

The return on education, even if it be considered solely in terms of productivity, is not something that can be estimated completely in terms of the return to individuals and of differential earnings. There is a further return in the shape of general adaptability and increased capacity for technological advance which, in the last analysis, is probably more important than what is measured within the system of relative prices. Education, in short, furnishes perhaps the most conspicuous example of the importance in social analysis of the difference between what economists call the "private" and the "social" net product of investment. . . . The difference as regards economic potential, between a tribe of savages and a civilized community depends much more on education than on material equipment. . . . If investment in higher education were seriously contracted, there would be a danger of a loss to the economy far greater than the measurable loss of the sum of the individual investments concerned.[30]

Since this paper deals with the economics of higher education, I have limited my discussion largely to this aspect of higher education as a social investment. Obviously, the concept of "social investment" has much broader connotations. Many of the arguments given above in support of an increase in Federal appropriations for higher education apply equally here. It would not be difficult to substantiate with much additional argument the overall value of higher education to our society.

WHAT CAN THE NATION AFFORD?

The best index of the prosperity and the economic potential in a country is the gross national product. Over a long period of years, the GNP has been expanding at the rate of 3 per cent or more per year. The 1964 Economic Report to the President of the United States predicts still further increases of similar proportions.

A distinction must be made between the ability of a government to provide appropriations for things, such as for higher education, and the gross national product; but the amount and rate of increase of the GNP is an indication of the potential revenues that can be collected by a government. In addition, certain of the expenditures of government are in fixed monetary values, and others of them have terminal dates. An increase in the productivity of taxes, therefore, provides the government with a margin of additional income in the expenditure of which there is some choice. This flexibility in revenues makes it possible to add new programs or to increase the portion of the income that is devoted to a

[30] *Higher Education,* Report of the Committee appointed by the Prime Minister under the Chairmanship of Lord Robbins, 1961–1963 (London: Her Majesty's Stationery Office, 1963), p. 205.

particular purpose. Another important factor is that in spite of increases in the total of the Federal budget, the expenditures in relation to GNP have declined. During the period from 1952 to 1959 the decline was from 20 per cent to 14 per cent.[31]

Higher education expenditures in relation to the GNP show some tendency to increase, but it is also clear that the amount devoted to higher education is a very tiny portion of the whole (see Table 5).

TABLE 5.   Total Expenditures for Higher Education in Relation to Gross National Product

| Year | GNP (billions of dollars) | Higher education | |
		Amount (millions of dollars)	Per cent
1930	$ 91.1	$ 508.5	0.56
1940	100.6	678.6	0.67
1950	284.6	2,259.9	0.79
1960	502.6	5,628.0	1.12
1962	554.9	7,077.0	1.28
1963	583.9		
1964	618.6		

SOURCES: U.S. Office of Education, *Higher Education*, October, 1963; *Federal Reserve Bulletin;* and Council for Financial Aid to Education, Inc.

The question then arises: What portion of the GNP should be devoted to higher education? The President's Committee (1957) recommended that the increase be from 0.68 per cent in 1953–1954 to about 1.10 per cent by 1970 (for educational and general expenses and plant). In Great Britain, the Robbins Committee recommended that the provision for higher education by 1980 should become 1.9 per cent of GNP as compared with 0.8 per cent in 1962–1963.[32] The past rate of growth in the United States suggests that a similar doubling for us by 1980 of the 1962 portion may be feasible. Small as that portion would be, the total amount probably would meet or exceed the requirements. If the rate of increase from 1940 to 1960 (67 per cent) were maintained, the percentage would reach 1.87 by 1980. Based on an assumed GNP of $900 billion, this would yield $17 billion for higher education.

The President's Committee calculated that to provide reasonably ade-

[31] Seymour E. Harris, "Higher Education: Resources and Finance (USA)" in *Economic Aspects of Higher Education* (Paris: Organization for Economic Cooperation and Development, 1964), p. 112.
[32] Robbins Committee Report, *op. cit.,* p. 207.

quately for higher education would require an annual expenditure of $34 per capita. The Committee contrasted this estimate with the per capita costs for a variety of necessities and luxuries, thus putting the figure in perspective as being a feasible goal and a relatively modest one. However, the rate of growth in the expenditures for higher education is somewhat in excess of that envisioned by the Committee.

Both measures of expenditures just given suggest that the total sums needed by higher education are reasonable, and that we can afford them without any serious hardship. The central question becomes one of relative values. The proposed larger expenditure admittedly does require that the American people place a greater value on higher education. They must be willing to tax themselves, provide gifts and bequests, and pay tuition charges and fees, and thus divert more of their own incomes to higher education. Again, to get a perspective on the problem, it is interesting to consider the conclusion of the Robbins Committee in Great Britain:

> The costs of the plan we have put forward are considerable. They involve an increase in the percentage of the national income devoted to higher education. They may involve increases in taxation, though whether this will be so depends upon the extent of other commitments, upon financial policy in general, and upon the increase of productivity. But we are convinced that no economic consideration need hinder their adoption if we as a nation desire the educational changes they will make possible. Whether we have them or not, is a question of choice. It is not a question of any technical or economic inability to achieve them.[33]

The implications of the foregoing analysis are that the interests of the nation coincide with the ability of our economy, and more especially, the ability of the Federal government, to provide the financial support needed by the colleges and universities of the nation.

[33] *Ibid.*, p. 216.

English Higher Education:
The Issues Involved

A. D. C. PETERSON, Director,
Department of Education, University of Oxford

INTRODUCTION

It is a great honor for a foreigner to be invited to take part in these discussions but I find it an equally great and difficult responsibility. Almost inevitably, in trying to portray the contemporary English scene, I shall have to touch superficially on many themes, each of which has been or will be discussed in much greater depth by individual American colleagues. Moreover there is the problem of language. Our two nations have been described as sister peoples united by all the ties of history and culture and divided only by the barrier of a common language. And this division is certainly as delusive as anywhere in the field of education. Let me begin therefore by a few words of definition. Though a Scot by birth I shall speak throughout of England and the English—and by this I mean the English and Welsh. This is not because, on the topic we are discussing, there are important differences between North and South of the border, although Scottish universities are more local, less exclusive, and cheaper than English ones, but because the two educational systems are quite separate. We therefore present our statistics in such a way that figures usually refer either to one section of the island or to the other. Thus, unless I specifically refer to "Britain," I shall be speaking of England and Wales. Secondly I shall use the term "tertiary education" to refer to education within the eighteen to twenty-two age group. "Secondary education" in England is a term used, rather eccentrically, to refer to all school education beyond the age of eleven. It extends, today, compulsorily to the age of fifteen and voluntarily for about 15 per cent of the age group to eighteen. Finally, to quote a well-worn phrase, it must be assumed in all that I say, unless specified otherwise, that the term "man" embraces "woman" and "boy" embraces "girl."

Let me start, then, with a brief analysis of the present level of our educational provision and go on from there to consider the likely scale and direction of expansion at the tertiary level.

THE PRESENT SITUATION

Traditionally there has been an important difference in England between the duration of compulsory education, of free education, and of available education.

In considering the extension of the educational period it is important to be sure which of the three we are talking about.

The present position is that full-time education is compulsory to fifteen (in 1971 this will be extended to sixteen) on a nationwide basis. It is free (technically speaking) to eighteen or nineteen (the end of secondary school) but in practice the section between fifteen and eighteen is highly selective. Only the children of the wealthier classes, and among them mainly the boys, are likely to continue in full-time education to the age of eighteen if their IQ falls below 120. There is nothing legally to prevent the youth of average ability remaining in the publicly maintained school until this age, but there is little inducement for him to do so. Where the secondary system has become comprehensive rather than selective the positive discouragement in the school system is less; but the social inducement to complete secondary education in terms of better job prospects, which has been so important in America, hardly exists yet in Britain, except for the gifted minority who are capable of passing the General Certificate of Education at Advanced Level, or those who complete the course at an independent and expensive "public schoool."

In the tertiary age range English statistics unfortunately deal with the age group eighteen to twenty, but since our tertiary education courses are normally of three years and the dropout in the third year (usually twenty to twenty-one) is very low, they may be taken to give a fair picture of the tertiary stage. This calculation shows approximately 30 per cent of the age group receiving some form of tertiary education in 1962 but the figure for those in full-time education is much lower, 6.56 per cent in universities, further education, and teacher training colleges combined.[1] The remainder were in part-time courses, usually consisting of evening study or of one full day a week at the technical colleges and colleges of further education.

It would seem, therefore, that if we apply Professor Martin Trow's admittedly "somewhat arbitrary" calculus, according to which the point of take-off into universal education in any level—primary, secondary, or tertiary—is reached when it absorbs 15 per cent of the age group, England is very far from universal tertiary education and only on the threshhold of establishing genuine universal secondary education. Yet it is commonly supposed that the publication of the Robbins Report in 1963 marked the British entry into this third phase.

These conflicting viewpoints are due, I would suggest, to two factors: the impossibility of applying the Trow formula, if I may call it by a name which I am sure its author would disclaim, to a managed society in which the growth of education is not a simple response to the demands of the educational market, and to a misreading of the Robbins Report. It is quite possible that what will happen in England is a deliberate forcing of the pace of expansion in the tertiary sector by government action, for which no parallels can be found in American experience, even before the natural curve of expansion in the secondary sector reaches the universal level. But this is not what the Robbins Report is about.

It is important to recognize that the recommendations of the Robbins Report are concerned solely with the expansion of opportunity in higher education for the same academically elite group as does at present receive it. Conclusive arguments are brought forward to show that by 1980 this group will be considerably larger, both absolutely and as a proportion of the total age group. I think that by its recommendations in favor of more "broad" or mixed university courses it recognizes that this ability group, although selected already, contains a proportion who are not and should not become "Ph.D. material." But the Report is not concerned with the possibility of providing tertiary education for a wider, because less aca-

---

[1] The difference between this figure and that of 8.5 per cent in the Robbins Report for those *entering* on higher education in this year is accounted for partly by an increase of 1.66 per cent in the figure for teacher training colleges, which were greatly expanded at this period, and partly by the inclusion of Scotland in the Robbins figures.

demically selected, group, and still less for the age group as a whole. Higher education is in fact defined in academic terms as being that which falls beyond the Advanced Level of the General Certificate of Education, and a special case has to be made for including in it the teacher training colleges, 40 per cent of whose entrants do not have an A-level qualification, although they have probably followed A-level courses. Another indication that the Report is concerned with education at a particular academic level rather than over a particular age range is that in calculating the "demand" it includes those who have reached this level after leaving school, irrespective of their age, but does not discuss whether it would be advisable to provide additional facilities for slower or less naturally specialized workers to reach it in some other institution, after the completion of a secondary school course. For the same reason the Report does not concern itself with other areas of tertiary education, referred to as "the initial stages of much professional and other education," nor with "nursing and some of the occupations associated with medicine."

In the political circumstances in which the Committee was working this attitude was not surprising. By their terms of reference they were instructed to inquire into "full-time higher education," and although it was open to them to give a less academically exclusive definition to "higher education," just as in fact they did devote considerable attention to part-time study, they decided not to do so.

For this decision they had two good reasons. The first was that the definition they adopted clearly fitted the intentions of the government which appointed them and the facts of the existing situation. "Higher education" had been interpreted in this sense for some years by the Ministry of Education, which preferred to describe tertiary education of a less academic type as "further education." Moreover, Britain had not yet achieved a full secondary education for more than 15 per cent of the age group, and to have suggested an expansion of educational opportunity in the eighteen to twenty age range for those to whom it had been denied between fifteen and eighteen would have been revolutionary.

Second was the climate of opinion in which the Committee began to work. They knew that if their recommendations were to have any hope of general acceptance they must not involve expense and expansion on a scale which would frighten the government and the public too much, and that if they were to have any chance of university acceptance they must demonstrate beyond all doubt that there was absolutely no "watering down" of academic standards. Nevertheless the Report does recommend that by 1980 we should be providing higher (not merely tertiary) education for 17 per cent of the age group, and this would bring us beyond Professor

Trow's point of take-off, twenty years before the end of the century. Moreover, it is very widely admitted that on the basis of "qualified student demand" on which their calculations were made this is much more likely to be an under- than an overestimate; and both general and university opinion have come to accept the Robbins estimates as reasonable.

The base from which we start is therefore a narrow one but the climate is clearly one of expansion. What are the factors in the social and economic structure which have led our planners to expectations very similar to those which many surveys show to have grown up in the minds of innumerable individual Americans?

SOCIAL AND ECONOMIC FACTORS FAVORING EXPANSION

It is particularly difficult here to avoid the repetition of truisms which have been repeated on both sides of the Atlantic until they are tedious. I shall try to do so by simply listing the obvious and agreed factors and concentrating my few remarks on divergencies. I take it, then, we can agree that the increasing complexity of technological processes and the shift in employment from agriculture, mining, and manufacturing to service occupations leaves progressively less opportunity of employment for the unskilled. Along with this we should probably recognize a growing sense of human equality which makes personal domestic service, once a major consumer of unskilled workers, no longer attractive. Michael Young's vision of a meritocracy enjoying a glut of domestic servants was intended as a nightmare rather than a prophecy. I am not one of those who see an increase in the number of cleaning women, even better-educated cleaning women, as a probable development.

In terms of economics, therefore, all Western societies are likely to need more people with a tertiary education. What is much more difficult to calculate is how many more and how much more education they will really *need*, simply in order to carry out their changing economic functions.

It is sometimes suggested that this is an unreal problem; that in fact the labor market cannot long absorb this age group, and that therefore we need not concern ourselves with speed or economy in giving them the necessary education or training, but might as well keep them in tertiary education even if this involves a very leisurely pace and much study which is directly relevant neither to their future employment nor to their personal and cultural life.

It is certainly a widely accepted principle in the sociology of education that however much educationists have pressed on cultural grounds for the gradual raising of the terminal age of secondary education, the decisive factor in bringing about this gradual rise has been the employment situation. Either there were no jobs for the adolescent in farm or factory, or organized labor was anxious to keep him off the labor market.

How far is this influence likely to operate in England to make us provide more places in college for the eighteen to twenty-two-year-olds because they are not wanted anywhere else? I should say not at all, at least until 1980. Our problem since World War II has not been one of unemployment, which runs at a level of 1 or 2 per cent, though in some sectors there may well be underemployment (i.e., three men doing one man's job). Nor can I find any indication in the figures that within the minimal degree of unemployment that we do have there is any tendency for the eighteen to twenty-year-old-group to be affected more than proportionately—if anything the reverse.

TABLE 1.   Unemployment of eighteen- to twenty-year-olds as a Percentage of total Unemployment

Year	Males	Females	Total
1962	13,028 (3.47%)	8,065 (2.15%)	375,027 (5.62%)
1963	14,507 (3.37%)	9,601 (2.23%)	430,192 (5.60%)
1964	9,306 (3.12%)	6,313 (2.12%)	298,379 (5.23%)

So far, in fact, the change in the employment pattern from manufacturing industries to services which has been so marked in the United States (a decrease of 5 per cent in the proportion of the work force engaged in manufacturing industries and a parallel increase of 6 per cent in services over the decade 1953–1963) is not nearly so pronounced in the British figures. Services did in fact increase their share by 3 per cent in this period but two-thirds of this came not from manufacturing but from agriculture, mining, construction, and public utilities. Manufacturing still absorbs 38 per cent of our working population as compared (1963) with 29 per cent in the United States. The trend is there, of course, but the question is how rapidly it will develop.

The official view is that there is no likelihood of this position changing in the near future. The first of the Ministry of Labour's Manpower Studies published in October, 1964, foresees no likelihood of a rising level of unemployment over the next five years. It suggests, on the contrary, that "the needs of an expanding economy will provide at least sufficient jobs in total for the additional number of workers foreseen"; while between 1968 and 1973 "a situation of overall shortage (of labour) is much more likely than one of surplus."

The economic pressure in England, therefore, is likely to be the genuine need for a better-educated working force, and not the need to keep this age group off the labor market.

The second of our truisms is that the age of automation is going to be an age of leisure. I wish I could think that this will develop as fast in England as some people seem to expect. Nevertheless, a very considerable shortening of working hours should take place within the period of our survey, and this faces the educational system with both an obligation and an opportunity. The wealth and the time will soon be available to produce a society with a genuine mass culture hitherto available only to the elite who sought it through tertiary education.

THE NATURE OF EXPANDED TERTIARY EDUCATION

We may accept, then, that social forces both economic and cultural are operating on English society, just as they have operated on American, to stimulate a great expansion of tertiary education. We are still deeply uncertain, however, as to the form which this expansion should take and within the debate which is going on I would single out two issues of primary importance. The first is this: Should we aim at a great expansion of full-time education within the age range eighteen to twenty-two? The second is: Should we aim at a much greater provision of part-time education, both within this age range and throughout adult life? It would be easy, of course, to say that we shall have to provide both, but since education in England is so largely and increasingly financed out of public funds the pattern of future educational provision is a matter for political decision. And politics are a matter of priorities. As Mendès-France said, to be a politician is to choose.

I would like to suggest, first, that there are certain good economic, cultural, and social reasons, where a choice has to be made, for choosing, in England at least, to extend part-time rather than full-time tertiary education, and, second, that there are certain specific factors in the English educational tradition which make such a choice probable. I do not mean by this to imply a definite commitment to the view that the part-time solution is, even for us, the better or the more likely one, but it is certainly an alternative that must be taken into account. Let me take, somewhat illogically, the second set of factors first. The economic reasons within our tradition are perhaps easiest to see. In many developed Western technological societies the average length of education and training before a young man becomes fully productive is increasing at one end of the life-span, while the proportion of retired people who have passed the age of production increases at the other. In a welfare economy the burden of producing the necessary wealth to keep both ends of the spectrum in reasonable comfort falls, through taxation, on a proportionately diminishing age-band. The situation becomes more marked as the age of marriage goes down and the productive section of society has to support not only the student but his wife and perhaps their first two children. This may not be a strong economic disincentive to the expansion and prolongation of full-time tertiary education where the students' living costs are a burden either on his own family, his own current earnings, or, through loans, his own future earnings. It is a strong disincentive in Britain, because of the tradition that the living costs of the student, as well as his tuition costs, should be provided by the state in its central or local incarnation.

The Robbins Committee found that "in none of the Western countries we visited are students so extensively assisted from public funds": yet the majority of the Anderson Committee recommended, in May, 1960, an increase in this assistance, namely that all students in universities should receive grants from public funds covering the whole of their living and tuition costs, irrespective of the parents' income. This recommendation was not, in fact, accepted, but may be by a Labour government. It was reckoned at that time that to implement it would only increase the national bill for student maintenance grants from £23.9 ($67.5) million per annum to £25 ($70.5) million. But it is worth considering that if England were to accept this sort of responsibility for 50 per cent of the age group over a four- instead of a three-year course, then the bill for student maintenance, in terms of costs prevailing in 1960, would be something in the nature of £300 ($850) million—approximately a quarter of the total national expenditure on education. If such a situation were to develop, therefore, it is likely that there would be strong opposition on political grounds to the expansion of full-time tertiary education on the scale which is contemplated in the United States.

It is perhaps worth trying to clarify here a convention which seems to me to be often overlooked in our use of the terms "full-time" and "part-time" education at this stage, and which perhaps diminishes the importance of the distinction. In England it is reasonably common for an eighteen- to twenty-year-old to be in employment for most of the year but to pursue his further education, for a number of hours in the day, days in the week, or weeks in the year: this we call "part-time education." In Europe, and I believe in America, it is much commoner than it is in England for a similar person to be primarily a student but to spend a number of hours in the day, days in the week, or weeks in the year in productive work: this we call "full-time education." Both are in fact combinations of tertiary education with productive work. The distinction is important but not absolute; and perhaps one of the reasons why we are drawn in England toward an expansion of part-time education is because our students have no such strong tradition of part-time productive work.

The second feature in our educational tradition likely to favor the extension of part-time rather than full-time tertiary education is the concept of a national responsibility to provide cultural and civic education for everybody, as well as intellectual and technical education for an elite, however large that elite may be. After all, the more education any society provides for the top 50 per cent, as it were, of the age group, the more pressing becomes the responsibility not to allow the development of a bottom 50 per cent of second-class citizens for whom no provision is made at that stage. To some extent, of course, this is bound up with the concept of tertiary education as a social service, freely available to all citizens, rather than a consumer good of which everybody gets as much as he wants and can afford (whether from his own resources or from scholarships, loans, and so on). This idea that some form of postsecondary education should be just as much compulsory and universal as secondary education itself is enshrined in the concept of the county college, first put on the Statute Book in the Fisher Act of 1918, recommended again in the Crowther Report of 1960, but never implemented in its compulsory and universal form. It was, of course, a concept that referred to postsecondary rather than tertiary education, but as the terminal date of universal secondary education creeps up toward the age of eighteen it becomes more and more relevant to the tertiary phase. We are, in fact, so accustomed to this kind of pattern in postschool education that it is natural for us when thinking of a massive expansion of tertiary education to turn our minds to what is familiar.[2]

A third feature in our tradition which I had intended to mention is the more custodial attitude which I supposed to be associated with English rather than either European or American institutions of tertiary education. I am not sure, after Howe's remarks, that you are not as overly custodial as we are. The danger of creating prolonged adolescence as

[2] Burton Clark (The Cooling Out Function in Higher Education) reports a similar attitude from California, where it is held that even high school graduates who cannot qualify for the State University should still have "the opportunity of attending a publicly supported institution of higher education," this being an essential part of the state's goal of guaranteeing equal educational opportunities to all its citizens.

opposed to "premature maturity" may be a problem more common to our two cultures than I had supposed. It seems to be clearly relevant to this choice between full-time and part-time education at this certain stage.

So far I have been discussing factors in the English educational tradition which are likely to influence us in this direction, although trends elsewhere and even some observable trends in England itself seem to be pointing in the direction of an increase in the proportion of full-time students. I turn now to the question whether this direction is not the right one, at least for us, to go in.

On the economic side the most important factor in the increased requirement for technical and technological training is likely to arise from changes in technology or business methods which render skills acquired at the beginning of a working life redundant, and at the same time impose the need to learn new ones. This seems to imply that both the risk of unemployment and the need for education are likely to arise at different stages in a man's working life but not particularly at the beginning of it. And this need can best be met by adequate schemes of redundancy pay and short, intensive periods of reeducation—periods certainly short enough to count under our definition as part time. It can, of course, be argued that a longer initial full-time education is required—to develop not knowledge or skills which may become redundant, but those powers and flexibility of the mind on which alone subsequent specialist reeducation can be based; and that, in order to counteract the lure of highly paid employment to young people at an age when this initial education is incomplete, structural unemployment should be artificially created at this age range by making it unattractive to firms to employ them. I would support this kind of action in England in the sixteen- to eighteen-year-old age range, but I am not at all satisfied that for most young people these powers and this flexibility are best developed after that age in the sort of custodial and academic atmosphere, largely isolated from productive work, which we in England associate with full-time tertiary education. This view about the practical value of extended full-time tertiary education was to some extent supported by Paul Chambers, the Chairman of I.C.I., in his Chuter Ede lecture.

If full-time initial education beyond this stage is not *necessary* for these practical economic purposes for more than a minority of the age group, then we shall perhaps do better to concentrate our limited resources on providing a first-class system of part-time education both at this and later stages.

The cultural argument is of course very similar. It is a commonplace that students whose interest is captured by cultural pursuits in their initial

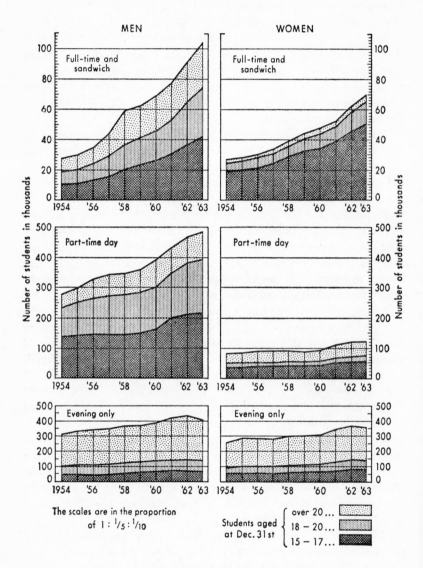

Figure 1. Students in grant-aided major establishments

tertiary education often drop them in later life while adults take to them long after they have left college; moreover, we shall, for the rest of this century, have a high proportion of older adults who have never had an opportunity of full-time tertiary education and who have as much claim on the educational resources of society as the young. The social argument I see as simply this: The more that the expansion of tertiary education is on a part-time basis and extended into working life the less will be the apparent and irremediable distinction between those who have received tertiary education and those who have not.

It is clearly of some significance also in assessing the relative probability of expansion in part-time or full-time tertiary education in England to look at the trend over the last ten years. Most part-time education is, of course, in the secondary sector, the fifteen-to-eighteen age group, 85 per cent of whom are not in full-time secondary education. Leaving these aside, we can identify fairly clearly what has been happening to the eighteen-to-twenty-year-olds. (The over-twenty group represents approximately 75 per cent of the figure enrolled in the eighteen-to-twenty age group.) This shows that while in 1953 the proportions of the eighteen-to-twenty age group enrolled in full-time, part-time day, and evening study were 0.8, 5.76, and 10.26 per cent, respectively, the figures in 1963 were 2.38, 9.84, and 11.65 per cent. While, therefore, the rate of growth in full-time courses is considerably faster than in part-time, the base from which part-time courses start is so very much higher that even assuming the uninterrupted influence of existing trends it seems likely that for the next two decades at least, part-time day courses will be in the lead. The sector which is static or actually in decline is tertiary education through evening study, and most English educationists would agree that this is a healthy development.

The second great question under debate is whether the whole range of tertiary education is to be equalized, or whether we are to maintain the

TABLE 2.   Proportion of the Eighteen-to-Twenty Age Group Taking Part in Further Education *

Class hours	1953	1958	1963
Full time	0.77	1.16	1.86
Sandwich	0.03	0.26	0.52
Part-time day	5.76	8.76	9.84
Evenings	10.26	11.97	11.65

* N.B. These figures exclude students at universities, teacher training colleges, and colleges maintained by individual ministries, i.e., Agriculture and Defence (*Statistics of Education 1963*, Part Two).

distinction between higher education, provided in universities, and further education provided in colleges and institutions of "subuniversity" or parauniversity level—for which maintenance grants, residence, full-time courses, and vacation grants are not at present provided on the university scale.

The Robbins Report has here thrown its influence into the scale of equalization, though not perhaps as emphatically as some of the equalizers would have wished. The colleges of advanced technology, which were established in 1956 and at that time refused the power to grant degrees, are to become, in accordance with the recommendations of the report, technological universities. But the critical issue, on which the debate is still raging, is the future of the teacher training colleges. These provide tertiary education for 54,000, compared with the present English and Welsh university population of 98,500. The Robbins Report recommends that their historic, but often purely formal, association with local education authorities should be broken; that they should be decisively accepted within the university orbit; that university degrees should be opened to an increasing proportion of their students; and that a number of them should widen the range of their courses to include preparation for careers other than teaching. What this amounts to is a planned development, under national control, very similar to that which has happened spontaneously to the teachers colleges in the United States. The opposition to this proposal is strong and in my opinion likely to be successful at least in the short run. It is based on two factors: the desire of the department of education and of the local authorities, who are the employers of teachers, to retain that control over the bulk of teacher training without which they could not plan in relation to national needs; and the reluctance of the universities to admit to their portals both a range of students who, they suspect—I believe wrongly—would be of lower academic ability, and a range of subjects such as housecraft, physical education, and child study which are not "disciplines" in the sense to which our universities have been accustomed.

It seems reasonable that in a society like ours, where the supply of teachers for the schools is regarded as a national responsibility and the teacher training colleges are nationally financed, the central government should wish to retain this control. The universities as a whole are jealous of their academic freedom and, if teacher training were absorbed into the university sector, would not take kindly to instructions from the central authority altering, for instance, the sex ratio in their intake or the balance between training for primary and secondary school work. Yet these are exactly the instructions which the central government would wish to give in accordance with its demographic surveys of the probable demand. This may be another example of the divergencies which arise as a result of our different systems of financing tertiary education. A market economy in tertiary education can leave the teacher training colleges free to respond, as flexibly as may be, to the changes in supply and demand: A managed economy implies a considerable degree of central planning. This controversy seems to me to illustrate well the problems of combining rational planning with institutional autonomy which Professor McConnell posed to us earlier.

We have already set up, as a result of the Robbins Report, a Council for National Academic Awards which is empowered to grant "degrees." This will presumably act as a sort of national accrediting agency to validate courses in a large number of what are at present "subuniversity" institutions, as being of an academic quality, equal to that of a university degree course. An alternative system therefore exists by which the teacher training colleges could be left under public control and yet empowered to grant degrees. This kind of gradual assimilation of the two levels in tertiary education rather than their equalization by promoting the various "colleges" to the independent status of the university world is the sort of development which may seem foreign to American experience but which is completely in accord with English tradition.

At the moment the equalizers and the separatists are still drawn up in opposite camps, but I should not be surprised, in the particular case of the teacher training colleges, to see a typical English compromise by which the Council for National Academic Awards would appoint the existing university institutes of education as its accrediting committees, and so preserve a link between the degrees awarded in teacher training colleges and those in universities, without actually absorbing the colleges into the university sector.

There are, of course, "equalizers" in England who would like to see the whole range of colleges follow the colleges of advanced technology into the university system and so produce as wide a range of autonomous degree-granting institutions as has developed in America. These people argue that nothing less will confer sufficient prestige on the subuniversity colleges and the courses they provide to enable them to play their proper role in the expansion of tertiary education. There is force in their argument, but the opposition is strong, and there is another model in the U.S.S.R. where the proportion of tertiary education allotted to universities, as opposed to professional institutes, is even lower than in England.

It seems to me probable, therefore, that the line dividing university from subuniversity professional tertiary education will be drawn, at least for the next decade and probably longer, between the colleges of advanced technology on the one hand and the teacher training colleges on the other.

All this may seem a typical English hierarchical structure, reminiscent of our tendency to recognize and perpetuate social and academic class distinctions that have long been abandoned elsewhere. But I think it is also a result of the financing of tertiary education from public sources. Whereas in America colleges and universities draw their finance from a wide variety of sources, fund-raising, fees, government contracts, and public funds, in England public funds have become almost the sole source of finance. In such circumstances the cost of equalization would fall on the taxpayer and since it would almost inevitably be equalization upwards the cost would be heavy. It is much cheaper to maintain two levels of tertiary education. Two figures are perhaps indicative of this kind of differentiation. The annual cost of a university place is reckoned by the Robbins Committee as £777 ($2,180), and that of a teacher training college place as £576 ($1,625). The average cost of student grants (1962–1963) was, for university students, £324 ($914), and in further education £266 ($750).

CONCLUSION

What, then, is the likely shape of tertiary education in Britain over the remainder of this century? And what are the implications for our economy? Burton Clark sees the developing American pattern as one of elite colleges, service institutions, and screening centers, all of these full-time, contributory one to another at the terminal stage and providing for more than half of the age group. The British pattern, I suggest—and this is one man's guess—will be closely parallel in function, though differing in structure and nomenclature, and taking a smaller proportion of the age group into full-time education.

Parallel to the elite colleges we shall have our expanded universities providing for between 15 and 20 per cent of the age group by 1980 but not expanding very rapidly after that; by the time these numbers are reached I think we shall have to consider very seriously the extent to which we provide residence in a university far from home and also the question of substantially switching the financial burden of students' living costs from the taxpayer to the student himself, either through his own earnings or a system of loans. I see Clark's service institutions as represented by a loosely coordinated group of "colleges" of subuniversity status, but entitled to grant degrees either through affiliation with a university or through the Council for National Academic Awards. These will include colleges of art and commerce, teacher training colleges, and possibly the Armed Service colleges. They will provide both part-time and full-time courses, leading to qualifications at different levels, and it is through them that I personally should hope to see better provision for the student whose study for a degree must be largely external, aided by television and correspondence courses, and often spread over a longer time period than the traditional three or four years of residence. It would be important that there should be a channel from them to universities at the graduate level. It is in these colleges that I should also expect the screening function of Clark's third tier to be carried out. I do not foresee the development in Britain of any separate institution at this level of the junior college type. We shall, I think, see the development within the school system in some areas of "Sixth Form colleges" with an age range of sixteen to nineteen which will be both terminal and contributory to the university and college systems which I have outlined.[3] We shall also see an increasing number of young people between the ages of seventeen and twenty completing full-time advanced secondary courses as well as subdegree-level courses in the colleges of further education and this is already providing an opportunity for experiment in mixing these younger students with mature adults in the way that Howe suggested. We may even implement the concept of the county college, but a lot of this work at all levels will be part time.

All these institutions, to some extent or another, sometimes overlapping in age range and in function, will help to provide both the screening process which we need to channel available talent to the universities and

[3] These Sixth Form colleges are the development which might be of most interest. The English Sixth Form traditionally is equivalent to grades eleven and twelve but largely under the pressure of competition to enter universities. It is imperceptibly expanding for the university preparatory half of its pupils to cover grade thirteen also. It's curriculum is appallingly overspecialized *but* it does provide that introduction to new *methods* of intellectual work which I gather Howe felt to be lacking in grade twelve of the high school.

Perhaps the most interesting experiment in this direction is the Atlantic College, because it looks to me almost exactly what Howe (and incidentally I, too) is asking for: age range seventeen to nineteen, a college type of approach to academic work, a curriculum broader than the normal English, combined with a program of fairly tough training in sea, cliff, and mountain rescue work, and first aid to take the place of high school athletics—and the student body drawn from something like fourteen different countries.

the short tertiary courses leading to subprofessional qualifications which the economy is likely to demand. But I cannot see any likelihood of half our age group claiming a college education, either in the sense of two years of full-time junior college or of a full tertiary education, within this century. Nor can I see any likelihood of any British government providing for it out of the public purse. Perhaps it is the improbability of the latter which inhibits the development of the former.

Observations and Comments

FRANK H. BOWLES, Vice President, Fund for the Advancement of Education

Each of the papers in this book was written on the assumption that universal higher education would develop within the next twenty years as a pattern within the American educational system—in other words, that it was on its way but still well over the horizon of events. However, when the papers are assembled and studied as chapters of a book they make it clear that the institutions, purposes, concepts, and attitudes of universal higher education already exist. It is only the enrollments, at present approaching 40 per cent of the age group, which fall short—but not very short—of the figure of 51 per cent which is stipulated in the definition. By 1980 at a conservative estimate and by 1975 at present rate of increase, the definition will be met in full.

It should not be surprising that we have come to the borders of universal higher education. The two principles on which it is based have been operating in America for twenty-five years. They are that entry to higher education is controlled by interest and ability, not by the form or content of previous formal education; and higher education is whatever we define it to be in terms of content, so long as it involves mature learning for the purpose of the intellectual development of the student.

The formal practice of universal higher education in the United States may be traced to the period of mobilization for World War II. During that time it became clear that the supply of individuals who were qualified through formal education to become either commissioned officers or technician specialists was too small to meet needs. The military answer to the discovery was to lower the formal requirements for entry and to select in terms of ability (so far as it could be measured) and individual capacity (so far as it could be judged). The men so selected were placed in concentrated programs of study and on completion of their programs took the appropriate rank or grade.

The program these men followed did not meet the definition of college courses. In no sense did those programs constitute a general or liberal education. They were short; they were limited in scope and vocational in purpose. But broadly speaking they were not inferior in content and standards to the higher education of the time. The proof lay in hundreds of thousands of these young men whose lives were changed by their wartime educational experiences. They had entered military service without hope of ever going to college. Their experience in military service established their capacity to do college work, the GI Bill of Rights supplied the possibility, and their subsequent performance in formal higher education established their intellectual right to the opportunity. The achievement was important in itself, but it had a larger importance. It made the nation aware of the nature and values of education, and this awareness was the first step in what has since become an educational revolution.

The first recognizable suggestion of universal higher education as a desirable goal for America appeared in the report of the President's Commission on Higher Education (1947) and provoked a memorable storm. The idea that half of the population could profit intellectually by study beyond secondary school was not greeted with universal approval. But despite harsh criticism it remained on the record to serve as a reminder for the future.

Thus by the end of the 1940s we had experimented successfully with the methods of universal higher education and had recognized and approved their implications in a report on education that went directly to our President. This meant, essentially, public acknowledgment and recommendation of the societal philosophy of educational purpose. The acceptance of the societal philosophy by the President's Commission did not displace the scholastic view which had long controlled an important sector of American education. Instead, in a remarkable exercise of educational pluralism, both philosophies were accepted, each as a control for its own form of educational expansion.

The societal view was responsible for a tremendous horizontal expansion. New institutions were created to offer programs that had not previously been considered as higher education. Entrance requirements were liberalized to allow new groups of students to enter, and college requirements were liberalized to enable students to search out their likes, dislikes, skills, and needs through a process of trial and error. This was a philosophy which emphasized mass culture, rather than the nurture of prospective graduate students, and laid more stress on student adjustment than on intellectual productivity. But at the same time it provided opportunities for those who had graduate schools or higher professional studies in view.

The scholastic view was responsible for a vertical expansion of our system, accompanied by a rigid application of standards. The colleges that were linked to the great university graduate and professional schools became more severe in their control of college preparation, and more specific in their direction of students toward graduate and professional schools. These are institutions which have no time for failure or uncertainty. Their stress is on study as a path to intellectual productivity. Culture is implicit rather than explicit in the curriculum.

The great problem, of course, has been to reconcile these two philosophies under one rubric of higher education. The problem within the problem has proved to be that of providing for movement between the two groups, and the solution which is generally accepted is that movement can take place when it is based on achievement. If students who fail of entry at one type of institution can have the assurance that they can try again when they have new achievement to support their effort, then different standards can exist simultaneously within one system and opportunity remains open to all students. This essentially has been the pattern of reconciliation.

If the reconciliation had not been accomplished, the reduction of movement between the two groups would have led to stratification and separation. Neither group could have drawn on the other, and the expansion of education which is a precondition for expansion of opportunity would have ceased. In such case, universal higher education could not be achieved.

But it must be clear that universal higher education is not, in itself, a goal of our educational system. The goals are intellectual, social, economic, cultural, political—the enlargement of knowledge, an open society, the advancement of the culture, freedom of opportunity, freedom of conscience and political expression—aspirations that are individual, and aspirations that are collective. These are goals, and it is to reach these goals that we expand our system. The fulfillment of the definitions of universal higher education will be an incident in the course of the expansion.

The consequences of the expansion are made clear by the several papers.

Moynihan presents a model of development which would achieve a postsecondary school enrollment of 50 per cent of the school age population by 1970. His model postulates the provision of universal opportunity for free public instruction for two years beyond the high school, plus sufficient financial aid to eliminate the economic deterrent for those with ability and desire to continue their education beyond this level. This, he estimates, could produce an enrollment of 1 million students beyond present projections. About 350,000 of these students would be enrolled in the upper two years of college and 240,000 of them might be expected to graduate.

Transferring these individuals from the labor force to higher education would free 400,000 jobs. This number would just about offset the number of unemployed youth in the same age group. In addition to the jobs freed by bringing their potential holders into college, about 150,000 jobs would be created by construction of the needed facilities, and 150,000 permanent jobs would be created for instructional services, maintenance, and operation. Beyond these immediate economic consequences, there are also long-term results. Assuming that over the twenty years from 1960 to 1980, 40 per cent of the labor force were to receive one year more of education than they otherwise would, the national product during that period could be increased by 1.4 per cent a year.

The model is presented in terms of decisive political action. It would require the formation of 100 new colleges a year, each with a capacity of 2,000 students.

Reynolds, discussing the possibility of a slower approach to enrolling a larger group comprising 70 per cent of the age group by 1974, estimates a need, by that date, to accommodate 2,240,000 additional students. This would require from 1,500 to 2,000 new community colleges, or an average of 30 to 40 for each of the fifty states. Assuming an average operating cost of $800 per student, the annual cost of operation of these colleges will be close to 2 billion dollars, and capital outlay for the physical plants will be between 4.5 and 6 billion dollars.

Haggerty, considering the provision of teachers for the larger enrollments, including the number of students who must be retained in high school in order to go on to college, estimates for 1965 to 1970 a need for 20,000 additional high school teachers and 25,000 additional college teachers a year. For 1970 to 1975, his figures call for 13,000 high school teachers and 22,000 college teachers a year, or a total for the ten-year period of 400,000 high school and college teachers for new enrollments. Needed replacements bring the number up to just under 2 million.

The figure is a large one, but it is not all of this story. In addition to the teachers, there are the guidance workers, administrators, librarians, and other professional academic personnel. Further, if schools or colleges, or both, should go into year-round operations, up to 30 per cent more new teachers would be required—another 120,000 over the ten years. The teacher requirement thus adds up to a very large percentage of all the young persons in the nation who finish college and begin working careers. However, as Haggerty points out, the problem of recruiting is not one of availability, for there are enough college graduates to fill teaching positions, but rather one of competition with other professions, which is partly a matter of salary and partly a matter of attracting college students to teaching as early as possible in their college careers.

Recruiting becomes entangled with teacher training. Howe remarks that a twelfth-grade teacher must be trained in accordance with certain requirements and must demonstrate his teaching skills before being allowed in a classroom, while a teacher in the thirteenth grade has no such requirements to meet and may be anyone whom the institution chooses.

He could also have remarked that it is customary for college teachers to have advanced degrees but that the custom is not always complied with in staffing the classes in the first two college years. There is therefore the question of whether the colleges mentioned by Moynihan and Reynolds may be staffed by teachers who have neither the advanced education of college teachers nor the professional skill of secondary school teachers. If such staffing were to be done on a large scale—and it is easy to imagine that it might often be—it would prove a sure way of discrediting universal higher education, or at least of delaying its acceptance.

Probably the most effective way to avoid poorly trained teachers will be to reach early decisions on what is to be taught, why, and to whom; for if we know the purpose of training, it is easier to train and easier to recruit for training. This is a curriculum problem.

The problem begins with determining the function of high school. If nearly all high school graduates are going to college, the terminal function of high school is correspondingly reduced. When this happens, most of the high school program must be devoted to general education and most of the terminal vocational courses moved up to the thirteenth and fourteenth grades. This creates problems for both levels of education. High schools must develop additional programs of general education for the students who can no longer be channeled into vocational courses; they must either retrain their vocational teachers to teach the general education program or add new staff to do so.

The shift will also affect the guidance function, for vocational guidance toward job placement at the end of high school will no longer be necessary save for a few students. Instead there will be the different and in some ways more demanding task of educational guidance to help students prepare for the college programs they require.

The new demands for educational guidance will, as Pearson has pointed out, require techniques and instruments which can be applied as early as grade seven to permit the development of guidance for each student paralleling his instruction throughout the last six years of his pre-college education. Such guidance programs will require measurements of ability and achievement which we simply do not now possess. The basic research necessary to their eventual development is now being suggested by discussions and investigations of the learning process, the development of linguistic skills, the effects of compensatory education, and the relationships between successful learning and motivation. However, most of this work is now directed toward young, deprived children. The problem of moving the locus of research to higher age levels, and generalizing results to cover the entire population of the upper grades, has not been approached.

The acceptance of the task of vocational guidance in the new colleges will be one consequence of what McConnell refers to as the shift from high school to college of the point at which students are distributed between employment and further education. He suggests that much of the guidance will be accomplished through the formation of specialized colleges such as technical institutes and the development of work-study programs such as are now used so successfully in England. He also points out the possibility of formalizing the extensive educational activities now carried on by large industrial firms.

But in addition to the guidance which is built into specialized institution and work-study programs, there is the problem of providing advice and direction for the hundreds of thousands of students who will enter universal higher education without any sense of direction or understanding of their own skills and abilities. The provision of professional assistance for them will be a major operation. Nevitt Sanford suggests that their adjustment to contemporary society will be an important mission for the new colleges. In fact, in his view, which he supports persuasively, it will be the most important mission of these institutions. If this is so, then the recruiting and training of student personnel officers will be an intricate operation, although perhaps no more intricate than inducing the students to make full and responsive use of their services.

The only estimates of the cost of universal higher education are based on projections of present figures. Reynolds and Henderson discuss cost but only Henderson has attempted to show costs for all of higher education. His figures suggest that higher education will cost the nation at least 12 billion dollars a year by 1970 for operating costs and upward of 2 billion dollars more for facilities.

It is doubtful that this figure presumes teacher salaries that compete with other professions, or that all the changes involved in universal higher education have been costed out and included in the estimate. Nor does it allow for the fact, which cannot be quantified, that the last million students who enter universal higher education in any decade—that is to say, the final group of marginal students who can qualify for some form of higher education—will be expensive to educate. Their academically useful skills will be more difficult to identify and apply; their motivation will require guidance and reinforcement; their achievement and maturity will come slowly. To put it in industrial terms, the cost of producing a unit of intellectual achievement from this raw material may be from three to five times as high as the cost per unit for the comparable number of students who, at the other end of the achievement scale, are best qualified for entry to higher education. Because of the probable errors of estimate which these and other factors introduce, it is necessary to raise both the lower and the upper limits and estimate an annual cost for higher education of not less than 13 nor more than 15 billion dollars for 1970. Projected to 1975, the upper limit becomes the lower limit and the figure is clearly established at not less than 15 nor more than 20 billion dollars a year, plus facilities costs. This is expensive, but not unbearable.

It is clear from the foregoing discussion and even clearer from the papers, which go into the details, that the arrival of universal higher education will present tangible, difficult, and costly problems. But it should also be clear that underneath them there is another layer of problems which are less tangible but even more difficult. They may be less, or more, costly, but we shall never be able to find out for there are few expenditures traceable directly to these problems, although many that will be affected by them.

The first problem is one which is implied in all of the papers—the question of the types of institutions required to serve the purposes of universal higher education. Some of the problems which the institution must meet have been discussed, but the models which could establish the nature of the task of founding and organizing have not been supplied. A first suggestion for such models was offered during the conference in an imaginative paper prepared by Dr. Harold Howe, which is here presented as part of the summary chapter.

Institution number one. This comprehensive community college serves a large area 60 miles in radius without a major urban center. It is a truly comprehensive school with a full range of student ability. It is large enough to offer a good program for all ability levels for at least 1,200 students. It is nonresidential and provides, at public expense, transportation for its students. It provides as much campus life as is possible in a nonresidential setting.

Institution number two. Primarily for the less able student in the urban centers, this school offers a combination of work and study. The student attends on a year-round basis with a month off and is able in two years of combined work and study to prepare for reasonably skilled employment. The school arranges for the job the student occupies while in school and checks on his performance with the employer. The school is perhaps a high efficiency institution with three groups of students going through it simultaneously—morning, afternoon, and evening. Formal education would have two aspects: general education and job-related study.

Institution number three. School three offers students a chance to live away from home in a residential setting and at public expense. Closely connected to the guidance services of high schools and the social work services of communities, this institution recognizes the needs of youngsters whose homes are so inadequate that continued residence there militates against success in education or employment. It has a special emphasis on counseling and on rebuilding skills. It might well start with grade ten and continue four years. If organized for older students, it would be financed by the Job Corps program.

Institution number four. This is a school closely oriented to a particular industry—a textile mill, a chemical plant, an atomic installation, a large food processing company. Specifically directed to the two objectives of improving the skills and background of the individual and making people employable in the local community, it would be partly financed by local or state taxes and partly by the industry which would take responsibility for the job-oriented aspects of training. Depending on circumstances, it might or might not be residential. Under some circumstances, it might be eligible for support under the federal poverty program. Students of all ages could attend, eighteen to fifty.

Institution number five. This school recognizes that some will wish to learn on their own with special help but without formal classes. It offers a combination of correspondence work and TV teaching. It provides validation of learning through examinations, and awards credit on the basis of the results. Studies offered at this school may be taken by regular high school students for completion of graduation requirements and by older students for a variety of purposes. The school provides counseling services but has no classrooms or campus. It makes arrangements, however, to bring together for joint studies students with similar interests. In addition, it maintains a file for tutors who are able to help students on a volunteer basis. Many of these volunteers are housewives, some are college professors, others are able undergraduates of four-year colleges.

Institution number six. This school for eighteen- to twenty-year-olds is denominational and uses church facilities normally only in use on Sunday. It is extremely flexible and puts an emphasis on individualized programs for its students. It depends on local industry for its vocational training and offers for a portion of each student's time a mixture of general education and group experience. It will have a hard time obtaining public funds but should be able to solve the problem by a program which makes payments directly to the students, such as the GI Bill.

Institution number seven. Operating in conjunction with a large university center, this two-year residential institution uses the general facilities of the university, that is, the library and labor sources and so on. While some students will go on from this institution to the upper university years, many will not. The focus will be upon general education combined with training for technical vocational specialties which do not require industrial facilities for laboratory purposes.

The 7 types of institutions described above are only a sampling of the variety of institutions among the 2,000 that the achievement of universal higher education will require, but they do suggest the complexities of the problems of planning and organization.

The listing of these models leads directly into a problem which Mc-Connell points out: the tendency of new institutions to imitate old institutions. He feels, and is able to cite examples to support his feelings, that institutions which may be created to meet the requirements of universal higher education will take on the characteristics of existing institutions and in time become indistinguishable from them. The problem is that of finding social supports for institutions of different types within a differentiated system. If the problem is not solved in the future—and it is certain that it has not been solved in the past—institutions will fail to provide the diversity of educational opportunity that our economy, culture, and polity require.

There are two other problems which follow from McConnell's point. One is the threat of disturbing the pluralistic relationship between the scholastic and the societal philosophies of education by an emphasis on mass culture which may suppress individuality and ultimately destroy the sense of style which marks the educated man. This eventuality has long been predicted as the end product of American education, and it is not a sufficient answer to the future threat to say that since it has not happened, it probably will not happen. The fact is that as we go into the next stage of expansion, the threat increases. We may avoid the catastrophe, but we cannot ignore it.

The other problem concerns the effort to maintain the institutional diversity and individuality that we cherish. Sanford's emphasis on the dimension of individual adjustment directs attention to the present unrest among American students which he, and others, suggests is in reality a question of student values in conflict with institutional values. His statement that the institution has an obligation to provide an ambience in which this conflict of values can be resolved is not, in its general wording, a new one. However, it is new and challenging in its emphasis.

It may be said that this premise of necessity for student adjustment to society is implicit in every institutional plan of organization and instruction, but that it is subordinated to the explicit necessity for student acquisition of knowledge and skills necessary for vocational or professional life. But if the premise of social adjustment is made explicit among institutional objectives, the organization, staff, and curriculum must be modified, and in addition, the whole question of the institution's present view of proper student values and adjustment comes into consideration. This, in brief, involves a shift in institutional emphasis of some proportions which might eventually lead to a form of polarization along the axis of student adjustment as a new but nonetheless real challenge to institutional individuality.

Still another of the hidden problems in the future of universal higher education is the question of whether our present educational skills will be equal to the demands placed upon them. The word "skills" is used in a broad sense to cover the provision and use of facilities and equipment; teaching methods; and other, less structured, methods of inducing learning. Our present methods may be classified under five general headings:

1. Teachers talking to students
2. Student use of written materials—books, periodicals, programmed instruction—to reinforce classroom instruction
3. Student learning by observation, practice, and experience in the laboratory and the field
4. Teacher criticism and evaluation of student response—verbal and written—to instruction
5. Student criticism of student learning

The use of these five methods presumes a balance between size of student body, size of teaching staff, provisions for classrooms, provisions for student use of written materials, provision for student learning by observation, and opportunity for reciprocal criticism.

The dynamics of institutional growth tend to destroy this balance by admitting too many students. This can be done because classrooms always will hold more and students and teachers can always be recruited, particularly if qualifications are leniently interpreted. But it is done at the cost of overloading the facilities—library, laboratories, student center, and dormitories—which support the other instructional methods. The overloading reduces their effectiveness and further reinforces the method of teachers talking to students.

Two problems which will be very serious ones in developing effective universal higher education arise from the effects these institutional dynamics will have on instruction and learning. First, research on the learning process suggests that instruction by teachers talking to students is an ineffective and expensive process when evaluated in terms of units of learning produced by the student per unit of expenditure. Studies in linguistics, in the development of skills, in the relation of environment to learning, in the relation of identity to learning—in short, into the learning process—indicate that the teacher, particularly when he is talking, is playing less of a role in learning than had generally been assumed.

Second, the same studies on the learning process emphasize the values of student learning through use of written materials, by practice and observation, and by criticism of student learning performance. Yet it is these very learning patterns which tend to lose support as institutions grow.

It may be argued that we do not know enough about the learning process to justify reducing the role of the classroom teacher. It may also be argued that mechanization, computerization, and other technological changes will reduce the unit cost of providing learning materials. Both of these are valid points, but they do not deal with the issue. The issue is that we will get poor learning results in universal higher education if we limit the planning and staffing of our future institutions to the patterns of our present ones. The list of problems could be prolonged almost indefinitely but it is already long enough to show the size of the task.

Yet if the problems are great, the hopes are greater. There is a hope that universal higher education may bring some of the same values in the seventies and eighties that the democratization of secondary education brought in the thirties and forties—better knowledge of living, better use of human resources, higher standards of family life, higher standards of employment and work, higher aspirations. Obviously these were not and are not educational goals. But neither is universal higher education an educational issue. It is no more—and no less—than one more American effort toward human betterment. Like all such efforts over our two centuries of national life, it will fall short of its goal, but it will reach farther than we can now see, and its values will be one of our legacies to the future.

Index